GENEALOGICAL DEMOGRAPHY

POPULATION AND SOCIAL STRUCTURE

Advances in Historical Demography

Under the Editorship of

E. A. HAMMEL

Department of Anthropology
University of California, Berkeley

Kenneth W. Wachter with *Eugene A. Hammel* and *Peter Laslett*, Statistical Studies of Historical Social Structure

Nancy Howell, Demography of the Dobe !Kung

Bennett Dyke and *Warren T. Morril* (Editors), Genealogical Demography

GENEALOGICAL DEMOGRAPHY

Edited by

Bennett Dyke

Warren T. Morrill

Department of Anthropology
The Pennsylvania State University
University Park, Pennsylvania

ACADEMIC PRESS   1980

A Subsidiary of Harcourt Brace Jovanovich, Publishers

NEW YORK   LONDON   TORONTO   SYDNEY   SAN FRANCISCO

Academic Press Rapid Manuscript Reproduction

Proceedings of a Symposium
Held at the Forty-Eighth Annual Meeting of the
American Association of Physical Anthropologists
San Francisco, April 5, 1979

ACADEMIC PRESS, INC.
111 Fifth Avenue, New York, New York 10003

United Kingdom Edition published by
ACADEMIC PRESS, INC. (LONDON) LTD.
24/28 Oval Road, London NW1   7DX

Library of Congress Cataloging in Publication Data
Main entry under title:

Genealogical demography.

(Population and social structure)
"Proceedings of a symposium held at the
forty-eighth annual meeting of the American
Association of Physical Anthropologists, San
Francisco, 5 April 1979."
Includes index.
1.   Demographic anthropology—Congresses.
2.   Genealogy—Congresses.   I.   Dyke, Bennett.
II.   Morrill, Warren T.   III.   American
Association of Physical Anthropologists.
IV.   Series.
GN33.5.G46   929'.1   80-17683
ISBN 0-12-226380-4

PRINTED IN THE UNITED STATES OF AMERICA

80 81 82 83   9 8 7 6 5 4 3 2 1

To the memory of Ralph Spielman

CONTENTS

CONTENTS

CONTRIBUTORS

Numbers in parentheses indicate the pages on which authors' contributions begin.

John W. Adams* (115) Department of Anthropology, University of South Carolina, Columbia, South Carolina 29208

Lee L. Bean (95) Department of Sociology, University of Utah, Salt Lake City, Utah 84143

Anthony J. Boyce* (197) Department of Biological Anthropology, University of Oxford, 58 Banbury Road, Oxford OX2 6QS, England

Ellen R. Brennan* (197) Department of Anthropology, University of Texas, Austin, Texas 78712

Ann W. Brittain* (157) Department of Anthropology, University of Tennessee, Knoxville, Tennessee 37916

Ranajit Chakraborty* (41, 63) Center for Demographic and Population Genetics, Graduate School of Biomedical Science, University of Texas, Houston, Texas 77025

George A. Collier* (23) Department of Anthropology, Stanford University, Stanford, California 94305

Eric J. Devor* (179) Epidemiology Section, Cancer Research and Treatment Center, The University of New Mexico, Albuquerque, New Mexico 87131

Sue M. Dintelman* (95) Department of Biophysics and Computing, University of Utah; LDS Hospital, Salt Lake City, Utah 84143

Bennett Dyke* (1) Department of Anthropology, The Pennsylvania State University, University Park, Pennsylvania 16802

Margaret I. Gradie (139) Department of Anthropology, University of Massachusetts, Amherst, Massachusetts 01002

Eugene A. Hammel* (209) Department of Anthropology, University of California, Berkeley, California 94720

Alice B. Kasakoff* (115) Department of Anthropology, University of South Carolina, Columbia, South Carolina 29208

Paul W. Leslie* (167) Department of Anthropology, State University of New York, Binghamton, New York 13001

Chad K. McDaniel* (209) Department of Anthropology, University of Missouri, Columbia, Missouri 65201

A. Timothy Maness (95) University of Utah, Salt Lake City, Utah 84143

Richard S. Meindl* (235) Department of Anthropology, Kent State University, Kent, Ohio 44240

Warren T. Morrill* (1) Department of Anthropology, The Pennsylvania State University, University Park, Pennsylvania 16802

*Asterisk denotes participant at the symposium.

Susan L. Norton* (11, 41, 63) Center for Demographic and Population Genetics, Graduate School of Biomedical Science, University of Texas, Houston, Texas 77025

David L. Rossmann* (41, 71) Center for Demographic and Population Genetics, Graduate School of Biomedical Science, University of Texas, Houston, Texas 77025

Mark H. Skolnick (95) Department of Biophysics and Computing, University of Utah; LDS Hospital, Salt Lake City, Utah 84143

Alan C. Swedlund* (139) Department of Anthropology, University of Massachusetts, Amherst, Massachusetts 01002

Kenneth W. Wachter* (85, 209) Graduate Group in Demography, University of California, 2234 Piedmont Avenue, Berkeley, California 94720

Kenneth M. Weiss* (41, 63) Center for Demographic and Population Genetics, Graduate School of Biomedical Science, University of Texas, Houston, Texas 77025

Peter L. Workman* (179) Department of Anthropology, University of New Mexico, Albuquerque, New Mexico 87131

PREFACE

In another book on demography, the authors credit the goddess of chance as the inspiration for the volume. This book on demography had its origin in a distinctly different manner. It has been clear for some time that there is a small group of individuals working in what we call here "genealogical demography." These individuals are widely dispersed geographically, and (as will be apparent from the papers collected here) are seeking answers to remarkably divergent questions about human population structure. They are held together, however, by a strong common interest in at least three fundamental issues:

1. These studies take into account attributes of the population and of the individual. This is in marked contrast to traditional demographic approaches in which only aggregate measures are of concern; it is also unlike many social and genetic studies that often treat individual attributes (particularly kinship relationships) without reference to demographic structure.

2. Data are usually taken from separate birth, death, and marriage registries, entries from which must be "linked" into single records for each individual. These individual records must further be linked with one another to find genealogical relationships. Linking in both senses is an intricate process, and a particularly tedious one for populations that are large enough to yield statistically reliable results at the aggregate level. Thus, methodological considerations take on great importance to those engaged in these studies.

3. Because of the often fragmentary nature of the data (small sample sizes, shallow genealogical depth, incomplete or inconsistent vital registration, etc.), many workers have resorted to what can be described very broadly as a modeling approach. That is, these studies often depend heavily upon stochastic and statistical models, computer simulations, and very standard demographic devices such as life tables and stable populations. Implicit in these methods is the recognition that making inferences directly from limited data is a risky process, and that it is often more appropriate to fit models that incorporate information from sources that are more complete and better understood.

Communication between members of the group has been informal and irregular, a situation that has led to countless promises and suggestions that a meeting be held during which recent results could be reported and notes could be compared. A tentative proposal to hold such a gathering at the 48th Annual Meeting of the American Association of Physical Anthropologists in San Francisco during the first week of April 1979 met with approval. The association program chairman, William Pollitzer, graciously made last-minute adjustments to the schedule, allocating to us an entire day for a symposium. Anthony J. Boyce and Alan C. Swedlund served as moderators of the morning and afternoon sessions, respectively.

The symposium met the expectations of the participants in a number of ways. Methodological similarities were abundantly evident, but it was also clear that the wide variety of problems being attacked had led to many new approaches and techniques. More important, perhaps, was the realization that despite the divergent goals and training of those presenting papers, communication was easy, and there was a strong sense of mutual appreciation for the work being carried on by the other participants.

It is appropriate to point out that the interdisciplinary nature of genealogical demography makes it quite difficult to place its practitioners in neat academic categories. By traditional standards, the contributors to this volume are working in such diverse areas as ethnology, population genetics, historiography, epidemiology, historical demography, and the like. Nonetheless, most consider themselves anthropologists of one variety or another, or at least have a strong anthropological interest. We wish to emphasize the anthropological connection, and to suggest that studies such as are represented here have important implications for anthropology: We are all convinced that any understanding of social behavior, culture history, and human biology rests on the data we collect. We are also convinced that generalizations about these subjects can be made only with the detailed, systematic, and scientific analyses of the data exemplified by the papers in this volume.

Anthropological exhortations aside, however, we hope that readers in other fields will find the work presented here as useful and stimulating as it has been for us.

We wish to thank Christopher M. Lynch, Peter R. Sieger, Christine A. Wilson, and Stephen L. Whittington for their invaluable help in preparing this manuscript. Financial help in this undertaking was provided by the College of the Liberal Arts of The Pennsylvania State University.

ETHNOGRAPHIC AND DOCUMENTARY DEMOGRAPHY

Warren T. Morrill
and
Bennett Dyke

Traditional anthropology has largely ignored demographic facts in the course of ethnographic analysis. One occasionally reads statements about the size of the ethnic group as a whole, "... the total Nuer population is round about 300,000 ...". There are sometimes demographic summaries of a page or two, but these are usually based on a census done by the ethnographer during field work and are limited to that period of a year or two. But all too often ethnographies do not have even estimates of the size of the community being studied, let alone rates of fertility, mortality, completed family size or other basic demographic information. Part of this deficiency can be explained by the traditional anthropological interest in the social system as a whole rather than the statistical analysis of the population who operate the system. Equally important is the difficulty which anthropologists have experienced in setting up categories for description which will allow comparable analyses. The debate on residence categories (Bohannan, 1957; Fischer, 1958, 1959; Goodenough, 1956; Raulet, 1959) is an example of the difficulties of getting agreement on categories in such a way that separate analyses can proceed from the same data base.

In the past decade, however, the literature gives evidence of an increasing awareness of the importance of demography. This recent ethnographic concern with such things as population size, density, sex ratios, etc. carries with it some risks.

If contemporary ethnographers are interested in undertaking basic demographic description of the populations they study, a question must be asked about the kinds of demographic information which can be provided by traditional approaches. More explicitly, what are the capabilities and limitations of ethnographic fieldwork in providing reliable demographic data?

Most anthropologists are well aware that genealogies are not pedigrees. That is, genealogical information collected in the traditional way from informants in other cultures does not necessarily represent the biological facts of descent and relatedness. Informants engage in the activities known to anthropologists as telescoping, clipping, and patching in order to distort the biological facts so that they can be used to rationalize the social, political or economic needs and desires of the informant or the group. In spite of these inadequacies, we are often stuck with informants as the sole source of genealogical

data.   If this information is to be used as a basis for demographic analysis, it is clearly important to make estimates of
its reliability.

     Here we present a comparison of two approaches which we
have termed "ethnographic" and "documentary" and try to show the
kind of differences which result from the two approaches. By
"ethnographic" we mean more or less traditional anthropological
approaches using informants.   By "documentary" we mean the use
of written records of birth, marriage, and death. We have compared the data gathered using each technique and suggest some
inferences which may be made from the comparison.

     The population we have used in this comparison is the
French-speaking population of St. Thomas, Virgin Islands. All
of the members of the population were born on the island of St.
Barthelemy, F.W.I. or, if born on St. Thomas, are descended from
persons who migrated from St. Barth to St. Thomas.   The
French-speaking population of St. Thomas is divided into two
communities which live on different sides of the island and
which are largely endogamous. Here we discuss only the population of Northside, St. Thomas. General ethnographic and demographic descriptions of the population have been published, and
only a sketch is necessary here (see Morrill and Dyke, 1965;
Dyke, 1970).

     The Northside population are speakers of a Creole native
to St. Barth. Most read and write some standard French and
many are bilingual in French and English. Virtually all married
persons live in single family houses, perhaps as the result of a
preservation of a St. Barth cultural trait which requires a man
to provide a house for his bride.   The houses on St. Thomas are
scattered along the slopes of the north side of the island, and
there are no nucleated settlements.   The community is small
enough so that every adult knows, by reputation at least, every
other adult. The Northside population is connected by kinship
and proximity to the population of one of the two parishes of
St. Barth, and neighbors on St. Thomas are often descendants of
persons who had been neighbors on St. Barth.

     One of the first tasks undertaken in the fieldwork was a
household census. This proceeded by visiting every house identifiable as belonging to the population. In each house the
household head or, more commonly, wife of the household head,
was asked a series of questions about the residents of the
house:

     1.   Name all the persons living in the house with
          their age, sex and relationship to head of
          household.

     2.   Name the parents of the household head, siblings
          of these parents, and the spouse of each sibling

of parent. Name children of siblings of parents
with their age, residence and spouse name.

3. Same for wife of household head.

4. Name siblings of household head, giving their
sexes, ages, spouses, children, and residences.

5. Same for wife and non-resident children of
household head.

In sum, an attempt was made to construct a complete genealogy of three generations' depth and to the first degree of
collaterality for every person in the household. Questions were
also asked about infant mortality and fetal loss and about
migratory history of any individual in the genealogy. In order
to increase the probablity of a complete sample of the population, each informant was asked to identify all other houses in
the neighborhood occupied by members of the population.

In addition to the household survey, we used another traditional technique for gaining informaton. Four individuals
were used as key informants. One was an aged but still active
woman who appeared to be knowledgeable about the population. A
second was a middle-aged married woman whose husband was repeatedly identified by others as a leader in the community. The
third was another man repeatedly identified as a leader. The
fourth was a young man born on St. Thomas who acted as a guide
and who identified houses as being occupied by members of the
population. The first three of these informants were questioned
repeatedly and at length about details of the genealogies
acquired from others and about the identification of individuals
who sometimes confused us by having married repeatedly, who had
names similar to others, or who had nicknames which led us to
consider them two persons instead of one. From the information
collected in the household survey we constructed a genealogy of
the entire population and checked it with informants. In addition we were able, from the genealogy and the raw field notes
from the household survey, to compile a list of present and past
residents of the community with birth and death dates approximated or known. This list of the population over three generations we refer to as the "informants" list. Fieldwork was carried out over a 3-month period in the summer of 1962. During
the course of field trips over the next 3 years, we also compiled a list which we refer to as the "records" list. This was
compiled by linking all available civil and religious records of
birth, baptism, marriage, death and taxes between 1870 and 1962.

The discrepancies between the "records" list and the
"informants" list give an indication of the kinds of demographic
information likely to be missed with a purely ethnographic
approach. There are net discrepancies between these lists, and
there are some patterns in the discrepancies.

    The net deficiencies   are in most cases   intuitively obvi-
ous.   The total size of the population is less   in the "informants" list than in the "records" list.   A number of persons are
simply missed by the ethnographic method.   This is possibly a
result of our simply missing certain households, or it could be
the the result of the informant's failure of memory in listing
persons such as siblings of parents.   Since there   are individuals who are missed in the ethnographic survey, it follows that
the figures for distribution of age and sex in the population at
any given time in the demographic history are likely to be erro-
neous.   This can be seen in Figure 1.

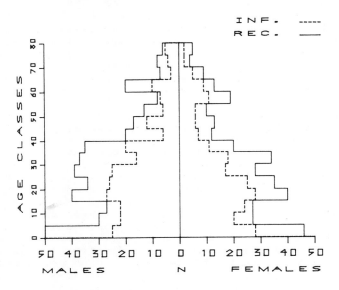

FIGURE 1.   Age-sex   structure   of   Northside in   1962   based   on
            record (outer   pyramid) and informant   sources (inner
            pyramid).

Quite clearly we missed an alarmingly large number of population
members (196 individuals, or about 25% of the total 1962 population of 740) in spite of a considerable effort to make a complete enumeration.

      As might be expected, the proportion of persons missing in
our field notes inceases as we move backwards in time and are
forced to rely increasingly upon the memories of a small number
of older informants.   This can be seen in Table 1. which shows
proportions of marriage-age individuals for whom at least one
member of various ancestor classes is known.   For each sex the
proportion calculated from record sources is given in the left
hand column, that from informant sources on the right.   (For

TABLE 1. Proportions of individuals for whom at least one of each ancestor class is known. Figures are for individuals of mating age (males 18 - 45, females 14 - 40) in the decade 1953 - 1962.

Ancestor	Males		Females	
Class	Rec.	Inf.	Rec.	Inf.
Parents	.986	.889	.969	.873
FF/MM	.779	.484	.813	.458
MF/MM	.797	.492	.917	.568
FFF/FFM	.318	.111	.378	.119
FMF/FMM	.291	.151	.318	.161
MFF/MFM	.470	.135	.563	.203
MMF/MMM	.525	.095	.641	.178
Numbers	217	126	192	118

example .986 of the males have one or both parents known according to the records, whereas informant sources show this proportion to be only .889.) These differences increase markedly with each ascending generation.

A technique common to many studies of genealogical demography consists in determining kin relationships between individuals by comparing the identity of their ancestors. For example, two persons are related as sibs if they have the same parents, or as mother's brother's child if MF of one is the same individual as FF of the other, etc. The "lineal truncation" of the genealogies shown in Table 1. has an important implication for the application of this technique.

Table 2 shows estimated proportions of female relatives of marriage-age males which can be determined from informant and from record sources. Proportions in this table are calculated by multiplying the appropriate entries in Table 1. For example, to find the average proportion of MBD's which can be determined from the genealogy based on our records, the proportion of males having known MF and/or MM (.797) is multiplied by the proportion of females having known FF and/or FM (.813), giving the figure .648 for MBD in Table 2, etc. Three cautions are required in interpreting the table: first, the entries represent _proportions_ of relatives who can be determined on the basis of a given mean genealogical depth, but they tell nothing about the _numbers_ of relatives who actually fill these genealogical positions. That is, although we can expect to find only .525 of male egos' DD's from the genealogy based on informant sources, the table gives no information about the mean number of DD's who may in fact have been present in the population. Second, we have treated all relationships as if they are full, even when they

TABLE 2. Proportions of female relatives of marriage-age males
which can be determined from genealogies based on
record (Rec.) and informant (Inf.) sources.

Relat-ionship	Source Rec.	Inf.	Relat-ionship	Source Rec.	Inf.
M	.986	.770	MBDD	.448	.089
Z	.955	.735	MZDD	.511	.087
D	.969	.636	FFBD	.258	.046
			FFZD	.29?	.059
FM	.765	.397	FMBD	.236	.062
MM	.788	.357	FMZD	.266	.080
			MFBD	.382	.057
FZ	.754	.398	MFZD	.431	.071
MZ	.772	.397	MMBD	.427	.041
			MMZD	.482	.052
BD	.801	.393			
ZD	.904	.483	FFBSD	.119	.013
			FFZSD	.101	.018
SD	.813	.407	FFBDD	.179	.015
DD	.917	.525	FFZDD	.204	.020
			FMBSD	.109	.018
FBD	.633	.215	FMZSD	.092	.024
FZD	.714	.266	FMBDD	.163	.020
MBD	.648	.218	FMZDD	.186	.027
MZD	.731	.273	MFBSD	.176	.014
			MFZSD	.149	.018
FBSD	.292	.055	MFBDD	.264	.020
FZSD	.247	.072	MFZDD	.301	.022
FBDD	.438	.088	MMBSD	.197	.011
FZDD	.499	.082	MMZSD	.167	.015
MBSD	.299	.058	MMBDD	.296	.015
MZSD	.253	.078	MMZDD	.337	.017

are traced through only a single member of an ancestral mated
pair; that is, no entry is made for half-sibs, half first cousins, etc. Third, the aggregate figures imply that all persons
have an equal proportion of known ancestry by class, which is
simply not the case.

Despite these cautions, it is clear from the table that
proportions of kin which can be determined from the genealogies
decrease rapidly with collateral distance.   We see an important
implication for the study of kinship in these figures: modest
lineal truncation of genealogies results in much greater loss of
information about collaterals.   This means that it is unlikely
that large numbers of otherwise unknown relationships will be
detected by matching for ancestry.   We feel, nevertheless, that
this technique is essential for purposes of validating relationships in the population as a whole.

As might be expected, comparison of the two sources of genealogical data reveals that discrepancies between lineal relatives known are magnified for the corresponding collateral relationships. For example, a weighted average of the last four rows of Table 1 (taking both sexes together) shows that informants provide knowledge of only about 33 percent of the great-grandparents known from our records (.143 /.435). But although the various second cousins may be determined by matching for the identities of these great-grandparents, comparison of the last sixteen pairs of entries in Table 2 indicates that informant sources give information on average for only about 9.5 percent of the second cousins detectable from our records (.018 /.190). There is thus no doubt that however low the figures in general, the record-based genealogy provides more information on kinship than does the one derived from informants. This has been important for us, not only in establishing general levels of kinship in the population, but also in identifying actual marriages between relatives. Informant genealogies revealed all three marriages of first cousins once removed, but only four of the eight first cousin and four of the six second cousin marriages found from our records.

The demographic consequences of these discrepancies can be seen in Figure 2, which shows population size over a 60-year period as constructed from the two sources. Our field notes report only 50% of the population found in the records for the year 1903. It is worth noting that the growth rate as calculated from field note sources is about 13% higher (.0283 per year) than that computed from the records (.0250 per year). We suggest that this is a general problem in demographic anthropology. That is, the failure to remember past population members will inflate growth rate estimates whenever informants are used as sources of demographic data.

We have made some attempt to understand why we found some individuals and missed others in our fieldwork, by comparing attributes of those who appeared in our "informants" list with those who did not. We have found the following differences:

1. As implied above, the likelihood of living persons being included in the "informants" list increases with year of birth. We also found that we missed significantly more individuals for whom no birth date at all was recorded. The reason for this lies in the fact that the earliest birth records available to us often give names and addresses of ego's parents, but not their ages. These parents were seldom known to informants, and were included in the "records" list but, of course, without birth dates.

2. Individuals who had died before 1962 were more likely to be included in the "informants" list the more recent the birth date. As with births, significantly more individuals were missed for whom no death date was recorded.

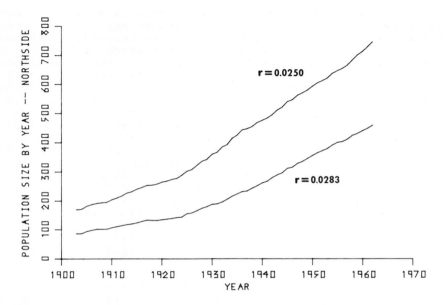

FIGURE 2.   Northside population size 1903 - 1962 based on record
            (upper curve) and informant sources (lower curve).

3.   Ego is more likely to have been included in our "informants"
     list if he or she has had children. In one way this is
     expected since the more children an individual has the more
     possible informants there are to report his existence. It
     is also possible that the parent of a large family may enjoy
     reputational prominence which will lead non-related persons
     to report him as a member of the community. There is, how-
     ever, a peculiarity in this deficiency. We have found that
     the probability of an Ego appearing in the "informants" list
     does not increase proportionally with the number of children
     he or she has had.

4.   Ego is more likely to have been included in our "informants"
     list if he or she has sibs, although _number_ of sibs does not
     affect this likelihood.

5.   We found no significant difference in distribution of resi-
     dences among those included in our "informants" list and
     those who were not. This of course tells us little about
     differences between the two groups, but it does lead us to
     believe that we sampled the population adequately with
     respect to residence, and that the deficiencies we have
     found are not simply the result of missing geographical sec-
     tions of the community.

Comparison of demographic data derived from a household survey conducted by an ethnographer with data derived from written records does not suggest that ethnography is useless. After all, in most anthropological populations there are no written records which would allow construction of a "records" list. It is quite likely, however, that patterned deficiencies will be present if this technique is used exclusively. These deficiencies suggest that ethnographers exercise some caution in generalizing about size, sex ratios, age, and rates of growth for populations for which only ethnographic evidence is available.

ACKNOWLEDGMENTS

Fieldwork was supported by NIMH Grant M-6843(A). We thank Jean W. MacCluer for her comments on the manuscript.

REFERENCES

Bohannan, P. 1957. An alternate residence classification. Amer. Anthropolgist 59: 126-131.

Dyke, B. 1970. La population de Northside dans l'ile Saint-Thomas. Population 25: 1197-1204.

Fischer, J.L. 1958. The classification of residence in censuses. Amer. Anthropologist 60: 508-517.

Fischer, J.L. 1959. Reply to Raulet. Amer. Anthropologist 61: 679-681.

Goodenough, W.H. 1956. Residence rules. Southwest Jour. Anthr. 12: 22.

Goodenough, W.H. 1964. "Introduction: Explorations in Cultural Anthropology". New York: McGraw-Hill.

Morrill, W.T. and B. Dyke 1965. A French community on St. Thomas. Caribbean Studies 5: 3-11.

Raulet, H.M. 1959. A note on Fischer's residence typology. Amer. Anthropologist 61: 108-112.

THE VITAL QUESTION: ARE RECONSTITUTED FAMILIES REPRESENTATIVE OF THE GENERAL POPULATION?

Susan L. Norton

Studies based on genealogies, pedigrees, or other family units assembled from vital records are becoming increasingly popular in fields as diverse as social history and genetic epidemiology. Generally speaking, the aim is to characterize numerically the population at some past time. The term "population," however, immediately raises one of the methodological issues that face such studies. In demographic and genetic work we are accustomed to defining a population as the group of people living in a given place at a given time. For example, the census, the classic demographic instrument, specifically enumerates the inhabitants of a locality on a particular day. In work using families reconstructed from vital records, including any kind of genealogy, reference to the population is much less unambiguous; it may be difficult to define clearly the group of people to whom the records relate. There are several ways in which genealogical studies may not yield accurate demographic statistics for the population they claim to be studying. For various technical reasons there may be problems of bias or error in the calculation of rates. For example, it may be difficult to determine the number of women at risk of having a child. Moreover, the entire vital registration system, at least as it is represented in a collection of linked records such as we are discussing, may not truly represent the population we assume it to cover. I will deal largely with this second source of error in the inference of population statistics from studies using linked vital records.

Studies based on vital events are indicative of the general population only insofar as the persons in that population make themselves known to the registration system. If vital events occur and are not registered, the persons involved will not be fully known to the study. Also, persons are noted only at the time of an event -- birth or baptism, marriage, death or burial. For all the years in between these dates -- and there are many in most person's lives, the vital registration system is silent. The census, on the other hand, is more aggressive -- not waiting for people to make themselves known by some demographic feat, but actively seeking them out, at a given time. If we assume the census encompasses the true "population," a comparison of census and vital registration results will shed light on the biases, if any, of the vital registration study. Often, of course, vital registration studies such as family reconstitution are undertaken precisely to provide demographic information when censuses are absent, so such comparisons are not usually made.

The state of Massachusetts provides a good opportunity for these studies. A civil vital registration system was established in 1639, almost at the colony's founding, and has continued in existence to the present day. Using the classic techniques of family reconstitution (Fleury and Henry, 1965) in a semi-automated way (cf. Rossmann, this volume), I have linked births, marriages, and deaths from the three contiguous towns of Boxford, Topsfield, and Wenham into family units. The records span the period from the founding of the towns in the seventeenth century to 1850. The census records used here are those of the federal government, which began a decennial enumeration in 1790. For seven censuses, covering the sixty years from 1790 through 1850, we can compare the population covered by the vital registration system, as revealed in the family reconstitution study, and that covered by the census. We will assume that the census covered virtually the entire population of the towns. While this claim cannot be rigorously proven, it is buttressed by an analysis revealing a reasonable age-sex structure for the towns over these censuses (although there is the possibility of underenumeration of children), and a notable lack of age-heaping in the 1850 census (Norton, 1979). The latter particularly suggests a population that was statistically sophisticated, which we would expect from the traditions of literacy and vital registration.

I have taken an extremely simple-minded approach to the study of this population. For the censuses from 1790 through 1840, the family was the unit of enumeration. A census entry consisted of the name of the family head and simple demographic information about the family as a whole. Early censuses contain only gross age divisions of the population and include almost no socioeconomic data. Information was reported by classes, such as the number of females in the family aged 16 to 25 or the number of males engaged in agriculture. Since the family is also the unit of reconstitution work, I have attempted to link each family listed on the nominal, manuscript census to the appropriate family reconstituted from the vital records. The name of the head of the family was the chief piece of identifying information; numbers and ages of family members would also be considered. Each census family can then be regarded as "linked" or "not linked," that is, included or not included as a family in the vital registration study. For 1850, individuals are enumerated and specific ages and occupations are given. Family membership is still shown, however, and for consistency I have continued for the most part to use the family unit. The method of analysis is to compare the census families linked and unlinked to the family reconstitution study, on characteristics described by the census. The census then is the basic source of information, and the vital registration is included solely as a dichotomy. A family enumerated in the census is either included or not included in the reconstitution study. In this way we can investigate the extent to which families included in a reconstitution study are systematically different from families in the

general population. I am not measuring directly any bias in
variables calculated from the reconstitution study, but am
determining the general characteristics of the families in the
reconstitution study as opposed to all families, as they are
described by the census. In this way we have an idea of the
type and extent of bias, if any, that may be present in a study
based solely on registration. We would like, of course, for
this bias to be relatively small, so that we can with reasonable
confidence make inferences from the registration study to the
entire population.

     The three towns considered here were all fairly small dur-
ing this period. Boxford's population in 1790 was 919, Topsfield's was 768 and Wenham's was only 492. By 1850, all three
towns had grown. Boxford increased slightly to 981, while Topsfield grew to 1,168 and Wenham to 973. Much of the remarkable
growth of Wenham occurred in the 1840's. The family reconstitution file consists of more than 4,400 nuclear families. Each
marriage record begins a family record, and births of children
and deaths of children and parents are added to this basic
record. A family record can also be established, according to
Henry, when a group of siblings ˙ can be identified without the
parents' marriage record. I have in my work established such
family records, but have not used them in this analysis. Any
procedure basing family records on the births of children, even
if a family record were established for each birth not linked to
a marriage, would bias the reconstitution study toward high fertility. In this study, then, I have used only family records
defined by a marriage.

     In considering links to the reconstructed genealogies, I
am counting only families headed by males. For all three towns
over all censuses, 378 of 3,152 families (11.99%) were headed by
women. Many of these appear to be widows. It is difficult to
make positive identification of many of these women in the
family reconstitution file; 59.52% of the female heads are
unlinked to the file. The ambiguity of women's names when marital status is unknown poses a particular problem. Throughout
this paper, then, we consider only male-headed families, which
are some 88% of the total. Of these, over all towns and censuses, 71.30% are linked to the reconstructed genealogy (see
Table 1). The percentage linked rises consistently from less
than 60% in the 1790 census to nearly 80% in the 1840 census,
then falls to 73% in the 1850 census. The rising percentage of
links, which occurs in all three towns individually as well as
in the totals, may represent an improvement of coverage in the
vital registration system or decreasing immigration to the
towns. The slight fall for the combined group in 1850 is particularly due to fewer links for Wenham (66%), which experienced
very rapid growth due to in-migration for the decade 1840-1850.
More detailed census analysis has shown that many of these
migrants were young men, and that many came from other states.
Most of these migrants would not be immediately represented in

TABLE 1. Percentage of census families linked to families
          reconstituted from vital records. N in each case is
          the number of census families headed by males.

	Boxford	Topsfield	Wenham	Total
1790				
%	51.47	70.40	50.00	58.57
N	136	125	60	321
1800				
%	58.91	76.69	53.33	64.69
N	129	133	75	337
1810				
%	62.69	78.36	67.50	69.83
N	134	134	80	348
1820				
%	69.78	74.31	74.42	72.63
N	139	144	86	369
1830				
%	71.53	77.46	76.00	74.87
N	144	142	100	386
1840				
%	77.91	80.10	80.00	79.34
N	163	196	125	484
1850				
%	73.05	79.33	65.58	73.35
N	167	208	154	529
Total				
%	67.09	77.08	68.38	71.30
N	1012	1082	680	2774

the vital registration system. Note that Topsfield in general
has the highest percentage of linked families; this is presumably because, as other census studies have shown, Topsfield has,
of the three towns, the lowest rate of immigration (Norton,
1979).

     We wish to establish whether the approximately 29% of the
families represented in the census but not in the vital records
are different in any important way from those seen in the vital
records.   In other words, would the families from the vital
records alone give a misleading picture of the population of the
town? In each case we will use a conservative test, comparing
linked and unlinked families. Since the linked are in fact some
70% of the general population, a comparison between linked and
unlinked overstates the difference between the linked families
and the general population. (The magnitude of the difference
between the values of a universe and one of two subsets of it
must be less than the magnitude of the difference between the
subsets).

TABLE 2.   Sizes of linked (L)   and unlinked (U) families, 1790-1850.

	Boxford		Topsfield		Wenham		Total	
	(L)	(U)	(L)	(U)	(L)	(U)	(L)	(U)
1790								
Mean	6.18	6.00	5.72	4.86	5.65	5.93	5.88	5.66
Number	74	62	89	36	31	29	194	127
Variance	5.96	9.38	5.59	5.89	3.84	6.64	5.45	7.91
1800								
Mean	6.32	5.73	5.50	5.40	4.76	5.67	5.66	5.62
Number	81	48	103	30	42	33	226	111
Variance	7.90	4.24	7.08	5.56	4.19	5.23	7.10	4.82
1810								
Mean	6.53	5.71	5.48	5.18	6.02	5.65	5.97	5.55
Number	86	48	106	28	54	26	246	102
Variance	6.51	6.81	5.91	5.71	5.68	7.60	6.24	6.63
1820								
Mean	6.26*	4.95	5.61	4.87	5.73	5.65	5.87*	5.08
Number	100	39	113	31	66	20	279	90
Variance	6.58	5.68	4.44	5.72	6.36	8.77	5.70	6.32
1830								
Mean	6.03*	4.82	6.16	6.60	5.44*	4.48	5.93*	5.27
Number	109	34	117	25	77	23	303	82
Variance	5.82	4.15	10.81	8.58	6.01	2.26	7.83	5.66
1840								
Mean	5.66*	4.44	5.01	4.79	5.05	4.09	5.24*	4.46
Number	136	27	167	28	102	23	405	78
Variance	5.86	4.18	6.97	6.10	5.37	4.81	6.26	5.01
1850								
Mean	5.07*	4.19	4.87	4.31	5.70*	4.53	5.14*	4.37
Number	135	32	179	29	103	51	417	112
Variance	5.09	4.22	5.17	4.79	6.94	4.41	5.67	4.40

Values separated by an asterisk (*) are significantly different, with p values less than 0.05.

Let us consider first the simplest and most important demographic variable, size of family.   In the census use, the definition of a family depends on living arrangements rather than on biological criteria. However, any variance between census-defined families and biological ones would presumably apply equally to the linked and unlinked groups.   In general, the families in the genealogy are somewhat larger than the unlinked ones.   The difference in family size reaches significance when all three towns are combined for each of the census years 1820, 1830, 1840 and 1850; for Boxford in 1820, 1830, 1840, and 1850, and for Wenham in 1830 and 1850 (see Table 2). The difference in family size is generally less than one person, or 15% to 20% of total family size.

TABLE 3. Number of children under 10 for linked (L) and
          unlinked (U) families 1800-1850.

	Boxford		Topsfield		Wenham		Total	
	(L)	(U)	(L)	(U)	(L)	(U)	(L)	(U)
1800								
Mean	1.78*	1.08	1.35	1.07	1.31	1.45	1.50	1.19
Number	81	48	103	30	42	33	226	111
Variance	2.80	1.78	1.80	2.34	1.93	1.82	2.21	1.94
1810								
Mean	1.74	1.38	1.51	1.39	1.98*	1.19	1.70*	1.33
Number	86	48	106	28	54	26	246	102
Variance	2.62	2.54	1.91	1.88	2.28	2.08	2.25	2.20
1820								
Mean	1.41*	0.74	1.35	1.16	1.45	1.05	1.40*	0.96
Number	100	39	113	31	66	20	279	90
Variance	2.41	1.41	2.14	1.47	1.64	1.73	2.10	1.50
1830								
Mean	1.29*	0.76	1.56	1.36	1.29	1.00	1.40*	1.01
Number	109	34	117	25	77	23	303	82
Variance	2.23	1.22	2.83	2.66	1.76	1.00	2.35	1.62
1840								
Mean	1.36*	0.63	1.12	1.39	1.15	0.91	1.21	0.99
Number	136	27	167	28	102	23	405	78
Variance	2.26	0.86	1.61	1.95	1.57	1.08	1.82	1.39
1850								
Mean	1.04	0.69	1.05	1.07	1.42*	0.98	1.14	0.92
Number	135	32	179	29	103	51	417	112
Variance	1.62	1.00	1.69	1.21	2.05	1.02	1.77	1.07
1850-own children								
Mean	0.97*	0.53	0.95	1.07	1.25	0.94	1.03	0.86
Number	135	32	179	29	103	51	417	112
Variance	1.63	0.97	1.62	1.21	1.92	1.06	1.70	1.10

Values separated by an   asterisk (*) are significantly
different, with p values less than 0.05.

     Insofar as family size is biological, then, the study from
vital records might overestimate the fertility of the total
population. We may be particularly interested in the extent of
this bias, since the study of fertility is one of the chief purposes of reconstitution work.   The possibility of bias can be
examined further by looking only at the number of children in

the linked and unlinked families. Again, we can deal only with
children residing with the family, rather than with the specific
children of the head of the family. The censuses of 1800, 1810
and 1820 used enumeration categories of 0-10 and 10-16 for children; in 1830 and 1840 the number of children was given in
five-year age categories, 0-5,etc. In 1850, precise ages were
given. I have used simply the number of children under ten as
the basis of comparison between linked and unlinked families.
Children between ten and sixteen would be less likely to be
residing at home, so the results would be less directly indicative of fertility. The figures are given in Table 3. In several cases, the linked families did have significantly more
children than the unlinked: for all three towns combined for
1810 to 1830, for Boxford in 1800, 1820, 1830 and 1840, and for
Wenham in 1810 and 1850. For 1850, individuals are listed by
name, but relationship to the head of the family is not given.
We can make simple assumptions about family relationships based
on names and ages. For example, in a family listing Thomas
Dodge, aged 25; Sarah Dodge, aged 22; Matilda Dodge, aged 4 and
John Dodge, aged 2, Matilda and John appear to be the children
of Thomas and Sarah. Using such asumptions, we can calculate
the number of "own children" in each family as distinguished
from the total number of children in residence with the family.
These results are also given in Table 3. Only in Boxford is the
number of own children in linked families significantly greater
than in unlinked ones.

      In general then, we can conclude that linked families are
usually somewhat larger than those not included in the vital
registration study. Part of the variation may be due to differing numbers of children, but living arrangements also appear to
play a role. The importance of differences in family size and
number of children depends on their magnitude; it is difficult
to make generalizations from this study, since, for the individual towns, the relatively small numbers mean that only large
differences will be statistically significant. Differences of
more than 50% in the number of children under ten are not unusual among those cases where a significant difference exists at
all. In many cases, however, no such significant difference is
found. The results suggest that caution should be used when
reconstitution studies are interpreted; biases in fertility
studies are certainly possible. Remember, however, that we are
using a conservative test comparing linked and unlinked families. If we assume as a worst-case analysis that the fertility
of the unlinked families is 50% less than that of the linked,
and that 70% of the population is linked, then the true fertility of the total population would be 15% less than the fertility
of the linked families. The difference in general between the
linked and unlinked families seems to be far less than than 50%, so
the corresponding difference between linked families and the
general population would be less than 15%.

TABLE 4. Number of linked (L) and unlinked (U) families with
          members in various occupations (see text for explana-
          tion).

	Boxford		Topsfield		Wenham		Total	
	(L)	(U)	(L)	(U)	(L)	(U)	(L)	(U)
1820								
Agriculture	57	16	61	21	40	9	158	46
Manufacturing	26	9	37	8	12	4	75	21
Other	5	0	9	0	1	1	15	1
Total	88	25	107	29	53	14	248	68
1840								
Agriculture	67	10	74	13	50	8	191	31
Manufacturing	39	10	54	7	40	10	133	27
Other	28	6	28	8	9	5	65	19
Total	134	26	156	28	99	23	389	77
1850								
Farmer	81	14	71	9	32	3	184	26
Shoemaker	31	11	65	8	45	21	141	40
Other	22	7	37	11	26	27	85	45
Total	134	32	173	28	103	51	410	111

Other measurements on which we can compare families linked
and not linked to the vital registration system are not directly
demographic, but can nevertheless contribute to our investiga-
tion. The only real indication of socioeconomic status in the
early censuses was a report of the employment of male family
members using crude occupational groupings for 1820 and 1840.
In 1850, specific occupations were recorded. In all three towns
the work was primarily agricultural throughout this period,
although shoemaking was also a major employment. The shoemaking
was done in the home or in small shops; this was before the time
of modern factory work in this trade (cf. Dawley, 1976). We
would expect that farmers, being more closely tied to the land
and hence more sedentary than other workers, would be more
likely than others to be represented in the vital registration
study, and this is indeed the case. Because of the way the census was reported, we must classify families rather than individuals as being in an employment class. If all the males in a
family, for example, are employed in agriculture, the family is
so counted in Table 4. Families in which men are reported in
more than one occupational grouping are included in the
"other" category. For 1850, the occupation of the head of the
family is taken. Using a Chi-squared test for association in
the table, statistical significance is found only for Wenham and
for all three towns combined in 1850. There is an excess of
farmers in the vital registration group. To the extent that

their families are different from the rest of the population,
the vital records study might be unrepresentative. Since most
of the population is linked, however, any bias would be quite
small. Moreover, no significant association between link status
and occupation was found in 1820 or in 1840.

A final point of comparison is the persistence of families
over several censuses. If the Nathaniel Dyer family appeared in
the 1800 census and again in the 1810 census, it can be said to
have persisted from one census to the next. If it also appeared
in the 1820 census, we can assume that it remained for twenty
years. In making claims that a family continued from census to
census there are some problems of identification, since the only
name is that of the head of the family. In many cases several
families will be headed by persons of the same name; often
these men will be fathers and sons, or cousins. The problem is
particularly acute for Wenham, where many persons bore the surname Dodge. One must attempt to age the family members in order
to identify the family from one census to the next. This is
particularly awkward given the crude age groupings of the early
censuses.

Persistence in the census is, of course, indication that
the family was in town for a prolonged period. We might hypothesize that many families not in the vital records but present
in the census were transient. Census persistence rates for
linked and unlinked families throw light on this issue. Over-
whelmingly we find that families who appear in the vital records
are more likely to persist to the next census than families who
do not. (See Table 5, and Figures 1 and 2). The difference
reaches statistical significance in many cases, especially for
the later censuses. This confirms our intuition. Differences
between the linked and unlinked over two censuses are especially
marked. Note that a fairly constant proportion of the linked
families remains for either one or two subsequent censuses,
while the persistence rates for the unlinked families generally
decline over the period. We know from Table 1 that the proportion of census families linked to the vital registration study
rises over time. The persistence rates indicate that those
unlinked are increasingly transient. The registration study
seems to be omitting fewer and fewer families who stayed in town
for more than ten or twenty years, and thus is becoming increasingly representative of at least the more stable part of the
population. However, a surprising number of families unlinked
to the vital registration system persist to the next census or
even for two censuses. These are families who are present in
the town for at least a decade or two without becoming identified in the family reconstitution file. Since a family is
established in this file through a marriage, migrant families
would often not be included. Such families, we must emphasize,
need not be very transient to be excluded. The presence of such
families weighs heavily in the problems of constructing the base
population at risk of any given vital event, in the classical
family reconstitution analyses (cf. Henry, 1970).

TABLE 5. Census persistence. Numbers (N) indicate numbers of linked (L) and unlinked (U) families which appear in the first and subsequent censuses of each set. Percentages are calculated from the first census in each set; an asterisk (*) indicates an association at the 5% level (see text for explanation).

Census	Boxford (L) N	%	Boxford (U) N	%	Topsfield (L) N	%	Topsfield (U) N	%	Wenham (L) N	%	Wenham (U) N	%	Total (L) N	%	Total (U) N	%
1790	74		62		89		36		31		29		194		127	
1800	49	66.2	37	59.7	72	80.9	21	58.3*	19	61.3	21	72.4	140	72.2	79	62.2
1810	35	47.3	21	33.9*	48	53.9	13	36.1	10	32.3	12	41.4	93	47.9	46	36.2*
1800	81		48		103		30		42		33		226		111	
1810	51	63.0	25	52.1	66	64.1	16	53.3	29	69.1	16	48.5	146	64.6	57	51.4*
1820	36	44.4	17	35.4	39	37.9	8	26.7	22	52.4	9	27.3*	97	42.9	34	30.6*
1810	86		48		106		28		54		26		246		102	
1820	53	61.6	23	47.9*	68	64.2	13	46.4	32	59.3	11	42.3	153	62.2	47	46.1*
1830	39	45.4	9	18.8*	48	45.3	7	25.0	24	44.4	5	19.2*	111	45.1	21	20.6*
1820	100		39		113		31		66		20		279		90	
1830	66	66.7	17	43.6*	68	60.2	9	29.0*	41	62.1	6	30.0*	175	62.7	32	35.6*
1840	45	45.0	5	12.8*	48	42.5	5	16.1*	34	51.5	3	15.0*	127	45.5	13	14.4*
1830	109		34		117		25		77		23		303		82	
1840	77	70.6	8	23.5*	77	65.8	8	32.0*	55	71.4	4	17.4*	209	69.0	20	24.4*
1850	49	45.0	3	8.8*	61	52.1	2	8.0*	34	44.2	1	4.4*	144	47.5	6	7.3*
1840	136		27		167		28		102		23		405		78	
1850	87	64.0	8	29.6*	119	71.3	6	21.4*	64	62.8	7	30.4*	270	66.7	21	26.9*

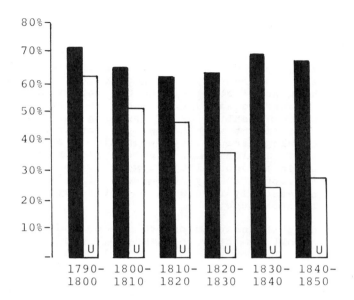

FIGURE 1.   Rates of persistence to next census for Boxford,
            Topsfield and Wenham combined, 1790-1840.   Based on
            linked (L) and unlinked (U) records.

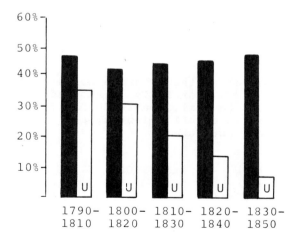

FIGURE 2.   Rates of persistence to   second subsequent census for
            Boxford, Topsfield and   Wenham combined, 1790-1840.
            Based on linked (L) and unlinked (U) records.

In general, I think these results are encouraging for work involving linked vital records. The families included tend to be somewhat larger, more agricultural and less transient than those families not included in the reconstitution; this is what we would have expected intuitively. These biases, however, do not appear to be very large. While they are at times statistically significant, they may well not be historically or genetically significant, at least in comparison to the ignorance we would face without such studies. On the other hand, the existence of such biases does suggest that we should be wary of overinterpreting our results, or of pushing our data beyond its useful limits. We might wish to be particularly cautious, for example, in comparing various socioeconomic classes, where differential rates of inclusion in the reconstitution study would be probable. As in all quantitative work, we must remember that even though the computer may crank out five decimal places, these are not necessarily five significant digits, either mathematically, or in substance.

In extending the conclusions of this study to other work, we should note that in these populations, and in Massachusetts as a whole, registration was well established. In situations where registration was less than adequate, discrepancies between the real and the studied populations may well be more pronounced. On the other hand, the mobility of this population is considerable, and might have been expected to compromise the representativeness of the reconstituted families. This does appear to have happened, but to a limited extent. We may draw some hope from this study that our studies involving linked records do in fact represent reasonably well the populations they purport to cover.

ACKNOWLEDGMENTS

This work was completed with the assistance of the following, whose support is gratefully acknowledged: a Fellowship from The Population Council, grant GM-19513 from the National Institute of General Medical Sciences, and grant CA-19311 from the National Cancer Institute.

REFERENCES

Dawley, A. 1976. "Class and Community: The Industrial Revolution in Lynn". Cambridge: Harvard University Press.
Fleury, M. and L. Henry 1965. "Nouveau manuel de depouillement et d'exploitation de l'etat civil ancien". Paris: L'Institut National d'Etudes Demographiques.
Henry, L. 1970. "Manuel de demographie historique". Geneva: Librairie Droz.
Norton, S.L. 1979. Unpublished observations.

THE KINPROGRAM: ACCOMPLISHMENTS AND PROSPECTS

George A. Collier

This is a description of the KINPROGRAM, a package of computer programs for the processing of genealogical censuses, such as those utilized by anthropologists, historians and demographers for the diachronic study of kinship, the family, human settlements and their continuous changes through time and space. The KINPROGRAM is not totally new. I have already developed and tested several major portions of the package having to do with kinship and demography. Yet, important segments having to do with kinship and settlement have still to be designed, coded and tested to enable full realization of the package's potential. However, the package as it presently exists may be of use to others seeking to process such data or to develop programs of their own for similar purposes. I wish, therefore, to make the KINPROGRAM available to others even while I continue to develop it in forthcoming years.

The KINPROGRAM processes genealogical census data of the kind anthropologists bring back from the field and historical demographers from the archive. Such data tie individuals to one another in a genealogical web, linking those who share households and allowing one to trace the changes in genealogical and household composition brought about by births, deaths, marriages, divorces, separations, arrivals, departures -- in short, by all those features ordinarily associated with the domestic cycle. Presently the KINPROGRAM compiles genealogies, traces kin relationships, reconstructs ancestry and summarizes demographic variables automatically for study populations of a size up to the several thousands, ordinarily too cumbersome to subject to similar analysis by hand.

The KINPROGRAM is no more, fundamentally, than a data moving program with some descriptive capabilities. The user supplies the program with a census in which genealogical relations, dates of vital events and residence histories are coded in convenient and simplified ways. The program does the work of interpreting the census and moving its data about in a manner that permits automatic construction of graphic displays useful in the analysis of the corpus.

In processing, the census corpus is first submitted to KININPT which reads the coded census material, checks for errors and converts the data into a standardized format that is saved on a disk storage file. The second step is to submit this file to TREES, which constructs genealogies of unilineal or bilateral descent while cross-referencing individuals to the genealogical

23

positions they hold in trees of which they are members. Other
existing modules which manipulate the disk-stored census file
are ANCES (to construct individuals' trees of ancestry), SEARCH
(to enable study of the census with regard to genealogical relations connecting individuals) and DEMOG (which builds population
pyramids and conventional measures of fertility and mortality
for the population over the span of time during which it was
censused.   I shall describe each of the existing modules in
turn.

KININPT

    Being the first step in KINPROGRAM processing, KININPT
receives the census as fixed-format data punched onto cards,
diagnoses the data for inadvertent omissions and inconsistencies, prints out information on each member of the census,
standardizes the census in a manner commensurate with other
modules and stores it in a disk file.

    KININPT has been designed to recognize many conventions in
the coding of census materials that greatly simplify preparation
into the fixed-format punch cards (or card images) required as
input for a census. The input deck supplies information on the
identity of individuals, their parentage, sex, dates of birth
and death, residence histories and marriages.

    Individuals in the census must be identified uniquely by
means of a 4-character code that the user may construct in any
convenient and consistent manner. The association of each code
name to its corresponding census member is facilitated by supplying the individual with an abbreviated name. Every individual should be identified and coded as a census member whose
existence indicates genealogical or residential connection
between other census members.

    Genealogical relations are made known to KININPT in part
by the indication of each individual's parentage. For example,
siblings can be recognized as such because they share at least
one parent. KININPT expects for each individual the designation
of father and mother through entry of their 4-character identifiers. If either parent is unknown, the corresponding input
field is simply left blank.   The relationship identified here
usually will be that of biological parentage, although sociological parentage can be substituted when appropriate.   Note that
parentage in no way implies marriage to the KINPROGRAM; marriage
is indicated by separate input (see below). Individuals' sex is
indicated as "M" or "F" in the input.

    KININPT expects each individual's date of birth and of
death if he is not living at the time of census collection.
These may be specified as 4-digit numbers. However, KININPT
also accepts dates written as values added to or subtracted from
letters that may serve as useful temporal anchoring points in

census collection. "D" stands for an individual's date of
death, "B" stands for his date of birth and "C" stands for the
date of census collection. The user can designate other letters
to correspond to specific years, for example "F" for the 1918
flu pandemic. Then, for example, if the birth date of an individual born 17 years before census collection is designated
"C-17", his death at age 5 could be written "B+5". The birth
and death of a person aged 15 at the time of the flu pandemic
dying in the epidemic might be written "F-15" and "F"
respectively.

A residence history is also supplied for each individual
if desired, consisting of a string of alternative dates and
locations marking his move from place to place. Locations are
4-character names or numbers corresponding to the lowest level
units for which spatial analysis will be relevant, usually house
sites. Thus a string "B,HS02,1917,HS03,1925,HS52,D" could be
the complete designation of residence history of an individual
we will call "John" for illustrative purposes, and the string
indicates that he was born into house HS02, that he moved to
HS03 in 1917 and to HS52 in 1925, where he lived until death.
Any of the conventions simplifying the construction of birth and
death dates can be used to write dates in a residence history.
KININPT also accomodates coding especially useful in writing
residence histories of persons moving together from one place to
another over long periods of time, usually in families. The
residence history of only one member of such a group need be
specified, and others can be designated as living "WITH" him
during portions of their life. In the example developed above,
for instance, the residence history of a child born in 1916 and
living with "John" until 1940, then moving to HS53 where he
lives at the time of censusing may be written "B,WITH John,1940,
HS53,C".

Finally, KININPT makes provision for inclusion of a field
of data for each individual that is of particular interest to
the user. Although this field is not analyzed by the KINPRO-
GRAM, it will be incorporated in output. It may be used to
carry any sort of socio-economic variable into the analysis of
kinship.

KININPT distinguishes marriage (a social bond) from the
sexual unions implied by parentage and thus requires separate
designation of marriages. Each marital dyad is designated by
the 4-character identifiers of the partners and by dates of the
marriage's inception and (if relevant) termination. There is no
bar to an individual being partner in any number of simultaneous
marriages.

As KININPT reads data on individuals and marriages, it
checks for errors and inconsistencies such as the use of the
same identifier for more than one census member, the lack of
correspondence between sex and parental role, illogical specifi-

cation of birth, death and marriage dates or of residence histories, and so forth. The module is user-oriented in its extensive utilization of error messages and diagnostics for defects
in the input which must be corrected before further processing
may be undertaken.

        When the census corpus has been found free of error,
KININPT creates data structures to tie together census members
is a web of kinship. The data structures, for instance, use one
system of pointers to link together an individual's successive
marriages, and another system to link together in order of birth
within sibling sets the offspring of an individual, and so
forth. Although initially time consuming, the construction of
this web of kinship need not be repeated by other KINPROGRAM
modules because the system of pointers is stored in a disk file
accessed by other modules.

TREES
‾‾‾‾‾
        TREES constructs genealogical trees of descent from the
data structures of a census corpus processed by KININPT. Ordinarily, TREES is the first module to be run after KININPT
because it generates cross-reference numbers for individuals
which are stored back in the data structures on disk, thus giving information to other modules about the connection of
individuals into trees of genealogical descent.

        TREES traces descent patrilineally, matrilineally or bila-
terally at the option of the user. The logic of constructing a
tree of patrilineal descent is related to the logic of tracing
unilineal ancestry. Every census member has just one father, be
he real or unknown. Patrilineal ancestry for a given individual
leads through a determinate chain of real fathers until an
unknown father is encountered.   Every census member, therefore,
is connected to a distinct, single unknown patrilineal ancestor
by a chain of ascent through known fathers.   Consequently, if
descent is traced patrilineally from each unknown father only
through males, then each census member must be included in
exactly one tree of patrilineal descent. Exactly parallel logic
corresponds to the construction of trees of matrilineal descent.

        TREES includes the algorithm for tracing descent in this
manner and for displaying trees of descent with graphics that
approximate those conventionally used (see Figure 1).

        A significant capability of TREES is its ability to con-
struct trees of descent for a population that take into account
only events of birth, death and marriage transpiring before a
date specified by the user. Thus, the same data structure may
be interpreted by TREES to depict genealogical relations between
members of a census as they existed in 1920, then in 1930, then
in 1940 and so on, thereby highlighting the processes of kinship
as they evolved from one decade to the next.

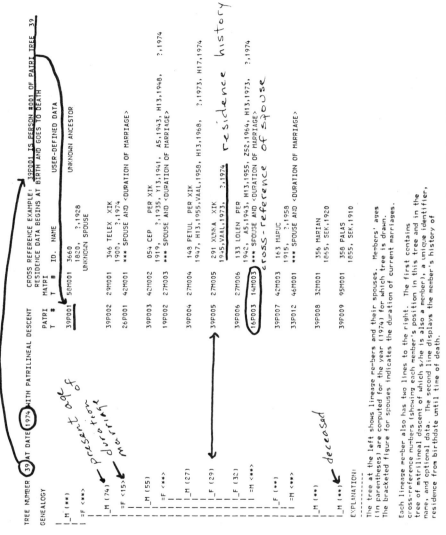

FIGURE 1.   Tree of patrilineal descent traced by TREES.

ANCES

ANCES has the simple function of displaying the ancestry of any given individual or set of individuals back through a maximum of six generations. ANCES thus complements the descent-tracing capabilities of TREES. An example of output created by ANCES is shown and explained in Figures 2 and 3.

SEARCH

SEARCH is the module which searches the genealogical corpus according to a user-defined algebraic expression of a kin relation, to discover individuals falling at a given date into that relation to a census member named in a list.

An algebraic system of notation for kinship relations was introduced to anthropology by Romney and D'Andrade in their 1964 article on the componential analysis of kinship systems. SEARCH makes use of an extended version of this system of notation. The notation can be broken down into a set of "operators" and "attributes", which alternate with one another in an expression representing a path of kin relations connecting one individual to the potentially many other census members related to him in the manner so specified. Operators include '+' ("go from child to parent"), 'O' ("go to sibling"), '-' ("go to a child") and '=' ("go to a spouse"), among others. Attributes include 'M' ("who is male"), 'F' ("who is female"), and 'A' ("who is of either sex"), among others. Thus the expression 'MOF-A' instructs SEARCH to start from an individual and seek out that person's "father's sisters' childrens' spouses." This example only hints at the flexibility and potential power of the notational algebra.

SEARCH also enables the KINPROGRAM user to designate a date at which the connections between kin must hold true in order for a path of search to pass through them.

SEARCH thus lends itself to a wide variety of analytical problems in which it is important to identify exhaustively all members of a census that are in a defined relationship of kinship to one another. It might be used, for example, to study the relationship of behavior to norms in a population that advocates a prescriptive marriage rule. SEARCH could automatically identify each census member's "eligible" marriage partners at the time of marriage to determine whether or not the actual spouse selected fell within that prescribed set.

DEMOG

DEMOG permits description of the vital behavior recorded in a census. Just how the techniques of demography are to be applied to a given case depends on answer to questions about the size, the accuracy, the completeness and the closure of a census

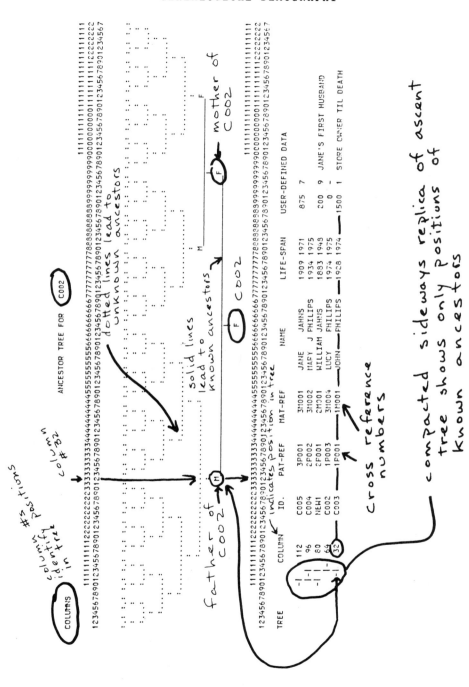

FIGURE 2. Annotated tree of ancestry created by ANCES.

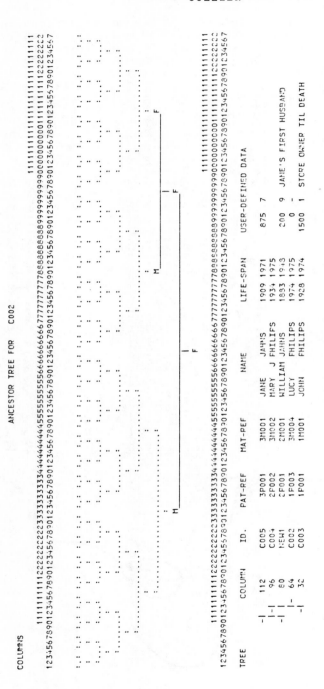

FIGURE 3. Tree created by ANCES (without annotation).

corpus. DEMOG is designed to examine a corpus at various dates
for which the conditions necessary for demographic analysis
might be met, to enumerate the censused population at those
dates, to assess mortality by the construction of appropriate
life tables, and to summarize fertility. DEMOG generates output
that can be used as input for more sophisticated analytic procedures such as those described in Keyfitz and Flieger's _Popula-
tion_: _Facts_ _and_ _Methods_ _of_ _Demography_ (1971. San Francisco:
W.H. Freeman and Co.). Thus, DEMOG serves as an interface
between the KINPROGRAM and more sophisticated demographic analysis, although it should be used as such only for censuses that
meet high standards of accuracy and completeness.

An important function of DEMOG is to allow for bounding of
the corpus to be examined demographically. Often a genealogical
census will include individuals solely for the purpose of tracing relations of kinship who should be excluded from consideration when studying a population's vital behavior because, for
example, they live in a different community. DEMOG allows the
user to build lists of individuals, either to exclude them from
the corpus for purposes of demographic analysis, or else to
limit application of demographic description to them alone.

A second important function of DEMOG is to allow for examination of a census at various moments in its history and over
periods of time ranging up to 20 years in length. Thus a corpus
which accurately and completely recorded vital behavior of a
population over a century could be submitted to DEMOG to generate automatically decade by decade summaries of its vital behavior.

How DEMOG works is illustrated by Figures 4-9 generated
from a small census drawn from my own research on a highland
Maya community of about 300 individuals studied during the
1966-73 period. As the figures show, DEMOG generated year-by-
year enumerations of population, births and deaths by age and
sex during this period, constructing a population pyramid for
each year. It summarized mortality over the entire seven-year
period through construction of life tables for males and for
females. It also cross-classified women living in 1973 by age
and parity and calculated age-specific birth rates observed over
the seven-year period.

One of the difficulties in demographic analysis of censuses collected by anthropologists and some family historians is
the problem posed by the small size of many populations so studied. However accurately and exhaustively censused, a small
population will exhibit greater variability in its vital behavior than will populations for which the law of large numbers
applies. Some low rates (for example, mortality between ages 10
and 50) may be difficult to estimate in such a population
because of the rarity of deaths in those cohorts. In the example illustrated in Figures 4-9, no male deaths were observed at

all between 1967 and 1973 in the 10-29 age cohorts. (Even crude
birth, a relatively high rate, fluctuated between a high of 56.7
in 1970 and a low of 20.2 in 1971!)

DEMOG incorporates two steps toward a solution of this
problem in its construction of life tables. One step is to base
the life table on population and deaths aggregated over all the
years of a time span specified by the user. The result is a
life table which is something of a hybrid between a period and a
generation life table in that it traces the fates of cohorts of
individuals over fairly long periods that are not usually entire
life spans. As the example illustrates, however, (see first
life table in Figure 7) even this aggregation may not reveal
observable mortality in some cohorts. A second step has been to
fit a cubic spline function to the observed mortality rates so
as to interpolate estimates of mortality for cohorts in which
none was observed (see second life table in Figure 7). Further
solutions to the small-numbers problem in DEMOG await design and
testing.

Plans for the full development of the KINPROGRAM

RESID and CORESID

KINPROGRAM data structures store residence histories of
individuals that can be manipulated to reconstruct the coresi-
dential patterns of groups of persons in clusters of settlement
locations. I will give priority to the design of modules that
manipulate and reconstruct residence patterns through time
because this step, more than any other increment to the KINPRO-
GRAM, will suit the package to a broader range of research on
domestic and residential group dynamics relevant to kinship and
the family. I plan the design of two complementary modules for
this purpose. The first, RESID, will focus on a defined location or small group of locations and automatically will generate
a diachronic account of all individuals ever residing there.
The second, CORESID, will focus on a defined individual or group
of individuals and automatically will generate a diachronic
account of all persons ever coresiding with them.

MAP

The potential is inherent in a KINPROGRAM census corpus
for the coupling of various analyses of kinship to settlement
pattern maps. An early version of the KINPROGRAM included the
printing of settlement maps in conjunction with the listing of
genealogical trees (see Figure 10), but this feature was set
aside in subsequent revisions and expansions of the program to
await further development. I propose to develop MAP eventually
as an adjunct to several of the modules.

Thus, MAP could be coupled to TREES to show not only the
evolution of genealogical relations, but also how their spatial

FIG. 4

FOR THE YEAR 1970

AGE	POPULATION MALE	POPULATION FEMALE	BIRTHS	DEATHS MALE	DEATHS FEMALE	AGE	MALES (EACH * = 1 PERSON)	FEMALES
UNKNOWN	0	0	0	0	0	UNKNOWN		
85	2	3	0	0	0	85	**	***
80	2	0	0	0	0	80	**	
75	5	3	0	0	0	75	*****	***
70	0	2	0	0	0	70		**
65	0	0	0	0	0	65		
60	4	2	0	0	0	60	****	**
55	4	5	0	0	0	55	****	*****
50	3	2	0	0	0	50	***	**
45	4	6	0	0	0	45	****	******
40	4	5	1	0	0	40	****	*****
35	4	5	0	0	0	35	****	*****
30	13	11	3	0	0	30	*************	***********
25	13	15	5	0	0	25	*************	***************
20	16	12	6	0	0	20	****************	************
15	15	16	2	0	0	15	***************	****************
10	19	16	0	0	0	10	*******************	****************
5	13	19	0	0	0	5	*************	*******************
1	25	15	0	0	0	1	*************************	***************
0	8	9	0	4	5	0	********	*********
TOTALS	154	146	17	4	5	TOTALS		
C.B.R. =	56.667	C.D.R. =	30.000	CHILD/WOMAN RATIO = 814.286				

FIG. 5

FOR THE YEAR 1971

AGE	POPULATION MALE	POPULATION FEMALE	BIRTHS	DEATHS MALE	DEATHS FEMALE	AGE	MALES (EACH * = 1 PERSON)	FEMALES
UNKNOWN	0	0	0	0	0	UNKNOWN		
85	2	3	0	0	0	85	**	***
80	3	0	0	0	0	80	***	
75	4	4	0	0	0	75	****	****
70	0	1	0	0	0	70		*
65	0	0	0	0	0	65		
60	4	3	0	0	0	60	****	***
55	4	4	0	0	0	55	****	****
50	3	4	0	1	0	50	***	****
45	4	5	0	0	0	45	****	*****
40	5	5	2	0	0	40	*****	*****
35	6	4	1	0	0	35	******	****
30	13	11	1	0	0	30	*************	***********
25	11	17	1	0	0	25	***********	*****************
20	19	14	1	0	0	20	*******************	**************
15	18	16	0	0	0	15	******************	****************
10	15	13	0	0	1	10	***************	*************
5	19	22	0	0	0	5	*******************	**********************
1	20	15	0	0	0	1	********************	***************
0	3	3	0	2	2	0	***	***
TOTALS	153	144	6	3	3	TOTALS		
C.B.R. =	20.202	C.D.R. =	20.202	CHILD/WOMAN RATIO = 569.444				

FIGURES 4 and 5. Output from DEMOG, showing changes in population structure of a village for 1970 and 1971.

FIG. 6

FOR THE YEAR 1972

AGE	POPULATION MALE	POPULATION FEMALE	BIRTHS	DEATHS MALE	DEATHS FEMALE	AGE
UNKNOWN	0	0	0	0	0	UNKNOWN
85	2	3	0	0	0	85
80	4	0	0	0	0	80
75	3	4	0	0	0	75
70	0	1	0	0	0	70
65	0	0	0	0	0	65
60	6	3	0	0	0	60
55	2	5	0	0	0	55
50	4	3	0	0	0	50
45	3	5	0	1	0	45
40	5	7	1	0	0	40
35	9	4	1	0	0	35
30	10	11	1	1	0	30
25	14	16	3	0	0	25
20	20	17	5	0	0	20
15	14	15	1	0	0	15
10	18	14	0	0	0	10
5	17	23	0	0	0	5
1	19	10	0	1	0	1
0	6	6	0	0	0	0
TOTALS	156	147	12	3	0	TOTALS

C.B.R. = 39.604 C.D.R. = 9.901 CHILD/WOMAN RATIO = 546.667

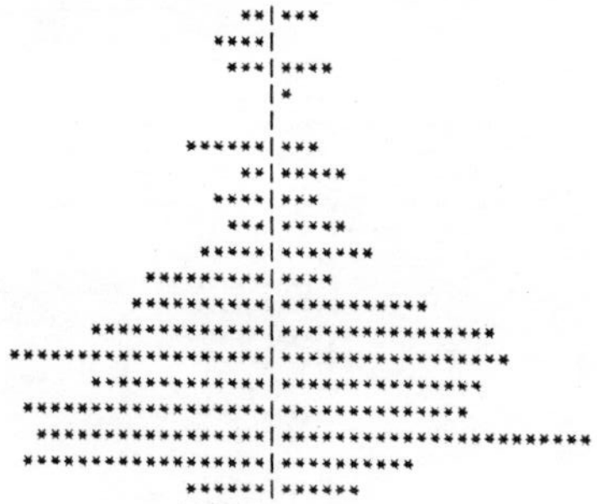

FIG. 7

FOR THE YEAR 1973

AGE	POPULATION MALE	POPULATION FEMALE	BIRTHS	DEATHS MALE	DEATHS FEMALE	AGE
UNKNOWN	0	0	0	0	0	UNKNOWN
85	2	3	0	0	0	85
80	4	0	0	0	0	80
75	3	4	0	0	0	75
70	0	1	0	0	0	70
65	1	2	0	0	0	65
60	5	2	0	0	0	60
55	2	5	0	0	0	55
50	4	4	0	0	0	50
45	3	3	0	0	0	45
40	4	9	1	0	0	40
35	10	5	1	0	0	35
30	8	13	4	0	0	30
25	18	14	1	0	0	25
20	17	16	4	0	0	20
15	18	14	2	0	0	15
10	14	18	0	0	0	10
5	22	19	0	0	0	5
1	18	15	0	0	0	1
0	9	4	0	1	0	0
TOTALS	162	151	13	1	0	TOTALS

C.B.R. = 41.534 C.D.R. = 3.195 CHILD/WOMAN RATIO = 821.622

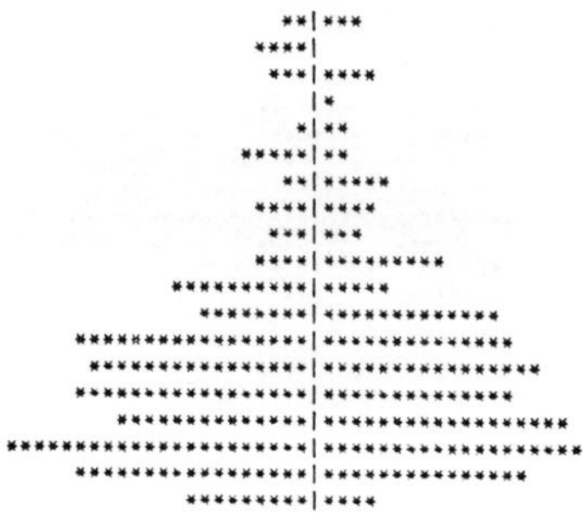

FIGURES 6 and 7. Output from DEMOG, showing changes in population structure of a village for 1972 and 1973.

REED-MERRILL LIFE TABLES USING OBSERVED AND INTERPOLATED M(X), FOR MALE POPULATION LIVING AND DYING FROM 1967 TO 1973

OBSERVED

AGES	PP	DC	M(X)	l(X)	D(X)	Q(X)	LL(X)	T(X)	E(X)
0	45	9	0.200000	100000	15527	0.155275	89131	4883275	48.883
1-4	139	3	0.021583	84473	6556	0.077606	324779	4794144	56.754
5-9	115	1	0.008696	77917	3321	0.042619	331883	4469836	57.361
10-14	119	0	0.000000	74596	0	0.000000	372981	4063082	54.803
15-19	116	0	0.000000	74596	0	0.000000	372981	3715101	49.803
20-24	125	0	0.000000	74596	0	0.000000	372981	3342120	44.803
25-29	85	0	0.000000	74596	0	0.000000	372981	2969135	39.803
30-34	75	2	0.026667	74596	9358	0.125349	349393	2591658	34.803
35-39	43	0	0.000000	65238	0	0.000000	328191	2345572	34.436
40-44	28	0	0.000000	65238	0	0.000000	328191	1920381	29.436
45-49	28	1	0.035714	65238	10738	0.164602	299345	1594190	24.436
50-54	23	1	0.043478	54500	10731	0.196904	245871	1294844	23.759
55-59	28	1	0.035714	43769	7204	0.164602	200032	1049172	23.971
60-64	22	0	0.000000	36564	0	0.000000	152821	848340	23.201
65-69	1	0	0.000000	36564	0	0.000000	152821	805519	18.201
70-74	11	1	0.090909	36564	13574	0.370488	148959	402698	13.201
75-79	27	0	0.000000	23018	0	0.000000	115088	398744	14.499
80-64	13	0	0.000000	23018	0	0.000000	115088	218655	9.499
85+	14	0	0.000000	23018	23108	1.000000	103579	103567	4.499

INTERPOLATED

AGES	PP	DC	M(X)	l(X)	D(X)	Q(X)	LL(X)	T(X)	E(X)
0	45	9	0.256310	100000	19449	0.194492	85338	5751445	57.414
1-4	139	3	0.032494	80551	9255	0.114805	305593	5605059	70.329
5-9	115	1	0.000662	71296	236	0.003307	355890	5361365	75.199
10-14	119	0	0.000011	71060	4	0.000056	355291	5005475	70.440
15-19	116	0	0.000000	71056	0	0.000000	355291	4850184	65.494
20-24	125	0	0.000000	71056	0	0.000000	355291	4294503	60.444
25-29	85	2	0.000002	71056	1	0.000010	355279	3959622	55.444
30-34	75	0	0.000033	71055	13	0.000183	355242	3504343	50.444
35-39	43	0	0.000321	71042	114	0.001601	354925	3229099	45.453
40-44	28	1	0.000305	70928	285	0.004718	353928	2874174	40.522
45-49	28	0	0.000818	70643	288	0.004083	352494	2520246	35.676
50-54	23	1	0.000510	70355	180	0.002549	351325	2167751	30.812
55-59	28	1	0.000296	70175	104	0.001479	350615	1816426	25.884
60-64	22	0	0.000242	70071	84	0.001210	350145	1495809	20.019
65-69	1	1	0.000425	69987	154	0.002122	349502	1115663	15.941
70-74	11	1	0.002411	69833	832	0.011988	347093	786101	10.970
75-79	27	0	0.067820	69001	19868	0.287943	295334	419004	6.072
80-64	13	0	1.000000	49133	49011	0.997521	123136	123670	2.517
85+	14	0	1.000000	122	122	1.000000	548	539	4.380

FIGURE 8. Life tables for males, prepared by DEMOG. Similar life tables are prepared for females.

BEGIN DEMOG TASK **FERTILITY

WOMEN ATTAINING AGE 15 OR MORE AFTER 1967
CROSS CLASSIFIED BY THEIR AGE IN 1973 OR AT DEATH IF DEAD BEFORE 1973
AND BY THE TOTAL NUMBER OF THEIR OFFSPRING AT THAT AGE

NUMBER OF OFFSPRING	15-19	20-24	25-29	30-34	35-39	40-44	45-49	50-54	55-59	60-64	65-69	70 AND OVER	UNKNOWN	MEAN AGE
0	12	5	3	-	1	1	-	-	3	-	-	4	-	34.66
1	3	2	2	-	1	-	-	-	-	-	-	1	-	30.22
2	-	6	3	5	1	1	-	-	1	1	-	1	-	29.94
3	-	3	2	2	-	-	-	1	1	-	-	1	-	35.30
4	-	-	2	6	3	-	-	-	-	-	-	1	-	37.79
5	-	-	2	-	-	-	1	-	-	-	-	-	-	45.17
6	-	-	-	1	-	2	-	2	-	1	-	2	-	52.78
7	-	-	-	-	-	-	1	-	1	1	1	1	-	61.67
8	-	-	-	-	-	2	1	-	-	-	-	-	-	43.13
9	-	-	-	-	-	1	-	-	-	-	-	-	-	43.00
10	-	-	-	-	-	-	-	-	-	-	-	-	-	43.00
11 OR MORE	-	-	-	-	-	-	-	-	-	-	-	-	-	0.00
MEAN PARITY	0.20	1.44	2.29	3.29	2.80	6.11	5.75	4.60	1.60	4.00	6.50	2.60	0.00	

FOR THESE SAME WOMEN
AGE SPECIFIC BIRTH RATES OBSERVED IN PERIOD FROM 1967 TO 1973

AGE OF MOTHER	OBSERVED BIRTH RATE
0	0.00
1- 4	0.00
5- 9	0.00
10-14	0.00
15-19	99.10
20-24	252.43
25-29	173.22
30-34	190.48
35-39	214.29
40-44	125.00
45-49	0.00
50-54	0.00
55-59	0.00
60-64	0.00
65-69	0.00
70-74	0.00
75-79	0.00
80-84	0.00
85+	0.00
UNKNOWN	0.00

TOTAL FERTILITY RATE BASED ON AGE-SPECIFIC RATES FOR COHORTS AGE 15 TO 49   T.F.R. = 5297.53

FIGURE 9.   Some of the fertility information summarized by DEMOG.

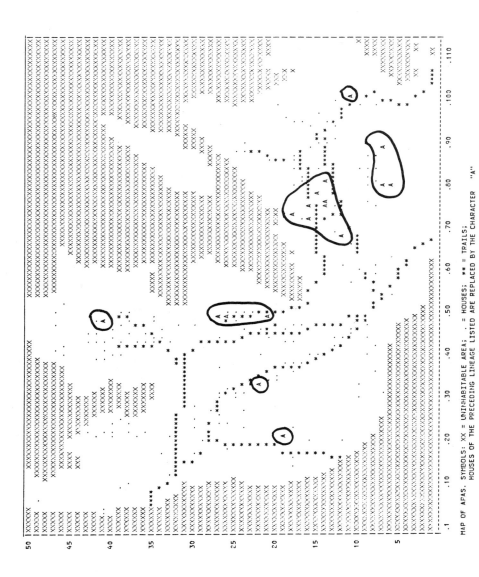

MAP OF APAS. SYMBOLS: XX = UNINHABITABLE AREA; . = HOUSES; ** = TRAILS;
HOUSES OF THE PRECEDING LINEAGE LISTED ARE REPLACED BY THE CHARACTER   "A"

FIGURE 10.   Settlement map produced by now-obsolete version of KINPROGRAM.

pattern changes through time. Or MAP could be coupled to SEARCH
to depict the residence patterns of kin falling into a designated relation to given census members. Or MAP could also com-
plement CORESID by showing the movement through space of groups
of people living together.

        Mapping need not be confined just to a local-level repre-
sentation of residences. I plan to construct MAP to allow for
designation of settlement locations in up to three base maps of
varying scale. If appropriate to a given census, for instance,
these scales might correspond to neighborhood, community and
regional settlement. By generating maps at all three scales,
the module might make apparent macro- as well as micro-spatial
patterning of kinship.

RELATE

        Discovering the relationships linking individuals to one
another is a recurrent problem of method in the analysis of kinship. Many kinship systems studied by social scientists incorporate explicit rules or implicit behavioral patterns which
delimit or proscribe kinship behaviors, such as marriage, on the
basis of individuals' prior relatedness. Measuring conformity
to such rules or assessing implicit, unrecognized behavioral
patterns of this sort requires a method for characterizing
individuals' prior relatedness. Sometimes the relation between
individuals seems self-evident, especially if they are genealogically very close to one another. However, the self-evidence of
a close connection between them may lead to overlooking other
less evident paths of kinship connecting them. Even moderate
separations in genealogical space can result in multiple and
potentially complex paths of interconnections. RELATE will be
designed to generate automatically the non-trivial connections
between any pair of census members.

        Thus RELATE will complement the existing SEARCH module.
Where SEARCH begins with an individual and discovers all census
members who are in a given, algebraically specified relation to
that individual, RELATE will begin with specified pairs of
individuals, will discover the distinct chains of relation
between them, and will display these chains in algebraic form.

System improvements

        A variety of overall modifications of the KINPROGRAM is
worth undertaking in conjunction with the development of new
modules.

        One simple modification will be to eliminate artificial
constraints on the size of census that can be processed. Existing modules have never been tested for reliability or efficiency
with censuses of over 5,000 members, and so the package incorporates an artificial cut-off at this level. Its data structures,

however, are inherently expandable within the limits imposed by
the hardware of a given computation facility.

I need to alter the representation of dates throughout the
KINPROGRAM. Presently, the system only codes dates conveniently
as years, whereas recording vital events at the level of precision of months and even exact days is important for many demographic analyses.

A more complicated improvement in the KINPROGRAM will permit easier specification of adoption. The present design of the
system hampers adequate handling of adoption. The system
expects each census member to have only one parent of either
sex. The user may, of course, designate social rather than biological parentage if appropriate, but cannot designate more than
one set of parents. Adoption can presently be handled by the
fiction of treating the adopted person as two individuals with
distinct parents but otherwise identical characteristics. But
this strategem entails awkwardness in the application of DEMOG
and other modules if adoption is frequent. I should like to
develop new coding throughout the KINPROGRAM to handle adoption
in a more realistic manner.

Users of DEMOG have suggested improvements that I will
incorporate into the module. One class of improvements will
increase the flexibility with which subsets of a census may be
designated for demographic analysis. At present, the user
defines these subsets by listing census members they include or
exclude. These lists may themselves result from application of
the SEARCH or TREES (or the future RESID and CORESID) modules.
What is not now possible is for these subsets to be identified
automatically from socio-economic characteristics of census members optionally supplied by the user and currently stored unan-
alyzed on disk. I should like to incorporate this capability
within DEMOG to help adapt it to particular users' needs. A
second class of improvements will be to incorporate additional
aids to demographic inference from small and incomplete censuses.

Availability of the KINPROGRAM

Existing modules of the KINPROGRAM are available from me
at Stanford in the form of PL/I language source decks written as
card images onto tape. I can supply users' manuals for these
modules at nominal cost. Unfortunately, I do not have the
resources to support others' use of the programs at their facilities. The KINPROGRAM has been tested and used on Stanford's
IBM 370-90 system, but I cannot guarantee the system to be free
of errors or "bugs", and the programs are offered only on a "use
at your own risk" basis.

I have had difficulty in obtaining funding for the full
development of the KINPROGRAM and thus plan to continue working

slowly on the development of additional modules and the making
of improvements in the system. I have no definite schedule for
the changes and additions I have proposed, but I shall be glad
to correspond with anyone interested in the unfolding of these
projects.

WHEREFORE ART THOU, ROMIO?
NAME FREQUENCY PATTERNS AND THEIR USE IN AUTOMATED GENEALOGY ASSEMBLY

Kenneth M. Weiss
David L. Rossmann
Ranajit Chakraborty
Susan L. Norton

"...The beginning of wisdom is to call things by their right names." (Chinese proverb)

How do people choose the names they give to their children? On first impulse this question might be relegated to the curio shop of sociology. However, when one has serious questions to ask of historical demographic data, one cannot fail to make a serious attempt at understanding the processes by which names are given, handed down, modified, misspelled and forgotten.

We are involved in a very large-scale study of genealogies in the U.S.-Mexico border city of Laredo, Texas. This Mexican-American population is well documented from the 18th century founding of the town to the present. This is because the vast majority of its people have been Roman Catholics, and the vital events of their lives have been recorded in the parish churches in Laredo. Our study uses these church records of births, deaths and marriages to construct extended genealogies by computer. Biomedical information, such as cause and age of death, will then be mapped onto these genealogies. We are interested in the nature and extent of the familial clustering of of major degenerative diseases, particularly cancers, in Laredo.

Before one can do epidemiological work, one must construct the genealogies from separate sets of vital records. This requires that one specify to the computer the algorithms by which uncertain or competing links between records are to be processed, the most likely links determined, and the final genealogies compiled. Thus, if we are searching for the birth record of an individual for whom we have a marriage, we look for the name and birthdate specified on the marriage record. Often there will be inexact matches (for example, because of spelling errors), or several records with the same name. The resolution of competing or uncertain links involves mainly name and date information.

Because the records are often handwritten in hard-to read script, and because literacy has been limited in the past, with spelling conventions often ignored, the resolution of uncertain

Genealogical Demography

name links is no trivial matter. It will be necessary to find
ways of establishing likelihoods that a name encountered in a
search is the name being sought. This involves a detailed statistical understanding of naming patterns in the history of this
population.

Patterned errors exist in many cases. Spanish orthographic
practices have changed systematically during the last century
('z' becoming 's', for example). Irish or German priests may
inadvertently have Anglicized some spellings, or may merely have
been sloppy or casual about spelling. This is a problem not
only because the names in the same lineage change with time, but
also because the spelling of an individual's name can change
within his or her lifetime. Spelling errors on baptismal
records may or may not be altered when it becomes necessary for
the individual to document him- or herself officially. (In this
area, official documentation may involve military registration,
legitimization of children, social security or other job-related
identification, land or inheritance actions, or proof of U.S.
citizenship in an area where illegal immigration has become a
major problem.)

In addition to these spelling changes are the problems of
hard-to-read handwriting, and typographical errors in transcrip-
tion for the computer. Thus it is clear that one must have a
firm understanding of which names actually exist and how they
are chosen, so that the probabilities of matching or not matching records can be computed and errors evaluated.

Starting from this point, we have begun to examine the way
in which names are distributed in Laredo and in other populations for contrast. We would like to be able to answer such
questions as: What is the probability that someone was named,
for example, Juanita Sanchez in the early 1900's? What is the
probability of more than one individual being born and given the
same name in a particular decade? Do names cluster in time?
Questions like these have been addressed along similar lines in
several other papers. The interested reader should consult the
following authors and their bibliographies for an introduction
to the literature regarding name distribution: Henry (1967,
1974); Dunkling (1976); Harris (1977) and Wrigley (1973). Skolnick (1974), Newcombe (1967) and Rossmann (1978) should be consulted for information regarding the computerized linkage of
historical and genealogical records. General discussions of
specific projects are also useful. These include the work in
Oxford (Acheson, 1964; Wrigley, 1973), in Italy (Skolnick,
1974), in Canada (Lavoie et al., 1972; Legare et al., 1972;
Beauchamp et al., 1973) and in Guam (Rossmann, 1978).

In order to answer these questions and to study the sociological behavior of names and the factors which may explain it,
we have extracted given names and surnames from the Laredo and
other records, and have statistically examined their distributions.

Methods of Analysis

Our primary data have been chosen for this analysis from the largest body of names we have computerized at this time. These are the names of the decedents on 56,000 death records for the population since 1897. They have been separated into girls' and boys' first names and into last names. The name groups are then roughly divided into generation-length intervals from 1897-1924, 1925-1949 and 1950-1977. The names in this set of files were checked to ensure that all were "valid" names, that is, that only proper alphabetic characters were present and that various vague categories (e.g. initials only) were eliminated. It must be remembered that these are large files which must be checked by machine. Our results are tentative in two senses. First, some typographical errors are certain to be identified in the future, whereupon these names will be eliminated or corrected. We expect that this will not be common since much screening has already taken place. The second problem involves large sets of spelling variants of names. These can be coalesced to see how the "core" name behaves, a process which will be discussed below.

The present population of Laredo is derived from a Spanish-speaking population, and there are many factors which affect the giving of Spanish names. By far the most important of these factors is the strong influence held by the Church over name choice in the population. In order to see if this fact affects the name pattern, or merely seems as if it ought to, we have constructed similar name statistics from two other sources. The first source includes names from the Church records of the Spanish-dominated population on the Pacific island of Guam, which were collected by David L. Rossmann for a study of neurological diseases. These names have been broken down by sex, first name and surname, and time period (-1899, 1900-1924, 1925-1949, 1950-1975). In addition, standardized names were determined for the Guam population to account for spelling variations. Standardized surnames have a file which can be analyzed separately. These names are taken from individuals baptized in Guam churches. For details see Rossmann (1978).

Finally, we have abstracted some information from First Names First, a book by Dunkling on naming patterns in England from 1850 to the present. This information will be used to contrast English naming patterns with those of the Spanish-speaking populations.

Our first treatment of the data was to sort names on the basis of how frequently they appeared in their respective lists, that is, to compute frequency distributions for each name list. It was immediately apparent that there are two kinds of names: those which occur only a few times (Rare Names) and those which are used often (Common Names). The borderline between these groups is somewhat vague, depending somewhat upon the use to

which one puts the whole distribution. However, at a given
point in the distribution one has clearly gone from one category
to the other. The number of copies of each name has risen to
more than ten, there are no longer names represented at each
frequency of repetitions in sequence, and each category with a
name in it has only one or two names. Thus while there are
great numbers of names with 1, 2, 3, 4, 5,... repetitions, when
one gets to 25, 26, 27 and so on, there are gaps (categories
with no names) and only a few names which appear in each represented category. Very quickly, gaps occur between frequencies
of represented names, and each category will contain only one
name. This situation will be discussed below. Here, however,
we stress that (1) there is a very large "spike" of names with
only one occurrence, and (2) there is a very long and irregular
"tail" of a few names with a large number of representations
each. The situation is such that the distribution is difficult
to represent graphically so that both the spike and the tail are
adequately pictured. It is also clear that different social
processes are responsible for the spike and for the tail.
Hence, we have analyzed each end of the distribution separately.
Although we initially attempted to fit standard probability distributions to these data, it became clear that this would be of
minimal use because the fits were poor and could not be interpreted in any case.

Rare Names

Rare Names include all names which appear only a few times
in any given list. Hence, it might well be expected that these
names constitute the more chaotic element of the sociology of
naming. All sorts of aberration, errors, variations and the
like will make up this list. There is no reason, other than an
a priori and somewhat mystic invocation of a "law" of large numbers, to expect any particular correspondence from one list to
another in regard to Rare Names.

The expectation is borne out in the sense that singleton
names and, often, names with only a few occurrences do not
appear from time period to time period. Naturally, there is no
correspondence between the Rare Names given to boys and those
given to girls, nor is there any correspondence between Rare
Names and surnames. Although it is not possible to reproduce
long name lists here, it is clear from looking at lists of Rare
Names that they include many spelling variants and unusual names
which, although always present in a population, never become
popular.

As different as the specific names in the Rare Name categories are, however, the expectation of no similarity in pattern
is not borne out in another very interesting sense. The shape
of the distributions of Rare Names (both boys' and girls') and
surnames from one time or population to another is similar.
This is represented schematically in Figure 1. Names with only

one occurrence produce a very marked "spike." This varies in
magnitude from one population to another. In Laredo, with very
little difference from time to time, this spike can represent
about 7% to 14% of all names, the former figure referring to
first names and the latter to surnames. After this spike of
singletons, which contains most of the miscellaneous and errone-
ous or aberrant names, there is a rapid drop-off in frequency.
Doubleton names represent about 2% of all names, trebleton names
about 1% and so on, in a pattern which rapidly becomes asymptotic to 0%. Thus, names with fifteen repetitions represent
only about 0.05% of all names, whether boys', girls' or surnames.

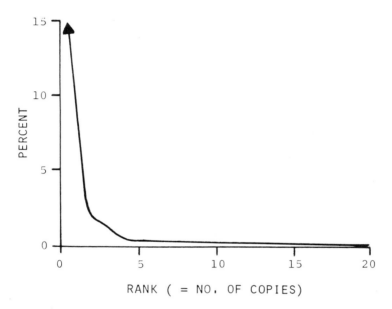

FIGURE 1. Distribution of Rare Names

     Table 1 shows this pattern for Laredo data. Because all
time periods were so clearly similar, the data have been aggregated. We have tried to represent this distribution with some
standard parametric probability distribution, in the hope that
perhaps the parameters of the fitted form would be interpretable
in some sociological terms. Unfortunately, we can fit these
Rare Names only with difficulty, and only with very general
exponential type distributions (Zipf's distribution fits best)
whose parameters are not interpretable. The problem is the very
marked spike. Perhaps some aggregation of spelling variants
might reduce the singleton spike and redistribute names into
other categories to produce a more gradually decreasing frequency pattern. Can we assume, however, that the sociological
process which leads one to choose the name Hermenegilda is the

TABLE 1.   Rare Name pattern -- percent of total names.

Male Given	Female Given	Surname
6.970	7.653	14.920
1.630	1.817	2.840
0.873	1.040	1.240
0.630	0.647	0.693
0.470	0.403	0.430
0.420	0.343	0.370
0.243	0.257	0.233
0.247	0.227	0.260
0.200	0.210	0.167
0.150	0.170	0.117
0.183	0.130	0.117
0.117	0.127	0.070
0.090	0.117	0.107
0.090	0.147	0.070
0.073	0.123	0.053
0.060	0.107	0.033
0.060	0.083	0.067
0.073	0.070	0.047
0.047	0.090	0.067
0.037	0.060	0.043

same as that for Hermenejilda? Or is the spelling variant part
of the parents' intent, for example, as a mark of distinction?

The generality of this result is seen when we look at Guam
names. Table 2 provides data on rare surnames, with time periods again aggregated because results were virtually identical.
For purposes of a genetic/family study (cf. Rossmann, this
volume) on Guam, names were eventually pooled according to
standardized spellings. We therefore have an opportunity to
examine the rare name distribution of actual and variant-aggre-
gated data. It is clear that except for a far smaller spike in
the names, the results for Guam are quite similar to those of
Laredo: a sharp spike declining after only two or three steps
to a fraction of a percent of all names, and then only very
slowly diminishing. It can also be seen that standardization of
names smooths out the distribution somewhat, but not dramatically except in the case of singleton and doubleton categories.

It is obvious that some social process is at work. This
is clear from the fact that although the specific names involved
change greatly, the shape of the distribution does not change.
In addition, boys' and girls' names and surnames behave similarly. But what is the process at work? It is difficult to

TABLE 2.   Guam Rare Surnames

Rank	Standardized Frequency	Percent	Unstandardized Frequency	Percent
1	64	1.17	107	1.96
2	26	0.48	39	0.71
3	17	0.31	23	0.42
4	8	0.15	8	0.14
5	9	0.16	12	0.22
6	10	0.18	15	0.27
7	5	0.09	6	0.11
8	1	0.02	6	0.11
9	4	0.07	6	0.11
10	4	0.07	4	0.07
11	1	0.02	1	0.02
12	0	0.00	2	0.04
13	2	0.04	2	0.04
14	2	0.04	3	0.06
15	2	0.04	1	0.02

| Total names | 209 | | 295 | |

imagine any specific factor, such as degree of striving for
originality, which could even begin to explain things.   It is
undoubtedly true that at least in some times and places, such as
in the U.S. in recent years, there is often a parental effort to
bestow unusual names on their children. This search for uniqueness can be manifested in deliberate unusual spellings of given
names.   It is interesting to note, however, that many times this
effort at uniqueness occurs quite often in the same population
at the same time, so that the same "unusual" name becomes common
(examples are given later in this paper).   This has been the
case in this country recently, for example, with names such as
Jason or Jessica, and parents are often upset to find that many
other children have turned up with those same "unique" names.
This process, however, would not affect last names, which are
inherited and change only as a result of stochastic "mutation,"
as in spelling changes or changes brought about by migration.
Perhaps in any reasonably complex society (although Guam is not
at all like Laredo) there is a level of noise in the system,
similar to the process of mutation keeping genetic variability
in a species; a certain proneness to make spelling errors or
unique names. Undoubtedly, such a process, combined with "large
numbers" exists. This explanation for names, however, is analo-
gous to the physician's diagnosis of "spontaneous remission" in
a recovered patient. It is an admission of ignorance clothed in
technical rhetoric.

Common Names

> "...Yet leaving here a name, I trust, that will not
> perish in the dust." (Southey)

Common Names are, for our purposes, those names which
appear a great many times in any given population (i.e. set of
records). There is, of course, an area of gradation from Rare
Names to Common Names, but we are interested in the rightmost
tail of the distribution, where approximately the top twenty
names are found. A few names occur at very high frequencies,
but because there is a low likelihood of finding a name with a
specific given frequency, a standard parametric probability distribution cannot fit. For example, although the name Juan may
have 647 copies, it is very unlikely to find a name with 646
copies, and the next most frequent name may have 538 copies.
Furthermore, the number of names with 127 copies, say, may be 1
or 0, which is the same number of names with 647 copies. The
frequency of names with given increasing numbers of copies does
not diminish asymptotically as would be required by a standard
distribution.

On _a priori_ grounds, we can see that the most common surnames at one time period would probably be nearly the most common in a subsequent period since they are inherited. Unless
migration is highly name-specific, or unless there is a large
name-specific difference in reproduction, a surname will persist. This can be quantified quite easily if we know the number
of parent couples with a particular surname and the family size
distribution, and we can make some assumptions about migration.
It is possible to compute the expected number of children having
the name in the next generation and its variance. (Variance is
the result of family size being a stochastic variable). In
fact, the study of surname extinction has been going on at least
since the work of Galton in the 19th century. In this century,
the great demographer A.J. Lotka was interested in the probabilities of family extinction with regard to the production of
orphans, among other issues. The result is that if a name is
common enough to begin with, it will remain so the vast majority
of times that such observations are made. Thus, the persistence
of common surnames is expected, and this is borne out in our
data.

Because of social factors such as contact and interaction
between parents, we might also expect that common first names
would persist over time. If there are many Robertos at Time 1
we may surmise that there will be many at Time 2, since people
will hear the name or know someone with it, and will bestow it
on their children. This appears to be the case in Laredo.

Figure 2 provides the distribution of common names. Since
it varies little no matter what time or name type we consider,
only one schematic figure is given. It is rather surprising to

find that not only do first names and surnames have similar distributions, but the shape of this distribution is very much like
that of Rare Names. If names are ordered by frequency rank, it
can be seen that the highest ranking name represents a very
sharp spike and that there is a rapid decline in frequency of
succeedingly less common names. In addition, there is a
"shoulder" in this decline with a subsequent asymptotic leveling
off.

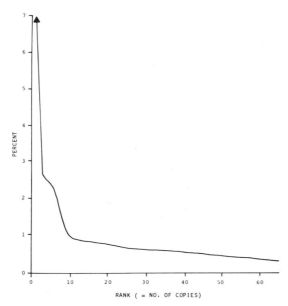

FIGURE 2.   Distribution of Common Names

        To see what is really happening with Common Names, it is
necessary to examine how the rank of _specific_ names changes over
time, and to note that the distribution keeps its shape. Tables
3, 4 and 5 provide this information for surnames and boys' and
girls' given names in Laredo, giving only the name rank and its
change over generations. Tables 6, 7 and 8 provide the actual
names involved. First, notice that the rank in the top ten
names changes very little. For surnames, as we noted, this is
the result of patronymy and the fact that heritable attributes
have slow stochastic evolution in sizeable populations (to bor-
row from the language of population genetics). Interestingly,
female and male given names behave similarly. This is at least
partially due to the strong influence of the Catholic Church in
Laredo. A common name in 1890 is still common in 1975.
Clearly, the influence of the Church is somewhat stronger on
girls' names than on boys' names, which results in a less pronounced spike and a slightly smoother frequency decline for
girls' names.

TABLE 3.   Surname rank change

1890	1925	1950
1	1	1
2	2	4
3	3	3
4	4	2
5	7	9
6	6	6
7	5	5
8	11	7
9	8	8
10	10	11
11	13	13
12	9	10
13	16	15
14	20	15

TABLE 4.   Rank change of female given names

1890	1925	1950
1	1	1
2	3	5
3	4	4
4	2	2
5	5	7
6	8	5
7	11	9
8	10	12
9	9	8
10	7	12
11	12	16
12	15	18
13	31	36
14	6	3
15	12	10

These "explanations" notwithstanding, it is quite interesting that such diverse units as boys' and girls' given names and surnames behave in such a statistically similar way over so long a time period. Why do people produce this J-shaped distribution of names, regardless of which specific names may hold given places? Statistical arguments based on genetics, where such J-shaped gene frequency distributions are often observed, may be successfully invoked for surnames (Chakraborty et al., this volume), but some sociological process must be posited for

TABLE 5.   Rank change of male given names

1890	1925	1950
1	1	1
2	2	2
3	5	4
4	3	5
5	4	3
6	7	7
7	6	6
8	12	11
9	10	12
10	8	21
11	21	25
12	18	15
13	14	19
14	24	33
15	40	33

TABLE 6.   Common surnames

Rank	1890 Name	%	1925 Name	%	1950 Name	%
1	Garcia	4.14	Garcia	3.63	Garcia	3.71
2	Martinez	3.87	Martinez	3.51	Gonzalez	3.25
3	Rodriguez	2.86	Rodriguez	3.21	Rodriguez	2.87
4	Gonzalez	2.79	Gonzalez	2.58	Martinez	2.78
5	Hernandez	2.13	Garza	1.98	Garza	2.52
6	Flores	1.90	Flores	1.91	Flores	1.62
7	Garza	1.88	Hernandez	1.54	Sanchez	1.58
8	Sanchez	1.41	Ramirez	1.37	Ramirez	1.50
9	Ramirez	1.24	Perez	1.25	Hernandez	1.43
10	Lopez	1.24	Lopez	1.22	Perez	1.42
11	Trevino	1.20	Sanchez	1.15	Lopez	1.36
12	Perez	1.05	Gutierrez	1.02	Villarreal	1.29
13	Pena	0.94	Villarreal	0.97	Trevino	1.10
14	Salinas	0.91	Trevino	0.97	Gutierrez	1.06
15	Villareal	0.82	Gomez	0.87	Pena	0.89

TABLE 7.   Common female given names

| | 1890 | | 1925 | | 1950 | |
Rank	Name	%	Name	%	Name	%
1	Maria	9.33	Maria	13.21	Maria	13.30
2	Juana	2.62	Guadalupe	2.26	Guadalupe	2.40
3	Francisca	2.59	Juana	2.24	Juanita	1.90
4	Guadalupe	2.37	Francisca	2.07	Francisca	1.80
5	Josefa	1.93	Josefa	1.51	Petra	1.28
6	Petra	1.82	Juanita	1.36	Juana	1.28
7	Antonia	1.75	Margarita	1.35	Josefa	1.21
8	Manuela	1.45	Petra	1.28	Dolores	1.19
9	Dolores	1.42	Dolores	1.16	Antonia	1.13
10	Margarita	1.26	Manuela	1.14	Rosa	1.12
11	Concepcion	1.18	Antonia	1.13	Mary	1.09
12	Paula	1.14	Rosa	1.07	Margarita	1.06
13	Refugia	1.10	Concepcion	1.07	Manuela	1.06
14	Juanita	1.00	Julia	1.06	Isabel	1.06
15	Isabel	0.94	Paula	1.03	Julia	1.03

TABLE 8.   Common male given names

| | 1890 | | 1925 | | 1950 | |
Rank	Name	%	Name	%	Name	%
1	Jose	6.98	Jose	7.16	Jose	7.01
2	Juan	4.39	Juan	4.98	Juan	4.50
3	Manuel	3.26	Francisco	2.64	Jesus	2.66
4	Francisco	3.10	Jesus	2.59	Manuel	2.47
5	Jesus	2.85	Manuel	2.45	Francisco	2.22
6	Antonio	2.60	Pedro	2.08	Pedro	2.06
7	Pedro	2.52	Antonio	1.91	Antonio	1.69
8	Guadalupe	1.30	Luis	1.36	John	1.16
9	Ramon	0.98	John	1.24	William	1.08
10	Luis	0.97	Ramon	1.18	James	1.05
11	Rafael	0.94	Roberto	1.15	Guadalupe	0.97
12	Pablo	0.94	Guadalupe	0.99	Ramon	0.86
13	Tomas	0.87	William	0.95	Roberto	0.83
14	Enrique	0.84	Tomas	0.89	Charles	0.83
15	Felipe	0.82	Andres	0.85	Pablo	0.82

given names. We cannot invent a compulsive persistence element
in human behavior (i.e., fidelity of given name from parent to
child), since the use of patronymic and matronymic given names
in this population is not frequent.

This fact can be seen more clearly in the data from Guam,
which is very different from that of Laredo. Table 9 provides
surname data to show that the general shape of the distribution
is quite similar to that found in Laredo, and that standardization has very little effect on Common Names. After all, it is
very difficult to argue, especially for surnames, that two
names, each with numerous copies, are merely accidental variants
of one another. When names are so frequent, they must be
treated as entities in their own right even if they originally
arose by spelling mutation.

TABLE 9. Common Names: Guam

Rank	Standardized Frequency	Percent	Unstandardized Frequency	Percent
1	549	10.03	548	10.02
2	414	7.56	414	7.57
3	361	6.60	354	6.47
4	242	4.42	242	4.42
5	203	3.71	170	3.11
6	168	3.07	166	3.04
7	164	3.00	160	2.93
8	154	2.81	152	2.78
9	144	2.63	132	2.41
10	133	2.43	128	2.34
11	126	2.30	126	2.30
12	122	2.23	122	2.23
13	115	2.10	115	2.10
14	109	1.99	107	1.96
15	107	1.96	98	1.79
Total names	209		295	

Tables 10 and 11 provide Guam unstandardized and standardized girls' given names respectively. Tables 12 and 13 provide
the same information for boys' names. In the first three time
periods, notice that girls' and, to a lesser extent, boys' names
are quite similar to those found in Laredo. The Spanish history
of Guam is clear in these names (Rossmann, 1978). However, this
history can hardly be invoked as an explanation for the distribution of Common Names. Should the reader be tempted to disa-
gree, he or she is invited to examine the 1975 column of these
tables. After World War II, the United States' presence on Guam
greatly increased, with the result that American names have
become fashionable. Yet while the names have changed, the dis-

TABLE 10. Common female unstandardized names: Guam

Rank	1900		1925		1950		1975	
1	Maria	100	Maria	75	Maria	84	Mary	49
2	Ana	36	Ana	49	Ana	40	Elizabeth	24
3	Dolores	31	Rosa	20	Rosa	27	Maria	18
4	Antonia	23	Dolores	20	Dolores	16	Julia	17
5	Josefa	20	Joaquina	17	Julia	13	Doris	16
6	Rosa	19	Carmen	16	Josefina	12	Rose	15
7	Carmen	18	Trinidad	11	Carmen	12	Dolores	13
8	Vicenta	17	Josefina	11	Isabel	11	Annie	13
9	Manuela	16	Rita	10	Teresita	8	Teresita	10
10	Joaquina	16	Concepcion	10	Rosita	7	Patricia	10
11	Juana	12	Isabel	9	Mary	7	Josephine	10
12	Nicolasa	10	Angelina	9	Guadalupe	7	Frances	10
13	Tomasa	9	Josefa	8	Virginia	6	Catherine	10
14	Rita	9	Antonia	8	Vicenta	6	Barbara	10
15	Luisa	9	Teresa	7	Rita	6	Ana	10
Total names	173		90		174		359	

TABLE 11. Common female standardized names: Guam

Rank	1900		1925		1950		1975	
1	Maria	107	Maria	75	Maria	93	Maria	79
2	Ana	36	Ana	49	Ana	49	Rosa	45
3	Dolores	31	Rosa	24	Rosa	40	Ana	37
4	Antonia	25	Dolores	20	Josefa	19	Elizabeth	28
5	Rosa	23	Josefa	19	Dolores	16	Teresa	22
6	Josefa	22	Joaquina	17	Juliana	14	Juliana	22
7	Carmen	18	Carmen	16	Carmen	12	Juana	22
8	Vicenta	17	Trinidad	11	Teresa	11	Elena	21
9	Manuela	16	Rita	10	Isabel	11	Catalina	19
10	Joaquina	16	Concepcion	10	Juana	9	Doris	16
11	Juana	12	Isabel	9	Florentina	8	Dolores	16
12	Teodora	11	Antonia	9	Matilde	7	Josefa	14
13	Nicolasa	10	Angela	9	Guadalupe	7	Evelyn	14
14	Luisa	10	Teresa	7	Antonia	7	Patricia	13
15	Tomasa	9	Luisa	5	Virginia	6	Francisca	13
Total names	140		76		119		195	

TABLE 12.   Common male unstandardized names: Guam

Rank	1900		1925		1950		1975	
1	Jose	101	Jose	87	Jose	82	Joseph	79
2	Juan	55	Juan	46	Jesus	66	John	64
3	Vicente	50	Vicente	45	Vicente	51	Vicente	42
4	Antonio	26	Jesus	40	Juan	48	Francisco	35
5	Felix	22	Joaquin	35	Francisco	48	Anthony	32
6	Francisco	21	Francisco	19	Joaquin	25	Jesse	28
7	Joaquin	20	Ignacio	18	Antonio	22	Jose	26
8	Pedro	19	Antonio	18	Ignacio	18	Peter	23
9	Ignacio	19	Pedro	12	Joseph	16	William	22
10	Manuel	18	Manuel	11	Tomas	14	Michael	22
11	Mariano	17	Mariano	8	Ramon	9	Kenneth	20
12	Domingo	13	Ramon	7	Pedro	8	David	17
13	Luis	12	Miguel	5	Mariano	8	Joaquin	16
14	Jesus	12	Luis	5	Manuel	6	Raymond	15
15	Felipe	12	Felix	5	Enrique	6	Juan	15
Total names		163		60		107		225

TABLE 13.   Common male standardized names: Guam

Rank	1900		1925		1950		1975	
1	Jose	101	Jose	87	Jose	99	Jose	114
2	Juan	55	Juan	46	Jesus	67	Juan	84
3	Vicente	50	Vicente	45	Juan	57	Francisco	53
4	Antonio	26	Jesus	40	Vicente	51	Vicente	51
5	Felix	22	Joaquin	35	Francisco	49	Jesus	46
6	Francisco	22	Francisco	19	Joaquin	26	Antonio	42
7	Joaquin	20	Antonio	19	Antonio	23	Ramon	26
8	Pedro	19	Ignacio	18	Ignacio	18	Pedro	25
9	Ignacio	19	Pedro	12	Tomas	16	Miguel	23
10	Manuel	18	Manuel	11	Carlos	11	Kenneth	22
11	Mariano	17	Mariano	8	Ramon	10	Guillermo	22
12	Domingo	13	Ramon	7	Eduardo	10	David	17
13	Luis	12	Enrique	6	Pedro	9	Joaquin	16
14	Felipe	12	Luis	5	Mariano	8	James	15
15	Jesus	12	Felix	5	Enrique	8	Tomas	14
							Daniel	14
Total names		140		56		79		147

tribution pattern persists. Thus, there is a social phenomenon
at work which is neither name nor culture specific. To further
illustrate this point, Tables 14 and 15 provide data drawn from
British given names since 1850 (Dunkling, 1976). Here it is
dramatically clear that although particular names in particular
places change almost completely, the distribution pattern
remains very similar to that seen in Laredo and Guam. In addition, the English pattern is basically the same shape as the
Guam and Laredo patterns. The tables show what has happened to
some of the very common names which rose and fell in favor during this time period.

While there are differences in the absolute magnitude of
the spikes in these distributions, it is clear that the members
of these cultures produce neither a flat name distribution, in
which each number of occurrences has about the same number of
names, nor a distribution peaked in the middle, where names with
intermediate numbers of occurrences are the most common.
Undoubtedly, the observed distributions can be fitted to stochastic models of "epidemic" or "contagious" type processes, in
which contact between individuals determines the likelihood of a
name being given. This does not in any way, however, help us to
understand why some names suddenly grow in frequency while others decline. Why, for example, doesn't Cuthbert ever take hold?

A Computer in Search of a Name

"...He said true things, but called them by wrong
names." (Browning)

It is clear that much remains to be learned about the naming practices of human beings in societies which do not have
strict naming prescriptions. However, what we wish to know
about name frequency distributions and their dynamics in a population must be determined at least in part by the reasons for
wanting to know these things. In the case of historical and
genealogical demography, there seem to be clear problems for
which at least a quantitative description is useful, if not an
understanding of the reasons for it.

1. Surnames behave like genes. Many geneticists and anthropol-
    ogists have used the presence of patronymy to estimate
    consanguinity, population size, heterogeneity of reproduc-
    tion, accumulation of genetic identity and probabilities
    of extinction.

2. Surnames can be used to match children with parents, and
    hence act as indicators of fertility.

3. Surnames can be used to gauge population growth.

4. Surnames can be used to study migration, especially in-mi-
    gration.

TABLE 14.   English male given names.

1850		1900		1975	
Name	%	Name	%	Name	%
William	14.49	William	8.97	Mark	4.26
John	12.41	John	7.76	Paul	4.24
George	7.88	George	6.09	Andrew	4.21
Thomas	7.88	Thomas	4.52	David	3.69
James	7.12	Charles	3.90	Richard	3.14
Henry	5.63	Frederick	3.76	Matthew	2.88
Charles	4.44	James	3.55	Daniel	2.86
Joseph	4.20	Albert	3.33	Darren	2.69
Robert	2.90	Ernest	2.69	Michael	2.55
Samuel	2.56	Robert	2.67	James	2.48
				Thomas	0.52
				Joseph	0.50
				George	0.21

TABLE 15.   English female given names.

1850		1900		1975	
Name	%	Name	%	Name	%
Mary	15.05	Florence	3.94	Sarah	3.71
Elizabeth	10.02	Mary	3.91	Nicola	3.40
Sarah	8.93	Alice	3.61	Claire	3.10
Ann	5.73	Annie	3.57	Emma	2.83
Eliza	4.37	Elsie	3.37	Joanne	2.71
Jane	4.29	Edith	3.37	Helen	2.26
Emma	3.93	Elizabeth	2.96	Lisa	2.24
Hannah	3.10	Doris	2.66	Michelle	1.88
Ellen	2.90	Ethel	2.46	Kate	1.86
Emily	2.32	Dorothy	2.46	Rachel	1.79
Florence	2.32	Sarah	1.52	Elizabeth	0.52
Alice	1.60			Ann	0.24
				Mary	0.14
				Alice	0.02

5.   Surnames can be used to infer relationships between popula-
     tions, if certain assumptions can be made about their
     origins.

6.   Common given names can be used in some cases to locate an
     individual in a given birth period with determinable prob-
     abilities, and hence can be used to facilitate computer-
     ized record linking and ordering.

7. In many cases spelling, especially of first names, can be used to date a person's time of birth.

8. Name frequencies may be used in automated record linking of separated files of birth, marriage and death records for the purpose of assembling genealogies by machine. This is the first major problem in our study of diseases in Laredo, and the major reason for our interest in naming statistics. Here there are several important questions we must ask in order to find a successful match among competing records, or to assess the problems to be expected in trying to find matching data in different records. Hand genealogical linking in smaller files will involve the same issues, but one must be much more specific and clear about decision-making criteria when programming a computer.

Problems in Automated Record Linking

    The difficulties in automated record linking are well known to those who have attempted it. (A good discussion of one method can be found in Skolnick, 1972; see Skolnick et al., 1977 and its references). Few researchers have yet become familiar with the procedures of automated record linking. However, many may try it in the near future as computing equipment becomes less expensive. Therefore, a brief discussion may be useful.

    If we are given a particular name and a time period in which to search (for example, when we are searching for the birth record of an individual we have accessed through his or her marriage record), we would like to know the a priori probability of finding that name in our list of birth records for the time period in question. How variable is this probability among all names in this time period? These questions are important because (1) it is very inefficient, and perhaps impossible, to search every list thoroughly for every possible error which could produce a slight mismatch among records, and (2) we must quantitatively assess the likelihood that, once found, a complete or partial match is actually the record being sought. Since the computer must determine all possible matches and then select the correct one, it is clear that we must design a search-and-evaluation algorithm which depends on the name structure being processed by the computer. In a time period for which multiple copies of the same whole name are unlikely, a name which is close to the one being sought might be assumed likely to be the "correct" name, and a link between the marriage and birth records might be made. On the other hand, if the name distribution leads us to expect to encounter many copies of the same name, we cannot use only the fact that we have found the name we are looking for to imply that a link between the records can be made. We must search more thoroughly through our birth records, access all possible records, and make a decision on the basis of other data.

Since all possible connections between partially matching records cannot be made (the computing requirements would be prohibitive) it is necessary to take into account many factors in designing search algorithms. In particular, the cost in time and programming complexity must be balanced against the increased accuracy provided by a more complex method. A general and comprehensive search being impossible, the task is to simplify in a way which is efficient and which minimizes both the number of correct links not made and the number of incorrect links made. The linking decisions will be made largely on the basis of partial matches, which is why a knowledge of the details of the data is important. If we know what kinds of problems might arise in a segment of data, we can design the search procedure to handle only those problems, thus simplifying matters greatly.

Errors in Records of Names

What is an "error" in historical/genealogical data? This is the major question in evaluating potential record matches. From a removed perspective, it seems that it might be easy to define various types of errors which could, in principle, be removed from the data or at least flagged as a signal that problems exist. Such errors would include: (1) typographical errors in computerizing records from the originals; (2) inadvertent spelling errors made by the official originally taking down the information; (3) unreadable handwriting; (4) misunderstanding of the information on the part of the recording official; (5) lack of care by the individuals or the officials in the actual spelling of information on the records; (6) "missense" changes, that is, changes such as letter substitutions or omissions which the individuals do not consider worth correcting or which, due to fashion, become acceptable ways of spelling names. There are probably other sources of error in addition to the above.

After the fact, it becomes impossible to determine when, or even if, most of these kinds of errors have occurred. This question is complex except in obvious cases in which bad handwriting or typographical errors can be spotted. An example might be the case of a name spelled incorrectly once on a record with the correct spelling appearing simultaneously on the same record. However, most changes in actual spelling due to the factors above cannot be identified if the individuals involved did not do so themselves when the records were being written. Thus, if a parent named Sanchez has a child whose baptismal record reads Sanches, and this situation is not later corrected, it often becomes the name used by the child. Is this an error? Does one correct or standardize the spelling? How does one differentiate among a change due to fashion, an inadvertent change, or two records which simply do not match because they are for different people?

It seems to us that in situations where handwriting may be difficult to read, where there may be illiteracy or casual attitudes toward spelling, or where records contain many variant spellings of names, that it is safest to assume that there is no "correct" spelling, and that all variants should be considered as one unit. This might be clearer if the issue is looked at the other way around. If there are many variants in a set of records (as there are), and if we know that spelling changes occur for many reasons (which we do), can we consider an <u>exact match</u> between records to be any more likely than a variant spelling?

Deciding what to do with uncertain links depends heavily on a statistical analysis of the name patterns, particularly of the variant categories as they change through time. We are forced to abandon any clear notion of the concept of "error" or of "sure" links in favor of a notion of probability or likelihood. This issue has been dealt with elsewhere by other historical demographers who have advanced various means to handle this problem (Skolnick, 1972; Wrigley, 1973).

A computer in search of a name must work by some specified statistical procedure. Such a procedure will be devised based on what we can perceive after the fact about the way in which names in a delimited population in the past were actually given. A person in search of a name works by some unspecified procedure based on what is perceived about the way names are being given to a changing, and hence open-ended, population of the future. There are many interesting mysteries in these processes. We hope to use the past behavior of parents in Laredo to construct the future behavior of our otherwise rather dull computer.

ACKNOWLEDGMENTS

Demographic Epidemiology of Aging and Disease, Paper No. 2. This work was accomplished with the help of the following federal grants, whose support is gratefully acknowledged: National Cancer Institute, CA-19311; National Institute of General Medicine Sciences, KO4 GM-00230 and GM-19513; and National Institute of Neurological and Communicative Diseases and Strokes, contract 74-C-913.

REFERENCES

Acheson, E. 1964. The Oxford record linkage study: A review of
     the method with some preliminary results. Proceedings of
     the Royal Society of Medicine 57:11.
Beauchamp, P., H. Charbonneau and Y. Lavoie 1973. Reconstitution
     automatique des familles par le programme "Hochelaga."
     Population 28e annee 1:39-57.
Dunkling, L. 1976. "First Names First". London.
Harris, A. 1977. Christian names in Solihull, Warwickshire, and
     Yardley, Worchestershire, 1540-1729. Local Population
     Studies 19:28-33.
Henry, L. 1967. "Manual de Demographie Historique". Paris:
     Librarie Droz.
Henry, L. 1974. "Noms et Prenoms". Dolhain, Belgium: Ordina
     Editions.
Lavoie, Y., P. Beauchamp and H. Charbonneau 1972. Automatic
     record linkage of nominal data: the experience of the
     17th Century Canadian censuses. Annual meetings of the
     Population Association of America.
Legare, J., Y. Lavoie and H. Charbonneau 1972. The early Cana-
     dian population: problems in automatic record linkage.
     The Canadian Historical Review LIII 4:427-442.
Newcombe, H. 1967. Record linking: the design of efficient sys-
     tems for linking records into individual and family histo-
     ries. American Journal of Human Genetics 19:335-359.
Rossmann, D. 1978. Increased fertility among amyotrophic lateral
     sclerosis and parkinsonism-dementia complex cases on the
     island of Guam. Ph.D. Thesis, University of Michigan.
Skolnick, M. 1974. The construction and analysis of genealogies
     from parish registers with a case study of Parma Valley,
     Italy. Ph.D. Thesis, Stanford University.
Wrigley, E. 1973. "Identifying People in the Past". London:
     Edward Arnold.

DISTRIBUTION OF LAST NAMES: A STOCHASTIC MODEL
FOR LIKELIHOOD DETERMINATION IN RECORD LINKING

Ranajit Chakraborty
Kenneth M. Weiss
David L. Rossmann
and
Susan L. Norton

INTRODUCTION

The study of last names got into the literature more than a century ago when G. H. Darwin (1875) recognized the parallelism of Y-chromosomal inheritance and transmission of paternally inherited surnames. Lotka (1931, 1939), on the other hand, treated the evolution of surnames based on the Galton-Watson branching process. The importance of last name distributions in Spanish-speaking cultures, where each person uses both paternal and maternal names (Shaw, 1960) for the study of human population structure has been emphasized by Yasuda and Morton (1967). The statistical properties of last name distributions and and their relevance in record linking purposes of genealogical research has been examined by Yasuda and Furusho (1971) and Yasuda et al. (1974). On the basis of these studies it was concluded that last name distribution and evolution can be analyzed by the theory of neutral mutations to predict the distributional form, immigration rate and extent of random isonymy (proportion of persons with the same surname). The distributional form and the probability of isonymous pairs should have direct relevance in likelihood determination of competing records for record linking purposes.

With this idea in mind as the data base of our Laredo genetic epidemiological study is progressing, we attempt here a preliminary analysis of last names for the time period over which the records are available to us. For comparison we also accumulated records on baptisms and burials in another Spanish culture population of Guam, which is smaller in size. In this preliminary report we emphasize the Guam data more because of its present time depth. In a later publication we will describe the features of the Laredo data to a fuller extent. In this report we attempted various statistical tests to examine the nature of name distribution. The change of such distributions over time is examined by constructing transition matrices from which the immigration rate estimation is attempted. An approximation of Karlin and McGregor's (1967) theory is worked out for some conditions which will be stated in the sequel.

AN INVENTORY OF THE AVAILABLE DATA

Data from Laredo, Texas

        At the present time there are twelve Catholic parishes in
the city of Laredo among which San Agustin is the largest and
oldest (established in 1767).   Throughout approximately the
first century of this city's existence, there was only one parish, namely San Agustin, and patently its records are central to
any effort to implement genealogical reconstruction of this
population. In Table 1 we present the number of records of each
kind available from all twelve parishes during the period 1875
to the present. When all records from the earlier time periods
are in our computer for detailed analysis in addition to these
figures we shall have 7,000 more baptism records, 1,400 more
marriage records, 4,000 burials and 2,600 confirmation records.
In the name of, say, baptism records apart from the child's
given name we also have available his/her middle name, paternal
and maternal last names. Similar information is also available
on each of his/her parents' and godparents' names which will all
be used to search for linking records.

Data from the Island of Guam

        The main source for the demographic history of Guam is a
set of records kept by the Catholic Church.   Rossmann (1978)
gives a detailed account of the records and describes various
characteristics and usefulness of these records for genealogical
reconstruction purposes which are also described by his presentation in this volume In Table 1 the approximate number of the
various kinds of records together with the time depth are presented. As in the case of the Laredo population, in this case
as well, the last-naming practice is to give both parental names
as is usual for most Spanish-speaking cultures.

TABLE 1. Vital and religious events recorded in Laredo and Guam

| | LAREDO | | GUAM | |
	Time Interval	No. of Records	Time Interval	No. of Records
Baptisms	Since 1875	120,000	1829-1973	5,500
Marriages	"	25,000	"	1,050
Burials	"	50,000	"	2,100
Confirmations	"	75,000	1920-1973	1,500

THE THEORY

Distribution of Surnames

If the transmission of last names follows the vertical mode of inheritance in family lines, as in the case of Spanish-speaking cultures where each individual carries the paternal as well as the maternal last name, the surname composition of a population at a given time point can be represented by the vector

$$M = (m_1, m_2, \ldots, m_r)$$

where m_i is the number of individuals carrying the ith specific surname. Note that some of these m_i values (but not all concurrently) may be zero in cases where such surnames are not represented at this point in time, and further Sum $m_i = N$, the total population size. In the case where r is large, so that the limiting form as $r \to \infty$ becomes appropriate and N, the population size is assumed to be constant over time. Following Karlin and McGregor (1967) we obtain the distribution of N_k, the number of surnames, each of which is represented by k copies in the population, as

$$E(N_k) = \frac{1}{k} \cdot \frac{Nv}{1-v} \cdot \frac{\left(\dfrac{N}{1-v} - (k+1) \right)}{\left(\dfrac{N}{1-v} - 1 \right)} \quad (N-k) \quad (N) \tag{1}$$

where v is a parameter that represents the joint effect of mutation and migration (or net immigration). In a short interval of time, ignoring the possibility of name spelling variations (an assumption which seems to be justified if names are standardized by combining spelling variants), v can be taken simply as the effect of immigration.

If N is rather large compared to k, that is, if equation (1) is used only to obtain the expected number of rare surnames, then by algebraic simplification (1) reduces to the form

$$E(N_k) = \frac{1}{k} \cdot \frac{Nv}{v} \cdot \prod_{i=1}^{k} \left(\frac{N+1-i}{\dfrac{N}{1-v} - i} \right)$$

$$\simeq \quad Nvk^{-1}(1-v)^{k-1} \tag{2}$$

It is easy to check that the total number of individuals, N, can be obtained by $\sum_k kE(N_k)$. Furthermore, if x_i represents the relative frequency of the ith surname in the population, the expected value of "random isonymy," i.e., the probability that the surnames of two individuals taken at random are identical is given by

$$I = E(\Sigma x_i^2) = \sum_k k^2 N_k / N^2$$
$$= \frac{1}{Nv} \tag{3}$$

Thus, if I is estimated from the data of name distributions from the observed values of N_k, then for known values of N, v may be estimated by $\hat{v} = (I \cdot N)^{-1}$.

Extinction Probability and Distribution of Progeny Size

If the progeny size distribution takes the form of a geometric distribution, i.e., the probability that an individual leaves r offspring for the next time period continuing the parental surname, P_r is given by

$$P_r = bc^{r-1}, \quad r = 1, 2, \ldots$$

With $P_0 = (1 - b - c)/(1 - c)$, the probability that a surname is extinct by n generations is given by

$$\phi_n = 1 - m^n(1 - P_0/c)/(m^n - P_0/c) \tag{4}$$

if the surname is represented by a single individual at the initial time period. In this formula, m represents the mean number of children per individual in a single time period. If there were k copies of the specific surname in the initial time period, the probability of extinction would be ϕ_n^k (Yasuda, et al. 1974). It is interesting to note that the expected time of extinction will be given, following the standard branching process treatment, by

$$E(T) = \sum_{k=1}^{\infty} \sum_{n=1}^{\infty} \frac{nNv}{k} \left[\left\{ 1 - m^n \left(\frac{1-s_0}{m^n - s_0} \right) \right\}^k - \left\{ 1 - m^{n-1} \left(\frac{1-s_0}{m^{n-1} - s_0} \right) \right\}^k \right] (1-v)^{k-1}$$

if the initial distribution of surnames is in the form of (2).

RESULTS AND CONCLUSIONS

As mentioned before, in this presentation we shall consider the data from Guam only for illustrative purposes. The baptism records in Guam are available from 1829. In order to understand the transition probability distribution of names from one generation to the next, we divided the entire time depth of 1825 to 1974 into six intervals each of 25 years length to represent a generation. The male childrens' paternal surnames were used to compare the observed distribution of surnames with the theoretical formula developed in the earlier section. Table 2 gives the observed data for 371 surnames found in the entire

---

TABLE 2. Comparison of the observed and expected distribution of last names on the island of Guam.

k	Observed N_k	Expected N_k
1	102	103.25
2	57	49.71
3	26	31.91
4	19	23.04
5	24	17.75
6	20	14.23
7	17	11.76
8	14	9.91
9	7	8.48
10	12	7.34
>10	73	93.62

Estimated random isonymy, $I = k^2 N_k / N^2 = 0.0097$

Total number of names, $N = k N_k = 2781$

$$\hat{v} = (I.N)^{-1} = 0.0371$$

---

time period from the male childrens' baptismal records. The last column of this table gives the expected N_k values as obtained by equation (2). The parameters N and v are estimated from the data as indicated in Table 2. The fit is reasonably satisfactory, the goodness of fit Chi-square being 19.21 with 9 degrees of freedom (P ≃ 0.025).

To test whether the transitions of surnames followed the theory described in the earlier section, we studied the probability of extinction for surnames from the baptism records of Guam for five generations separately. As noted by Yasuda et al. (1974), the expected probability of extinction depends on the parameters of the progeny size distribution, which are computed for our data in Table 3. These parameters apply for male children only, and a sex ratio of 1:1 is assumed.

TABLE 3.   Parameters of offspring size distributions.

Probability of k offspring, $P_k = bc^{k-1}$, $k \geq 1$

$$P_0 = (1 - b - c)/1 - c$$

Estimated $P_0 = 24/75 = 0.32$

$m = 1.1067$, assuming sex ratio 1:1

$b = (1 - P_0)^2/m = 0.4178$

$c = 1 - (1 - P_0)/m = 0.3856$

With these parameters the expected probabilities of extinction are computed by ϕ_n^k where ϕ is given by equation (4) for any value of k, the number of individuals with a specified surname at the start.   Since the number of observed cases is rather small for each value of k, we pooled the observations into two categories: k = 1 ~ 5, and k = 6 ~ 10.   The expectations corresponding to these categories are computed by the formula $\sum_k E(N_k)\phi_n^k$ where $E(N_k)$ values are given by equation (2).

The results are shown in Table 4.

TABLE 4.   Extinction of surnames after a given number of generations as a function of the number of people carrying these surnames at the start.

Number of Individuals with Surname at the Start		Extinction Probability After n Generations				
		n = 1	n = 2	n = 3	n = 4	n = 5
1 - 5	Obs.	0.3108	0.3725	0.4658	0.4773	0.4444
	Exp	0.2748	0.3467	0.4422	0.4804	0.5206
6 - 10	Obs	0.0000	0.0263	0.0385	0.0833	0.0000
	Exp	0.0024	0.0197	0.0324	0.0698	0.0857

As seen from Table 4, the agreement between the observed and expected probabilities is quite satisfactory although no statistical test for such agreement is made.

In conclusion we may say that the application of the Karlin-McGregor theory (Karlin and McGregor, 1967) to this study of surname distributions is based on approximations which are dif-

ficult to assert in practice.   However, the thesis that surname
evolution is similar to   gene evolution, as   seen in   the Parma
Valley data of Yasuda et.al. (1974), seems to hold for the
island of Guam as well. This finding can be fruitfully utilized
in determining the   likelihood of observing a given surname for
record linking purposes.

ACKNOWLEDGMENTS

Demographic Epidemiology of Aging and Disease Paper No. 3.
Research supported by U.S. Public Health Service Grants CA-19311
and GM-19513 from the National Institutes of Health.

REFERENCES

Darwin, G.H. 1875. Marriage between first cousins in England and
      their effects. J. Statis. Soc. 38: 153-184.
Karlin, S. and J. McGregor 1967. The number of mutant forms
      maintained in a population. Fifth Berkeley Symp. Math.
      Stat. Prob. 4: 415-438.
Lotka, A.J. 1931. The extinction of families. J. Wash. Acad.
      Sci. 21: 377.
Lotka, A.J. 1931. "Theorie analytique des associations biologi-
      ques, deuxieme partie". Paris: Hermann and Cie.
Rossmann, D.L. 1978. Increased   fertility among Amyotropic
      Lateral Sclerosis and Parkinsonism-Dementia complex cases
      on the island of Guam. Unpublished Ph.D. Dissertation,
      University of Michigan.
Rossmann, D.L. 1980. A semi-automated approach to genealogical
      reconstruction using "small" lists of vital events. (This
      volume).
Shaw, R.E. 1960. An index of consanguinity based on the use of
      the surname in Spanish-speaking countries. J. Hered. 51:
      221-230.
Yasuda, N., L.L. Cavalli-Sforza, M. Skolnick and A. Moroni 1974.
      The evolution of surnames: An analysis of their distribu-
      tion and extinction. Theor. Pop. Biol. 5: 123-142.
Yasuda, N. and T. Furusho 1971. Random and nonrandom inbreeding
      revealed from isonymy study in small cities of Japan. Hum.
      Genet. 23: 303-316.
Yasuda, N. and N.E. Morton 1967. Studies on human population
      structure. In "Third International Congr. Human Genet-
      ics". Baltimore: Johns Hopkins Univ. Press., 249-265.

A SEMI-AUTOMATED APPROACH TO GENEALOGICAL RECONSTRUCTION USING "SMALL" LISTS OF VITAL EVENTS

David L. Rossmann

Record linking is essentially a tedious and mechanical task. Names, dates and such have to be compared, and decisions made and recorded. In a really large study a totally automated approach to record linkage is mandatory. For example, the Laredo cancer epidemiology project involves hundreds of thousands of vital events, and we are developing methods to link them completely by machine. Other large studies have used their own automated methods (e.g. Skolnick, 1973, 1974). When small bodies of data are involved, well-defined procedures exist for manual record linkage (Fleury and Henry, 1965; Henry, 1970). Such methods of linking, in which the computer is at most an auxiliary tool, have been used in many historical studies (e.g. Gautier and Henry, 1958; Goubert, 1960; Wrigley, 1966; Norton, 1971). However, purely manual methods are very time-consuming, and as the number of records mounts into the thousands the task can become daunting.

Another avenue which we might explore is a semi-automatic approach to record linkage. We will attempt to marry the strong points of man and machine in a straightforward solution. The computer can handle large bodies of data and present it, organized in various ways, in a short period of time. It is also extremely accurate and consistent, not apt to lose or forget about any record it has stored. When it comes to deciding which records should be linked together, though, the complexity of the program which the machine requires increases tremendously. A decision about the linkage of two records can be thought of as a process of pattern recognition, the pattern being constructed from the names and dates in the records. Humans are intuitively very quick at recognizing patterns while machines must usually depend on exhaustive searches, so the decision-making in this type of record linkage is often done more efficiently by a human. The methods to be followed in the making of these decisions are just those well-defined ones developed by the workers in manual record linkage.

The process of record linkage is thus split in two. You make all the linkage decisions, have your hands on the data and control it at all times. The computer's task in this process is twofold. First, it stores all the records and the interconnections between them which develop as a result of your decisions. Second, it presents the record to you in a form which aids you in reaching those linkage decisions.

Genealogical Demography

The approach which I will describe is suitable for the linkage of small to moderate sized sets of vital events. I am sure it is not unique to me, but has probably been used in one form or another by others in the past. It can be used by anyone who can program in a language such as FORTRAN and has access to a file structuring method, which is nearly universally available on large computers and on most small ones as well. Thus, this method may be useful to many workers comtemplating or designing linkage studies of moderate size.

The approach was developed in connection with a study of two neurological diseases on the island of Guam. These diseases, amyotrophic lateral sclerosis (ALS) and parkinsonism-dementia (PD), occur at very high frequencies, accounting for one in four deaths of adult native Guamanians. They strike at an advanced age, from the mid-forties to mid-fifties, and are nearly always fatal within three to four years. While the diseases have probably been endemic on Guam for a long period of time, they were not recognized by the medical establishment until after World War II; so we have only thirty years of data on the affected individuals. The diseases cluster in families, and because of this were originally thought to be genetic in origin. However, the disease status of the offspring of cases is unknown, because nearly all of them have not yet reached the age of high risk of developing the diseases. Testing a genetic hypothesis, then, is very difficult. By reconstructing the genealogy of the population, we hoped to clarify the role of genetics in the causation of these diseases.

The main source for the demographic history of Guam is a set of records kept by the Catholic Church. In the 16th century, the Council of Trent decreed that each baptism, marriage or burial sanctioned by the Church be registered in the parish. When Jesuit missionaries came to Guam in the latter half of the 17th century they brought this tradition. Unfortunately, most of the Church records on Guam were destroyed during the Japanese occupation of the island in World War II. One book of records from the town of Agat survived, and most of the records from Umatac and Merizo were preserved. This is a fortunate coincidence, since Umatac and Merizo, especially the former, have the island's highest rates of ALS/PD. Umatac and Merizo have often been served by one priest, since they are small villages which are geographically close, and their records are intermingled in the surviving books.

The records of marriages and deaths in Umatac and Merizo begin in 1829 and are continuous to approximately 1862. At this point there is a break in the records of about thirty years because apparently a book, or books, was lost. The records resume in 1892 and are continuous to 1942, the beginning of the Japanese occupation of Guam. No records were kept during the occupation. The records extend from the end of World War II to the present. The earliest extant baptismal records are from

TABLE 1.   An example of a 19th century baptismal record in Span-
           ish. The names have been changed to maintain the con-
           fidentiality of the records.

Jose Lopez   En el ano del Senor mil ochocientos
indio, nino de   ochenta y cuarto dia doce de Abril. Io
Juan y de   Fr. Mariano Martinez de la Virgin del
Maria Portillo   Carmen, Agustino, Recoleto y Cura propio
                            de los pueblos de Merizo y Umata, pro-
                            vincia de las Islas Marianas, Diocesis
                            de Cebu, bautize solemnemente y puse los
                            Santos oleos en esta Iglesia de me cargo
                            a un nino que nacio a las siete del dia
                            diez de dicho mes, a qui en puse por
Nacio el dia   nombre Jose y es el undecimo hijo legi-
10 de Abril   timo y de legitimo matrimonio de Juan
de 1884 y fue   Lopez indio natural de Umata de oficio
bautisada el 12   Labrador y de Maria Portillo india
de id. id.   natural de Umata de oficio Labradora y
                            empadronados en el Barangay numero unico
                            de D. Juan Ramos. Abuelos paternos Mar-
                            iano Lopez indio natural de Agana de
                            oficio Labrador y Teresa Blanco india
                            natural de Umata de oficio Labradora y
                            ambos ya difuntos. Abuelos maternos
                            Luis Portillo indio natural de Umata de
                            oficio Labrador y Ana Palomino india
                            natural de Umata de oficio Labradora y
                            ambos tambien difuntos. Fue su padrino
                            Jose Calderon indio natural de Agana de
                            oficio Tabanero. I por verdad la firmo.

                                   (Signed) Mariano Martinez

1837. There is no break in the baptismal records in the late
1800's, and the only break which does occur is during World War
II. The total number of vital events for the entire period is
about 11,000. Records before 1935 were kept in Spanish, and
those of baptism, marriage and death were written out by the
priest in paragraph form, relatively standard for each type of
record, describing the event with the names of those involved
and the relevant places and dates. Unusual occurrences such as
a baptism by someone other than a priest were noted. (See Table
1 for an example of a pre-1935 baptismal record, Table 2 for for
an example of a pre-1935 marriage record, and Table 3 for an
example of a pre-1935 burial record). Since 1935 the records
have been kept in books formatted for each type of record, and
the priest merely fills in the names of the people involved and
the dates and places of the events.   This format has reduced
considerably the amount of information contained in the records.

TABLE 2.   An example of a 19th century marriage record in Span-
           ish. The names have been changed to maintain the con-
           fidentiality of the records.

Juan Lopez   En treinta dias del mes de Mayo de esta
con Maria   ano de mil ochocientos cincuenta y dos.
Portillo   Io Fr. Manuel de la Encarnacion Cura
                              Parraco de esta Villa de Umata corridas
                              las proclamas y no habiendo resultado
                              impedimento alguno, autorize el matrimo-
                              nio que <u>infacie</u> <u>Ecleria</u> <u>et</u> <u>coram</u> <u>testi-</u>
                              <u>bus</u> contrajo Juan Lopez soltero hijo de
                              Mariano y de Teresa Blanco con Maria
                              Portillo viuda hija de Luis y de Ana
                              Palomino los que fueron sui testigos y
                              Padrinos Joaquin Andujar y Filomena Gar-
                              cia, por lo que les di las benediciones
                              nupciales y para que conste lo firmo.

                                   (Signed) Manuel de la Encarnacion

TABLE 3.   An example of a 19th century burial record in Spanish.
           The names have been changed to maintain the confiden-
           tiality of the records.

Jesus Andujar   En vienta dias del mes de Agosto de mil
                              ochocientos cincuenta y cinco se enterre
                              en esta Cemeterio de Sn. Dimas de Mer-
                              izo el Cadaver de Jesus Andujar parbulo,
                              hijo de Joaquin y de Filomena Garcia
                              vecinos de Merizo. I para que conste lo
                              firmo.

                                   (Signed) Juan Fernandez

The computer's bookkeeping task involves both the storage of the
records and links, and the presentation of this data in a form
which is of use to the human in making the linkage decisions.
The programs which are needed to organize the data in various
useful ways are quite straightforward. In nearly all cases they
are simply sorts of the different types of records, baptisms,
marriages and burials, on the various pieces of information
these records hold in common. The results are lists of records
in which potential links are grouped together. You then decide
which links to make. The other half of the computer's task is
to keep track of all the records and all the linkage decisions

you have made. This task can be managed efficiently with a
judicious choice of what method to use in storing the records in
the computer. The records will need to be accessed in two ways.
The production of sorted lists will require the access of all
records, while the assignment and checking of linkage decisions
requires individual access to each record. An indexed sequential file structure satisfies both of these requirements. In an
indexed sequential file the records are stored in sequential
order. An index is also constructed which points to the location of each record based on the "key", which is an item of
information from the record. The data can be accessed sequen-
tially when one needs to examine all of it, and if an individual
record is required it can be retrieved by supplying the record's
key. This key can be any piece of information in the record
which will allow its identification, such as a name or an arbitrarily assigned number.

The storage of the linkage decisions is another part of
the computer's task. One way of storing these links would be to
create a new record whenever a link was made, which incorporated
information from the linked records, and then to eliminate these
original records. This saves space in the computer. If you
decide to break this link at some point in the future, though,
you might have some difficulty recovering the original unlinked
records, and the linking and unlinking processes would involve
moving a large amount of data. A simpler way to handle this
problem is to provide a space in each of the records for pointers to other records linked to this one. The obvious choice for
a pointer in indexed sequential files is the key of the record.
When you make a link, the key of each linked record is written
in the appropriate position of the other record (for an example
see Figure 1). If, in the future, you must break this link it
is only necessary to change one part of the record, the key,
without disturbing at all any of the data which originally made
up this record.

When you design the structure of the records in the
indexed sequential files, some thought should be given not only
to what they contain originally, but also to what they will need
to contain in the future. Throughout the linkage process you
will be adding information to the original data. Place should
be provided for this new information. You will have to provide
space for pointers to other linked records. If name variants or
misspellings are a problem you will probably want to provide
space for a standardized spelling for the names in the records,
or for some coded version of the name. As records are linked
together, you may want to allow space for some calculated
values, such as the age at marriage or birth interval, that will
be used often in analysis. This will spare you recalculations
in the future. The linkage process is going to add quite a lot
of new information to the data, so it is wise to plan ahead for
it, and not become locked into the punched card format you may
have used to enter the records into the computer.

```
+-------------------+                    +-------------------+
| Before Linkage    |                    |  After Linkage    |
+-------------------+                    +-------------------+
```

Baptism record [key 2435]		Description		Baptism record [key 2435]	
Word	Contents			Word	Contents
1	JOSE	First name		1	JOSE
2	LUNA	Middle name		2	LUNA
3	GOMEZ	Last name		3	GOMEZ
.				.	
.				.	
.				.	
12	2435100345	Baptism file key *1,000,000 + baptism identification number		12	2435100345
.				.	
.				.	
19	0	Burial file key *1,000,000 + burial identification number		19	3134500067
.				.	
.				.	

Burial record [key 3134]		Description		Burial record [key 3134]	
Word	Contents			Word	Contents
1	JOSE	First name		1	JOSE
2	LUNA	Middle name		2	LUNA
3	GOMEZ	Last name		3	GOMEZ
.				.	
.				.	
.				.	
12	0	Baptism file key *1,000,000 + baptism identification number		12	2435100345
.				.	
.				.	
19	3134500067	Burial file key *1,000,000 + burial identification number		19	3134500067
.				.	
.				.	

Records of Jose Luna Gomez, born 10 February 1840, died 7
June 1882. Baptism ID number 100345; baptism file key 2435.
Burial ID number 500067; burial file key 3134.

FIGURE 1. Illustration of link between baptism and burial
          records.

A link between any pair of vital records is one of two basic types. The records either report on one individual at different times in his life (e.g. the link between his baptism record and the record of his marriage), or they report on two individuals who are related (e.g. the link between the baptism record of a child and the record of marriage of his parents). The former type will be designated an intra-individual link, while the latter will be termed an intra-familial link. In the search for links, all information held in common by the two records is considered. This information is usually the name of the individual(s) being reported on and the names of his parents, possibly with other relatives' names. Because of this, this type of linkage is known as nominal record linkage. If the names match between records and the dates are congruent (e.g. for an intra-individual baptism-marriage link the baptism occurs more than fifteen but less than fifty years before marriage) the link is accepted. As the linkage proceeds, more complex comparisons involving groups of records are also made.

The linkage process, then, is primarily a process of comparing names. Dates and places may also be available, but they are used mostly as a final check on the validity of a potential link which arises due to an identity of names. The Guamanian naming convention, which provides that an individual's mother's maiden surname become his middle name, greatly increases the discriminating power of an individual's full name over that which is the case, for example, in the United States. In the U.S., the middle name most often is only another given name, and is frequently recorded on records subsequent to birth as simply an initial. In these circumstances the middle name provides very little additional information when using names to link records; one has usually only two names to work with, the given name and the surname. The Guamanian system, on the other hand, provides three useful names which are recorded in full on most records, and the middle as well as the last name provides genealogical information. Moreover, until recently, a married woman has continued to use her full original name throughout life, rather than adopting her husband's surname. The Guam church records also provide the full names of quite a number of relatives (i.e. parents and grandparents on birth and burial records) so that one often may have as many as eleven names (the individual's three names, both parents' given and middle names, and the four grandparents' given names) to compare when evaluating a link. This increases greatly the certainty of each link over the case where one has only the given name and surname of an individual and the given names of his parents to compare in linking. In fact, the three-generation depth of information in many of these records allows the incorporation in pedigrees of persons for whom no record reports individually but whose existence is known due to appearances as a relative on other records.

To cope with the variant spellings in the Guam records, a standard form of every name was chosen and assigned to each name

(cf. Weiss et al. and Chakraborty et al., this volume). Space
was saved for these standard spellings at the time of file creation, and the indexed sequential file structure made the standard name assignment relatively simple. All non-blank names were
extracted from the files and written into one of three files:
male given names, female given names or surnames. These three
files were sorted into alphabetic order. There were 21,471 male
given names, 22,822 female given names and 31,773 surnames. The
files were printed out and the standard spellings were chosen
manually. These names were then added to the three name files.
The files were separated into files based on which type of
record the name was taken from (baptism, marriage, etc.). The
standard names were then added to the indexed sequential files.
Thus standard spellings were quickly provided for all 76,065
names at one time.

        As provision was made for a standard spelling for each
name, an absolute date was provided for each calendar date in
the records. This absolute date is the cumulative number of
days which have elapsed from January 1, 1601 to the date of the
event. (This starting date was chosen arbitrarily). The difference between any two dates is then simply found by subtracting
the absolute dates. Using this method all ages and intervals
which are calculated for each record in the files are in days.

        As an example of how you would use this method to discover
and then make links between vital events, we will examine the
intra-familial link between a child's baptism record and his
parents' marriage record. If the baptism and marriage records
are sorted together, with spouses' names from the marriage
record matched with the parents' names from the baptism record
(see Table 4), the resulting list will contain a natural clumping of marriage records with the baptism records of the children
who were produced by that marriage. When a link is made, the
key of the marriage record can be entered into each of the baptism records to which it is linked. This list will also provide
a natural clumping of siblings for which there is no associated
marriage record, either because of immigration of the parents
into the study area or missing marriage records. The Guam
records required extensive use of these sibling sets because
there was a thirty year gap in the marriage and burial records
during the latter half of the 19th century. Nuclear families
can be reconstructed either from links of baptism to marriage
records or simply from baptism records. The search for links
should be treated as an iterative process. After the obvious
links have been made the process is repeated, searching for the
less obvious links.

        With the determination of a set of definite links a new
file will need to be constructed. Each record in this file is
patterned on the family reconstitution form of the manual record
linker. It brings together all of the information about a
nuclear family which has been built up during the linkage pro-

TABLE 4.   Names used and order of sort for the   baptism to mar-
           riage record intra-familial link

                                  Name

Order	Baptismal record	Marriage record
1	Surname	Groom's surname
2	Middle name	Bride's surname
3	Father's middle name	Groom's middle name
4	Mother's middle name	Bride's middle name
5	Father's given name	Groom's given name
6	Mother's given name	Bride's given name
7	Father's FA given name	Groom's FA given name
8	Father's MO given name	Groom's MO given name
9	Mother's FA given name	Bride's FA given name
10	Mother's MO given name	Bride's MO given name

cess. The information in it is abstracted from the individual
records of baptism, marriage and burial which have been linked
together. It is not simply the final step of the linkage process, though, but an integral part of it. These records contain
considerably more information than the individual records of
vital events and greatly aid the decision-making process for
records which had no obvious links in the first part of the
linkage. Take, for example, an illegitimate individual. On his
baptismal record his surname is that of his father. The mother
subsequently marries. When this individual marries, the surname
on the marriage record is the surname of his mother's husband,
who may or may not be his father; and his mother's surname,
which was his surname on his baptismal record, is now his middle
name. When the marriage and baptismal records are first compared for an intra-individual link, they appear not to link
because the surname and middle name do not match, and there is
no father listed on the baptismal record, but a father is listed
on the marriage record. The facts that the given name and the
mother's name match between the two records and that the dates
are reasonable imply that the link is possible, but are not
enough to make the link. After the nuclear family file has been
constructed, however, more information is available in evaluating this link. Since the mother's subsequent marriage is indicated on the nuclear family record in which the child's baptismal record occurs, the name of her husband is known. When this
new information is included in the comparison of the original
baptismal and marriage records, all names match and the link can
be made.

     This file is also useful for bridging gaps in the records.
The sets of siblings without an associated parents' marriage

record can define a family record here. Information about the
parents is available from the siblings' baptism records and can
be used to search for the families in which the parents appear
as children. If these families are discovered, the siblings are
thereby linked to their grandparents even though the marriage of
their parents is missing from the records. In the Guam records,
this procedure allowed the filling in of the thirty year gap of
missing marriage records. No break in the genealogies occurred,
some of which extend over eight generations.

        The information contained in the family reconstitution
form file created from the Guam records is listed in Table 5.
Table 6 provides the sequence of linkage steps which leads to
the construction of the file.

        This family reconstitution form file can be the final pro-
duct of the semi-automatic linkage method as it is for the
manual linkage method. These records provide a great deal of
information as they are a distillation of all the information in
the original records plus the new information developed during
the linkage process. They were extremely useful in the Guam
study, in examining the fertility of cases in relation to that
of unaffected individuals. These family reconstitution form
records contain all the necessary information for such an analysis. They include the dates of birth and death of all the
offspring of a nuclear family, as well as calculated values such
as the interval between births and the age of the parents at the
birth of each child.

TABLE 5. Contents of a single record in the family reconstitu-
          tion form file (FRF)

Part I. General Information about the FRF
Words 1-9. Include:
    FRF key *1,000,000 + FRF ID number
    Marriage file key *1,000,000 + marriage ID number
        for associated marriage
    Date of marriage
    Length of marriage
    Number of children

Part II. Information Relating to Husband
Words 10-54. Include:
    Name
    Parents' and grandparents' names
    Date and place of birth or baptism

TABLE 5. (continued...)

      Age at marriage
      Date and place of confirmation
      Date and place of death or burial
      Age at death or burial
      Information from NINCDS family history records,
         including ALS/PD diagnosis
      Key and ID numbers for birth, confirmation, death
         and other marriage records, and for parents'
         FRF record

Part III. Information Relating to Wife
Words 55-99.
      (This is nearly identical to information
      included for husband)

Part IV. For EACH Child
Words 1-37. Include:
    Name
    Sex
    Date and place of birth or baptism
    Date and place of confirmation
    Age at confirmation
    Date and place of first marriage
    Age at first marriage
    Date and place of death or burial
    Age at death or burial
    Interval to previous birth
    Rank of birth in family (1st, 2nd, etc.)
    Legitimacy
    Information from NINCDS family history records,
       including ALS/PD diagnosis
    Keys and ID numbers for birth, confirmation, mar-
       riage and death records, and for FRF record
       associated with child's own marriage

The 11,000 records of vital events from Umatac and Merizo were linked to form 2,068 nuclear families. These families contained 6,588 children of which 6,037 were derived from one or more vital records while 551 were identified due to their presence as relatives (parents or grandparents) on one or more vital records. Of the 3,724 parents of the 2,068 nuclear families (there aren't 4,136 parents because some of the nuclear families are illegitimate with only the mother listed) 2,451 appear as children in other nuclear families. So there are 7,861 unique individuals in the family reconstitution form file covering the period from roughly 1830 to 1972. The 1970 population of Umatac and Merizo was about 2,500 individuals.

TABLE 6. Construction of the family reconstitution form file.

Phase I
A. Links (intra-familial) are established between:
   1. Baptism and marriage records of parents of bap-
     tized individual
   2. Baptisms relating to sibs
B. Links (intra-individual) are established between
   baptism and non-baptism records relating to same
   individual:
   3. Baptism and marriage of baptized individual
   4. Baptism and confirmation
   5. Baptism and notice of marriage
   6. Baptism and burial
C. Links (intra-individual) are established between
   non-baptism records relating to same individual:
   7. Marriage and burial
   8. Marriage and marriage (implies remarriage of
     individual)
   9. Confirmation and marriage
   10. Confirmation and burial

Creation of the FRF file. A family record is established for each marriage record, notice of marriage and
sibset group.

Phase II
A. Use of full information provided by FRF record to:
   1. Search for additional baptism, confirmation,
     marriage and burial links to those individuals
     who are on an FRF record as either a parent or
     a child
   2. Create new sibsets in which individuals are
     defined by non-baptism records
B. Addition of new FRF records for remaining, singleton baptisms. Links made between:
   3. Confirmation and burial records and parents of
     new FRF records
   4. Parents of new FRF records and their parents'
     FRF records
C. Addition of children to existng FRF records. These
   children have no baptism record but are defined
   by confirmation, marriage or death records, or
   their presence as parents on other FRF records.

Calculations made on FRF file. These include age at
marriage and death calculated from linked records,
duration of marriage and interval between births.

The reconstructed genealogies have proven quite beneficial to the continuing study of ALS/PD on Guam. They have provided a possible explanation of the high frequency of the diseases on the island (Rossmann, 1978). The semi-automatic method used here is a straightforward and easily implemented technique for the linkage of other small to moderate sized sets of vital events.

ACKNOWLEDGMENTS

This work was completed with the assistance of the following, whose support is gratefully acknowledged: a Fellowship from the Population Council; the National Institute of Neurological and Communicative Disorders and Stroke, contract 74-C-913; the National Cancer Institute, grant CA-19311 and the National Institute of General Medical Sciences, grant GM-19513.

REFERENCES

Fleury, M. and L. Henry 1965. "Nouveau manuel de depouillement et d'exploitation de l'etat civil ancien". Paris: L'Institut National d'Etudes Demographiques.

Gautier, E. and L. Henry 1958. "La population de Crulai, paroisse normande: Etude historique". Paris: L'Institut National d'Etudes Demographiques.

Goubert, P. 1960. "Beauvais et le Beauvaisis de 1600 a 1730, contribution a l'histoire sociale de la France du XVIIe siecle". Paris: Ecole Pratique des Hautes Etudes -- VIe Section, Centre de Recherches Historiques.

Henry, L. 1970. "Manuel de demographie historique". Geneva: Librairie Droz.

Norton, S.L. 1971. Population growth in Colonial America: A study of Ipswich, Massachusetts. Population Studies 25: 433-452.

Rossmann, D.L. 1978. Increased fertility among amyotrophic lateral sclerosis and parkinsonism-dementia complex cases on the island of Guam. Ph.D. Dissertation, The University of Michigan.

Skolnick, M. 1973 The resolution of ambiguities in record linkage. In "Identifying People in the Past". pp. 102-127, E.A. Wrigley (ed.) London: Edward Arnold.

Skolnick, M. 1974. The construction and analysis of genealogies from parish registers with a case study of Parma Valley, Italy. Ph.D. Dissertation, Stanford University.

Wrigley, E.A. 1966. Family limitation in pre-industrial England. Economic History Review 19: 82-109.

ANCESTORS AT THE NORMAN CONQUEST

Kenneth W. Wachter

There are few illustrations of the inevitability of math in history so apt as the popular puzzle about the number of ancestors anyone had during some great historical event like the Norman Conquest. Each of us has two parents. If we reason that two parents mean four grandparents, eight great grandparents, and twice as many ancestors more each generation back, then each of us should have had a thousand million ancestors alive when William the Conqueror stumbled up the sands toward Hastings. Carrying the fallacy a step further, the ancestors of an English person of today would have been so numerous at the time the Emperor Hadrian visited his northern province that there would have been one ancestor for every square inch of surface area of the globe -- land and ocean.

The flaw in this reasoning, saving us from having such a myriad of ancestors, is not hard to pinpoint. People can marry their cousins, and so the distinct positions in a pedigree need not be filled by distinct men and women. But the question remains, how many distinct ancestors is a person likely to have had at any time? For how many generations back does the number of distinct ancestors grow larger? When does it start to shrink? Can a typical person expect to be descended, back beyond some date in the past, from the whole population of his country of origin, or at least from everyone in the population who had descendants? In this chapter we offer answers to these questions on the basis of a simple probability model. The exercise is an amusing one, and it exemplifies points of contact between model building and less formal varieties of speculation.

As a genealogist constructs a family tree, working backwards through time, he is effectively choosing for each individual in the tree two people out of some pool of possible candidates to record as the individual's parents. If the individual is generation $g = 0$, then at generation $g = 1$ there is one father and one mother. At generation $g = 2$ there are $2^2 = 4$ positions in the family tree, 2 for males, 2 for females. At generation $g = 3$ there are 2^3 positions in all in the tree, 2^2 of them for males and 2^2 of them for females. Thus g generations back there are 2^g positions in the tree, 2^{g-1} for males

Genealogical Demography

and 2^{g-1} for females. We shall suppose that the 2^{g-1} postions

for males are filled by m(g) distinct male ancestors and the

2^{g-1} positions for females are filled by f(g) females. To fill

the 2^{g+1} slots in the tree for generation g+1, the genealogist
must find m(g) + f(g) fathers for all the distinct males and
females of generation g. We suppose that he must find these
fathers out of some collection of x(g+1) men. He must also find
m(g) + f(g) mothers out of some collection of y(g+1) women. Of
these fathers, some m(g+1) will be distinct men, and of the
mothers some f(g+1) will be distinct women. What we want is a
model which allows us to calculate expected values for the numbers m(1), f(1), m(2), f(2),... going back in time.

Whenever two slots in a family tree are filled by the same
person, it means that further down the tree a couple who married
were in fact cousins. It seems sensible to distinguish between
two sorts of cousin marriage, close and distant, and this distinction forms an essential step in our analysis. Marriages of
close cousins, on the one hand, presumably involve a conscious
choice of a cousin as a marriage partner, and they may reflect
social preference for cousin marriage, desires to keep property
in families, special opportunities for acquaintanceship and
affiliation through a kin network, and similar social factors.
Such choice would be systematic rather than random. Marriages
of distant cousins, on the other hand, must often arise from
accident, without the couple knowing of the kin relationship.
If a bride's and groom's ancestors come from the same country,
there being only a limited number of people alive at any point
in the past in that country, then chances are that the couple
have ancestors in common. Duplicate people in the slots in the
family tree are likely to occur at random, with more of these
random duplications the larger the number of slots to be filled
and the smaller the pool of people in the population from which
these slots must be filled. A probability model ought to be
able to predict chances of various numbers of duplications. On
these grounds we propose to regard close cousin marriage as a
systematic process and distant cousin marriage as a random process.

We should mention that there are arguments for opposite
points of view, emphasizing the random character of close cousin
marriage or the systematic character of distant cousin marriage.
For close cousin marriage, Gilbert and Hammel (1966) have
demonstrated by microsimulation that in one society where elaborate cousin-preference systems have been supposed, a simple random model based on geographic propinquity would explain a large
fraction of the observed close cousin marriage. For distant
cousin marriage, it is easy to hypothesize patterns of social or
geographical stratification which would severely restrict the
pool of plausible candidates from among whom not only each per-

son's parents but his or her more distant forebears would be found. Such statification would give less scope to randomness. Geneticists interested in coefficients of inbreeding more complicated than our simple measure, the number of distinct ancestors, have collected some data on consanguinity in western societies. This work in summarized in Chapters 7 and 8 of Bodmer and Cavalli-Sforza (1971), but strictness of stratification over long time periods is not readily estimable from it. For some groups, stratification may have been so rigid, pervasive and prolonged as to be an important determinant of distant cousin marriage, but it is hard to imagine this being true for a majority of any national population.

A genealogist filling in a family tree who talks of a choice of parents or a pool of candidates eligible to be ancestors is adopting an artificial but a useful point of view. In the world where clocks run forward, brides choose grooms and grooms choose brides or parents choose them for them, but the effect, as we should see it if we ran the clock backward, is that children acquire parents, and more and more branches grow on the genealogical tree.

It may be right not only to think of the branches of the tree as spreading but to think of the ancestors on it spreading out through the country and through society. Even if the chance of mobility at any one generation is small, over many generations it can add up to a lot of movement. Furthermore, evidence is coming to light that geographical mobility may not have been infrequent, even in rural villages centuries ago. Chapter 2 of Laslett (1977) contains interesting material along these lines. Immigration and emigration do complicate matters, and we shall restrict our treatment of ancestors to the case of an English person of wholly English ancestry. For such a person, we shall assume that over the span of time back to 1500 ancestors diffuse through most regions of the country and most social classes. This assumption may be wrong, but it is a good one for a first attack.

In our model we measure time in generations, each generation lasting 30 years. This is a handy figure. It would be elementary to change our calculations to allow for some change in the span of a generation as we go back in time, if we could agree on some account of how the span has changed. More effort would be involved in allowing for random spans of generation, letting the same person appear not only at different positions in the genealogical tree but at different levels. Such duplications between levels imply marriages between distant cousins "several times removed," as the phrase goes in some dialects. These certainly occur, although it is not obvious that the total number of distant cousin marriages is much altered by letting them occur between cousins several times removed.

For times when the number of ancestors is large enough for
a random model of "parent choice" to be appropriate, we formu-
late our model in the following way: Consider m(g) distinct
males and f(g) distinct females in the tree at the g-th generation back.   At generation g+1 we have x(g+1) males and y(g+1)
females from whom the parents of these people must be drawn.
Think of distributing m(g) + f(g) "fatherhood markers" among the
x(g+1) males, just as we might distribute m + f balls among x
bins. More than one ball may go into the same bin. The first
ball may land in any of x bins, the second again in any of x
bins, and so there are $x^m x^f$ possible combinations of balls in
bins or fatherhood markers on eligible males. If we distribute
balls among bins at random, giving each of the $x^m x^f$ combinations
an equal chance, the probability of obtaining exactly u nonempty
bins, or exactly u distinct fathers, is given by a formula on
pages 60 and 102 of Feller (1968), namely

$$\frac{x!}{u!(x-u)!} \sum_{x=0}^{u} \frac{(-1)^k u!(u-k)^{m+f}}{k!(u-k)!x^{m+f}}$$

This is the probability that m(g+1) be equal to u given m(g) and
f(g) in our model, in other words, the probability of having
exactly u distinct male ancestors at the next generation back.
The same formula applies to motherhood markers and female ancestors.

    For this probability distribution the mean of u equals the
expression

$$x - x(1 - 1/x)^{m+f}$$

Using exp[z] to stand for the constant e raised to the z-th
power, the quantity x{1 - exp[(-m-f)/x]} is an excellent approximation to this mean when x is large.   Thus, given m(g) and
f(g), the expectations of m(g+1) and f(g+1) are the following
functions of the sizes x(g+1) and y(g+1) of the pools of eligible fathers and mothers:

    Em(g+1) = x(g+1){1 - exp[(-m(g) - f(g))/x(g+1)]},

    Ef(g+1) = y(g+1){1 - exp[(-m(g) - f(g))/y(g+1)]}.

    Under the model just cited for m + f balls in x bins, the
number of empty bins x - u has an approximately Poisson probability distribution when m + f and x are large. Its variance is
therefore close to its mean.   Its standard deviation, being
close to the square root of its mean, is very small relative to

the mean, less than one thousandth of the mean for x in the millions, the range of values of x that we shall have. Thus for
our purposes it is fair to identify the random variables m(g)
and f(g) with their mean values. Then assuming a sex ratio
close to 1.00 for the sizes of the pools x(g) and y(g), we have
approximate equality at every generation between the number of
distinct male ancestors m(g) and the number of distinct female
ancestors f(g), and we may replace m(g) + f(g) by 2m(g) and
write our recurrence equation in the form

$$m(g+1)/x(g+1) = 1 - \exp[-2(m(g)/x(g)).(x(g)/x(g+1))]$$

The quantity m(g)/x(g) is the proportion that actual ancestors
form out of the pool of those eligible to be ancestors at the
g-th generation. The equation expresses this proportion as a
function of its previous value and the growth rate x(g+1)/x(g)
of the pool.

    We might be concerned that the probability distribution
from Feller puts no constraint on the ratio of children m(g) +
f(g) to parents m(g+1) + f(g+1). Our model might be unrealistic
in producing arbitrarily large family sizes. It is a relief to
notice, therefore, that the small standard deviation relative to
the mean insures us that the probability of ratios out of line
with the growth rate of the pool itself is negligible. Were we
not using total population or some other pool that grew primarily by natural increase, the average family size in the model
might stray from the plausible range [1].

    We have now formulated our model for the effects of dis-
tant cousin marriage. We still need some assumptions about the
effects of close cousin marriage. In the absence of better
information on this subject, the author has consulted his own
family tree researched by his mother. The first place where two
slots are filled by the same person occurs six generations back,
where a man named Ebenezer appears twice, being the grandfather
of both Tabitha and Thomas Bishop, who are man and wife. Each
of Ebenezer's parents of course then occurs twice, so there are

only 2^6 - 1 or 63 distinct males and 2^6 - 1 or 63 distinct

females, making 2^7 - 2 = 126 distinct people at the seventh generation due to this close cousin marriage. Whether two duplications after a stretch of six generations back from the first are
too many or too few is hard to say. Other duplications occur
further back in this tree. Pending better evidence, we shall
allow 63 instead of 64 male ancestors at the seventh generation,
and again allow 63 instead of 64 distinct male ancestors for
each of these 63 males back another six generations to the thirteenth. We do the same for females. These are our fixed allow-
ances for close cousin marriage. Beyond the thirteenth generation back, the total number of ancestors is large enough that
the number of duplications predicted by the random model for

distant cousin marriage eclipses these adjustments. We shift to
the random model at g = 13 with m(g) = 63 x 63 = 3969 and f(g) =
63 x 63 = 3969, proceeding on from there.

We begin our calculations with a child born in England of
wholly English ancestry around 1947 who reaches the age of 30 in
1977. We trace the values of m(g) back at intervals of 30
years. Assuming wide diffusion of ancestors throughout the
society and the country by 1600, we take x(g) + y(g) to be the
total population of England for all earlier years. If desired,
these values could be reduced by guesses at the numbers of
infertile men and women, members of religious orders, and others
not eligible to be the parents of each generation. Since there
is wide uncertainty in the total population figures themselves,
such guesses are not likely to improve our answers very much.
We might consider taking the adult population at each 30-year
interval instead of the total population. Taking total population, however, gives some leeway for the differing ages of marriage and childbirth among different members of the family tree.

In order to carry out our exercise, we need guesses at the
population of England in medieval times. Unfortunately, all
such guesses are speculative. We have taken the values back to
1230 from the graph on page 386 and the remarks on page 387 of
Hollingsworth (1969) and for dates before that we have interpolated between estimates of Josiah Russell (1948). The most
accurate estimates pertain to 1377 and 1347. Although we should
not trust any of the figures too far, they suffice for our purposes.

The results of our calculations appear in Table 1. The
last column shows the generation g. The first column shows an
average date when the ancestors in this generation are reaching
the age of 30, and the second column shows our guess at the
total English population x(g) + y(g) at this year. The third
column shows our estimate of the number of distinct ancestors
m(g) + f(g) = 2m(g). The proportion of ancestors in the pool,
m(g)/x(g), occupies the fourth column and the rate of growth of
the pool, x(g+1)/x(g) the fifth column. Raising e to the power
given by minus twice the fourth column divided by the fifth
column and subtracting the result from unity gives the entry in
the next row in the fourth column. In this way, given the population figures, we generate the next row of the table from the
preceeding row. The seventh column shows 2^g, the total number
of distinct slots in the family tree.

The outcomes of our model are intriguing. Around the dis-
covery of America, our individual has more than 60,000 distinct
ancestors. Some 95% of the slots in the family tree at this
level are still filled by different people. But back as far as
the time of Wycliffe and the Peasants' Revolt, at the twentieth
generation, the number of distinct ancestors has grown beyond
600,000, and nearly a third of the slots in the tree are filled

TABLE 1.   Predictions of numbers of distinct ancestors   at each
           generation.

Date	x(g)+y(g)	m(g)+f(g)	$\frac{m(g)}{x(G)}$	$\frac{x(g+1)}{x(g)}$	2^g	g
1947	———	2	———	———	2	1
1587	3,500,000	7,938	.0022	.829	8,192	13
1557	2,900,000	15,833	.0054	.759	16,384	14
1527	2,200,000	31,438	.0142	.773	32,768	15
1497	1,700,000	61,728	.0363	.765	65,536	16
1467	1,300,000	117,776	.0905	.923	131,072	17
1437	1,200,000	213,874	.1782	1.167	262,144	18
1437	1,200,000	213,874	.1782	1.167	262,144	18
1407	1,400,000	368,579	.2632	1.607	542,288	19
1377	2,250,000	628,576	.2793	1.622	1,048,576	20
1347	3,650,000	1,063,510	.2913	.877	2,097,152	21
1317	3,200,000	1,553,820	.4855	.906	4,194,304	22
1287	2,900,000	1,906,866	.6575	.931	8,388,608	23
1257	2,700,000	2,042,455	.7564	.926	16,777,216	24
1227	2,500,000	2,012,114	.8048	.800	33,554,432	25
1197	2,000,000	1,732,588	.8662	.850	67,108,864	26
1167	1,700,000	1,478,584	.8697	.824	134,217,728	27
1137	1,400,000	1,230,650	.8790	.929	268,435,456	28
1107	1,300,000	1,104,255	.8494	.846	536,870,912	29
1077	1,100,000	952,279	.8657	———	1,073,741,824	30

by duplicate people. Just before the Black Death, nearly 30% of
the 3,650,000 inhabitants of England turn up as ancestors. Moving back through the reign of King John, we find the number of
ancestors starting to decline from its high point of around 2
million. Each person in the tree is occupying an average of 16
slots. The effect of distant cousin marriage on the numbers of
distinct ancestors is becoming enormous. By then 80% of the
population were ancestors of our single individual.

     With 80% already ancestors under King John, we might
expect that the whole population would be turning up as ancestors a few generations further back. Surprisingly, the proportion in the fourth column of our table never rises to 100%. In
fact, it oscillates around 85% for all the generations of Plan-
tagenet and Norman kings. Our individual is likely to be
descended from only about 85% of the population at the Norman
Conquest. The relatively constant proportion around 85% is a
kind of equilibrium level, built into our formulas for m(g).
The numbers of distinct ancestors get smaller as the population
gets smaller. But the proportion around 85%, once achieved,
persists as we go back in time, in spite of the changes in population size and the perpetual rule of two parents for each
child.

Thus our model leads us to imagine the population of
Domesday England divided into two groups, the ancestors and the
nonancestors of our individual. Five-sixths of the population
are relations, one-sixth are of no particular kin.   Of course
the relations are not some identifiable group of the population
like the Saxons or the husbandmen and servants. The assumptions
of our model imply that the group is a random sample out of the
whole population. Some other breakdown between five-sixths and
one-sixth of the population is defined by the ancestry of any
other English person. It seems likely that if people are not
siblings or bilateral cross cousins, the groups they define are
almost certain to be different, although we have not proved this
result in our model. Far enough back in time, when the population is very small, it must start to be common for ancestor
groups to coincide.

We have framed our discussion in terms of England and a
person of English ancestry back to the Norman Conquest. The
methods we have developed, of course, can be applied to the
ancestors of other nations and races, so far as an identifiable
pool of potential ancestors can be determined. It is strange to
think of ourselves within our population today as divided into
two groups insofar as we are or are not the ancestors of some
specific unknown person in the distant future. It is also
strange to think of the links which tie each of us by descent to
most but not all of the population of our country of origin in
the far past, to a group special in no way except in having one
of us as their common descendant. Each link between parent and
child is intimate and full of emotional associations, and only
30 such links back in time bring us to each ancestor at the Norman Conquest. Yet, these ancestors together, a random five-
sixths of the population, seem almost beyond picturing. Each of
us is connected to the historical past in many ways -- through
the language we speak, the changed face of the earth around us,
the institutions we act within, our store of knowledge, images,
emotions, and preconceptions. The "ties of blood," that is, of
genes and lineal descent, in some sense the most real of all
connections, are also the most mystical. Always hard to grasp
imaginatively, they become still more elusive when a statistical
element enters, when they connect us with millions of people, a
part of the whole population that we can count but not identify.
Our exercise in modelling numbers of ancestors opens the way to
piquant speculations.

ACKNOWLEDGMENTS

This paper has appeared as Chapter 9 (pp. 153 - 161) of "Statistical Studies of Historical Social Structure", by Kenneth W. Wachter with Eugene A. Hammel and Peter Laslett, published by Academic Press, 1978.

NOTE

[1] A model assuming a constant pool based on the same probabilities for balls in bins is given by von Schelling (1944). Schelling, however, allows one person to have four or more parents if that person occupies two or more slots. I am indebted for this reference to Dr. Kai Albertson of the Marselisborg Hospital in Aarhus, Denmark.

REFERENCES

Bodmer, Walter, and L. Cavalli-Sforza. 1971. "The Genetics of Human Populations". New York: W.H.Freeman.
Feller, William. 1968. "An Introduction to Probability Theory and Its Applications". Volume 1, Third Edition. New York: Wiley.
Gilbert, John, and Eugene Hammel. 1966. Computer analysis of problems in kinship and social structure. American Anthropologist. 68:71-93.
Hollingsworth, Thomas H. 1969. "Historical Demography". London: Hodder and Stoughton.
Laslett, Peter. 1977 "Family Life and Illicit Love in Earlier Generations". Cambridge: Cambridge University Press.
Russell, Josiah C. 1948. "British Medieval Population". Alberquerque: University of New Mexico Press.
von Schelling, H. 1944. Die Ahnenschwundregel. Der Erbarzt 12:113-122.

GENISYS: A GENEALOGICAL INFORMATION SYSTEM

Sue M. Dintelman
A. Timothy Maness
Mark H. Skolnick
and
Lee L. Bean

1. Introduction

Most utilization of computers in demographic applications
has been in the development of independent programs to assemble,
access and analyze data files. Each application usually maintains its own files and develops the programs necessary to
access and analyze them, even though similar programs may exist
for other data files. In addition, any change in a data file,
for example compacting (shortening the records of) a file by
coding a certain field rather than maintaining it as a text
string, usually causes changes to be made in existing programs.

A general data base system may be used to simplify the use
of computers in demographic applications by protecting programs
from changes in the structure of a file and by minimizing the
programming effort necessary to analyze data. The Genealogical
Information System, GENISYS, described in this paper is this
type of general data base system and is being developed for the
analysis of a genealogical data base.

The Utah Mormon Genealogy Project, for which GENISYS is
being developed, has a data base of approximately 1.75 million
records which represents one million individuals linked in genealogies. The project has its own Data General Eclipse Model
S/250 computer using the AOS operating system for input, editing
and analysis of the data base.

The file structure of the data base has been described by
Skolnick et al. (1979). Originally, access to the data base was
by a set of FORTRAN-callable subroutines, the Genealogical Data
Interface specifically where in a record a particular data item
was located, the user still had to be a FORTRAN programmer with
a detailed understanding of the structure of the file.

A system developed using GDI, the Demographic Utility
Package (DUP), was a first attempt to provide a higher level,
easier to use interface. DUP automatically assembles the information about nuclear families. The DUP user, although a FORTRAN
programmer, no longer needs to be concerned with the details of
the file structure. DUP, however, does not provide the ability
to assemble family groups larger than nuclear families, and it

was clear that extending DUP to include more capabilities would
lead to severe performance problems.

It was at this point that GENISYS was proposed to meet the
following needs:

a. A high-level query language to allow researchers to
    access data without having to have an extensive program-
    ming background.

b. The ability to do varied data analysis on selected data
    sets, thus minimizing the programming necessary for new
    techniques and allowing already existing analysis rout-
    ines to be used on all types of data.

c. The ability to add new data to existing files and new
    files for new applications.

d. To improve the performance of the data access programs
    to permit, at worst, overnight turn around on requests.

2. GENISYS Overview

GENISYS is a multiprocess, multiuser system written in
FORTRAN. It includes query facilities for accessing data files
and several functions to define and maintain data files.
Because our current application does not need to be sensitive to
updating, the present version of GENISYS does not contain data
modification capabilities.

Providing a high-level query language and providing efficient access to data are often opposing goals. One approach to
implementing a query language is to provide general subroutines
to analyze the query and to access the data base using a
selected access path. This approach can lead to considerable
inefficiency both in time and memory required, because the capability to perform all the operations anticipated must exist even
though any one query being processed requires only certain operations. GENISYS uses the approach suggested by Lorie and Wade
(1977) and produces a data access program specific for each
query. That is, after the query is analyzed and an access path
is determined, a FORTRAN program is generated containing only
the statements necessary to access the specific fields of the
specific files required. This technique allows data to be
accessed at the most primitive and therefore most efficient
level, independent of the level of the data language. The use
of this technique allows GENISYS to include a very high-level
query language while providing efficient access to the data
base.

To avoid accessing all records in a file to locate records
meeting some criteria, a data base system usually includes
indexes over certain fields. An index maintains an association

between a field value and all records which contain that value,
so only records with the desired value need to be accessed. The
indexed fields of a data base are usually chosen to optimize the
most frequent queries. Because of the wide variety and changing
nature of the queries used in our application, general indexes
are not used. Indexes over a large number of fields would be
required, and the time and space necessary for creating and
maintaining them is prohibitive. At present GENISYS uses bitmaps as the major accessing technique. A _bitmap_ is a file of
bits parallel to a physical file with set bits indicating
records which meet some specified criteria. Figure 1 shows a
bitmap with the set bits indicating individuals born between
1850 and 1899 in Utah. Bitmaps serve as indexes for specific
values of specific fields. If the bitmap required for a query
does not exist, it may be easily and quickly created using a
program generated specifically to produce the required bitmap.

```
     Bitmap                    INDIVIDUAL File
      File

                       Birthyear      Birthstate
     +---+         +------+----------+---------------+-----+
     | 0 |         | ...  | 1836     | New York  | ... |
     | 0 |         | ...  | 1901     | Utah      | ... |
     | 0 |         | ...  | 1905     | Utah      | ... |
     | 1 |         | ...  | 1851     | Utah      | ... |
     | 0 |         | ...  | 1860     | Idaho     | ... |
     | 1 |         | ...  | 1872     | Utah      | ... |
     | 1 |         | ...  | 1898     | Utah      | ... |
     | 0 |         | ...  | 1874     | Nevada    | ... |
     | 0 |         | ...  | 1906     | Utah      | ... |
     +---+         +------+----------+---------------+-----+
```

FIGURE 1. Use of a bitmap.

     The details of the system structure of GENISYS and the use
of automatic program generation to create both query-specific
data access programs and query-specific access paths (bitmaps)
may be found in Maness et al. (1979).

3. Data Model

     If a change in the physical structure of a file requires
changes in a program accessing the file, the program is said to
be _data dependent_. In a data base system, user programs do not
access data directly but make use of a data interface. A _data
interface_ allows programs to be written which are more _data
independent_ because the programs may access data without regard
for the physical properties of the data. Depending on the level
of the data interface, programs written using the data interface
are unaffected by changes in the data format, location or storage structure of data. A _data model_ is the information content
of a data base as it is represented by the data base interface.
The Genealogical Data Interface (GDI) and the Demographic Util-

ity Package (DUP) described above use data models which provide
some degree of data independence, but one of the design goals of
GENISYS was to provide more data independence and therefore a
higher level data model is required.

The data model chosen for GENISYS is the relational data
model developed by Codd (1970).   The relational model of data
allows a higher degree of data independence, and the tabular
structure used to represent the data is easy for non-programmers
to understand and use.

The model consists of the information needed by a specific
application organized into one or more logical files. A logical
file may be represented as a table with rows and columns. The
columns, which are named, are called fields and the rows are
called records. Figure 2 illustrates some of the contents of
the data base used by the Utah Mormon Genealogy Project. The
INDIVIDUAL file contains for each individual a record with a
number of demographic and medical attributes. The MARRIAGE file
consists of a record for each marriage.

INDIVIDUAL

```
+----------+----------+---+-----+------+-----+-----+-----+
|INDIVIDUAL|PARENT    |   |BIRTH|BIRTH |BIRTH|DEATH|DEATH|
|    #     |MARRIAGE #|SEX|YEAR |COUNTY|STATE|CAUSE|YEAR |
+----------+----------+---+-----+------+-----+-----+-----+
```

MARRIAGE

```
+--------+--------+----+----+---+-----+---+---+---+--------+
| MAR-   |HUSBAND |WIFE|    |   |     |   |   |   | NUMBER |
|RIAGE #|IND. #  |IND#|CITY|CO.|STATE|DAY|MO.|YR.|CHILDREN|
+--------+--------+----+----+---+-----+---+---+---+--------+
```

FIGURE 2.   Example data base.

It is a property of a logical file that there are no
duplicate records. This implies that there is a field or a combination of fields which uniquely determines a record.   This
field (or fields) is called the primary key of the logical file.
The primary key of the INDIVIDUAL file is the INDIVIDUAL#, a
number that is assigned based on the individual's first name,
last name, birth year and birth month.   Either the INDIVIDUAL#
or the value of these four fields could be used as the key, as
there is a one-to-one correspondence between them. The INDIVID-
UAL# is simply a more convenient way to specify a record. Similarly, the primary key of the MARRIAGE file is the MARRIAGE#,
which corresponds to each unique pair of individual spouse identifiers, the HUSBAND INDIVIDUAL# and the WIFE INDIVIDUAL#. A
MARRIAGE# is used in the INDIVIDUAL record to specify the marriage of an individual's parents. An important point to note is
that the definition of the logical files of the data model does

not indicate the number or contents of _physical_ files on secondary storage devices. Some fields (such as cause of death) are,
in fact, stored in separate physical files.

     Some types of data analysis involve information in a sin-
gle logical file, but more often information is needed from more
than one logical file. GENISYS uses a technique similar to that
in the Link and Selector Language, LSL (Tsichnitzis, 1976), to
simplify the formulation of queries involving more than one logical file. A set of one-way _links_ between files may be defined.
Figure 3 lists the links that are used in the genealogical
application. For example, the CHILDREN link is a one-to-many
link from the MARRIAGE record of the parents to the INDIVIDUAL
records of their children.   This use of links is a modification
of the relational model. GENISYS, then, uses a relational-like,
rather than a true relational data model.

```
+------------------------------------------------------------------+
|                                                                  |
|   Link Name            Type                 Relations            |
|                                                                  |
|   MARRIAGE             1 : N          INDIVIDUAL to MARRIAGE      |
|   PARENT MARRIAGE      1 : 1          INDIVIDUAL to MARRIAGE      |
|   CHILDREN             1 : N          MARRIAGE to INDIVIDUAL      |
|   HUSBAND              1 : 1          MARRIAGE to INDIVIDUAL      |
|   WIFE                 1 : 1          MARRIAGE to INDIVIDUAL      |
|                                                                  |
+------------------------------------------------------------------+
```

FIGURE 3.   Defined links.

4.   Query Facilities

     The data language of GENISYS is the GENISYS Query Lan-
guage, GQL, and is based primarily on the language SEQUEL 2
(Chamberlin et al., 1976). In this section several examples of
GQL statements illustrating the main features of the query language will be given.   Section 5 contains examples of queries
used in demographic studies.

     Each GQL statement has a similar format and consists of a
SELECT clause and an optional WHERE clause.   The SELECT clause
determines the type of processing to be done, and the WHERE
clause specifies the records or sets of records which are needed
for processing. Each GQL statement results in a file that may
be used as the subject of subsequent queries.

4.1. Single File Queries

     Figure 4 is a GQL statement which results in a file con-
sisting of the birth and death years for all women (SEX=0) born
in Utah. The SELECT clause may contain a list of field names or
expressions involving field names. The predicates of the WHERE
clause are the criteria used to specify needed records. A pred-
icate may compare a field to a constant (BIRTHYEAR > 1850) or

compare two fields in a record (DEATHSTATE = BIRTHSTATE). Predicates may be connected by AND and OR, NOT may be used to negate
predicates, and parentheses may be used to establish precedence.

```
+------------------------------------------+
|   SELECT BIRTHYEAR, DEATHYEAR            |
|   WHERE BIRTHSTATE = 'UTAH' AND SEX = 0  |
+------------------------------------------+
```

FIGURE 4.   GQL statement.

4.2.   Synonyms and Macros

Queries may use predefined _synonyms_ to increase readability.   The text of a synonym is simply substituted in place of
the synonym name, therefore the text need not conform to any
syntactic entity of a query statement.   Figure 5 illustrates the
use of synonyms. 'AGEATDEATH' is a synonym for for the expression 'DEATHYEAR - BIRTHYEAR' and FEMALE is a synonym for '0'.
Synonyms may be defined by the user for his private use or
defined by the data base administrator for everyone to use.

```
+-------------------------------------------------+
|   SELECT CAUSEOFDEATH, AGEATDEATH               |
|   WHERE DEATHYEAR >= 1950 AND DEATHYEAR < 1955  |
|     AND DEATHCOUNTY = 'KANE' AND SEX = FEMALE   |
+-------------------------------------------------+
```

FIGURE 5.   Use of synonyms.

Macros are essentially synonyms with parameters. Figure
6 illustrates the use of the macro 'LOCALPOPULATION' to specify
a group of individuals. The values 'WEBER', 1850 and 1899 are
substituted for the corresponding dummy arguments ↑1, ↑2 and ↑3
in the text of 'LOCALPOPULATION'.   The modified text is inserted
into the query text replacing 'LOCALPOPULATION' and the list of
parameters.

```
+-------------------------------------------------------------+
|LOCALPOPULATION = BIRTHSTATE = 'UTAH' AND BIRTHCOUNTY = ↑1|
|                  AND BIRTHYEAR >= ↑2 AND BIRTHYEAR <= ↑3   |
|                                                             |
|SELECT AGEATDEATH                                            |
|WHERE LOCALPOPULATION ('WEBER', 1850,1899)                   |
+-------------------------------------------------------------+
```

FIGURE 6.   Use of macros.

4.3.   Forming Groups

In most instances it is more useful to select an aggregate
property of a data set rather than the raw data itself. GQL
provides a way to use functions to compute properties of other

groups.   In Figure   7 the   properties are   the frequency   count
(COUNT) of   individuals and the   average (AVERAGE) age   at death
for the specified population.

```
+----------------------------------------------------------+
|   SELECT COUNT (INDIVIDUALS), AVERAGE (AGEATDEATH)   |
|   WHERE LOCALPOPULATION ('KANE', 1850, 1899)        |
+----------------------------------------------------------+
```

FIGURE 7.   Aggregate functions.

Aggregate properties   of a   relation may   also be   grouped
according to the   values of a field.   Figure 8   shows a grouping
of the   average   age at death   according to sex,   birth cohort and
birth county.   Figure 9 illustrates   the file   produced   by this
query.   After the keyword BY is the expression used to determine
the group   (i.e., BIRTHYEAR),   followed by   the range   specifier
which is   the description   of the   groups.   The range   specifier
(1850...1899,10)   in the   example gives   a minimum and   maximum
value and   the increment to be   used in forming the   groups.   In
this case there are five 10-year   birth cohorts.   A range specifier may also indicate groups based on upper and lower bounds of
each group   [(<14),   (>= 15,   <19), (>=   20, <30)]   or specific
values for each group ('UTAH', 'NEVADA',   'IDAHO').

```
+----------------------------------------------------------+
|        SELECT AVERAGE (AGEATDEATH) BY SEX BY             |
|                                                          |
|        BIRTHYEAR (1850...1899,10) BY BIRTHCOUNTY         |
|                                                          |
|        WHERE BIRTHSTATE = 'UTAH'                         |
+----------------------------------------------------------+
```

FIGURE 8.   Grouping by properties.

AVERAGE AGE AT DEATH	SEX	BIRTH COHORT	BIRTH COUNTY
54.2	M	1850 - 1859	Salt Lake
55.6	F	1850 - 1859	Salt Lake
55.1	M	1860 - 1869	Salt Lake
56.4	F	1860 - 1869	Salt Lake
.	.	.	.
.	.	.	.
.	.	.	.
56.7	M	1890 - 1899	Weber
58.2	F	1890 - 1899	Weber

FIGURE 9.   Structure of result file for query of Figure 8.

If for any individual record the computed value does not fall into any of the given categories, the record is not considered. If a range specifier is not given, as in the case of BIRTHCOUNTY, the full range of values encountered in the file is assumed.

4.4. Multiple File Queries

Figure 10 illustrates the use of a link specifier to extract the birthyear for a group of individuals and their mothers. Note that the use of synonyms may be used to increase readability. For example, 'PARENT MARRIAGE WIFE' may be replaced with the synonym 'MOTHER'. For any 1:N link, a link qualifier may be used to specify which of the N associated records should be selected. The query of Figure 11 selects the birthyear and number of male children of a set of women. At present, the link qualifiers allowed in GENISYS are key words (MALE, FIRST, etc.), but eventually general boolean expressions will be used.

```
+--------------------------------------------------------+
| SELECT BIRTHYEAR, PARENTMARRIAGE WIFE BIRTHYEAR         |
| WHERE AGEATDEATH < 5 AND BIRTHSTATE = 'UTAH'            |
+--------------------------------------------------------+
```

FIGURE 10. Use of link specifiers.

```
+--------------------------------------------------------+
| SELECT BIRTHYEAR, COUNT (MARRIAGE MALE CHILDREN)        |
| WHERE BIRTHYEAR > 1900 AND SEX = FEMALE                 |
+--------------------------------------------------------+
```

FIGURE 11. Use of link qualifier.

The query of Figure 12 illustrates the use of the aggregate function AVERAGE applied not to a group as specified in a BY clause, but to a group of linked records, in this case the children of the specified individuals. For each woman born in Utah after 1850, a record is created in the result file with her age at marriage and the average age at death of her children.

```
+------------------------------------------------------------+
|SELECT AGEATMARRIAGE,AVERAGE(MARRIAGE CHILDREN AGEATDEATH)  |
| WHERE MARRIAGE PLACE = 'UTAH' AND BIRTHYEAR > 1850          |
|      AND SEX = FEMALE                                       |
+------------------------------------------------------------+
```

FIGURE 12. Alternate placement of aggregate function.

4.5. Program Fragments

The aggregate functions used in GENISYS are not built-in functions, rather they are names associated with program frag-

ments. A <u>program fragment</u> is the outline of the FORTRAN code
needed for performing a specified algorithm. Program fragments,
like synonyms and macros, may be locally defined by the user or
globally defined by the data base administrator. A program
fragment consists of three sections, INITialization, LOOP and
END. These three sections correspond to the location in the
data access program where the code is to be placed. The statements in the INIT section are placed before the start of the
data access loop, the LOOP statements are placed inside the data
access loop after a new record is accessed, and the END code is
placed after the termination of the loop. Figure 13 shows the
definition of the AVERAGE program fragment. In the example of
Figure 8, the data access loop for the function AVERAGE is the
loop that accesses individuals of the specified population. The
data access loop for the query of Figure 12, however, is the
loop accessing children of a specified individual. The INIT
statements in this case are placed after a record meeting the
WHERE clause criteria is accessed, but before the 'MARRIAGE
CHILDREN' link specifier is processed. The LOOP code is placed
inside the loop that accesses children, and the END code is
placed after the last child is accessed. Figure 14 contrasts
the placement of program fragment code in these two examples.
The heavy lines indicate the data access loops.

```
+------------------------------------------+
|                                          |
|         AVERAGE (X)                       |
|         % INIT                            |
|            SUM = 0                         |
|            COUNT = 0                       |
|                                          |
|         % LOOP                            |
|            SUM = SUM + X                   |
|            COUNT = COUNT + 1               |
|                                          |
|         % END                             |
|            AVERAGE = SUM/COUNT             |
|                                          |
+------------------------------------------+
```

FIGURE 13. Definition of AVERAGE program fragment.

A program fragment contains only the definition of an
algorithm. The use of the program fragment determines (1) where
the code is inserted in the data access program and (2) which
field names or expressions are bound to the dummy arguments. In
addition, any necessary subscripting is done automatically in
the case of SELECT...BY constructs. For example, the query of
Figure 8 must accumulate sums and counts for each combination of
sex, birth cohort and birth county in order to compute the average. Figure 15 shows the expanded version of the AVERAGE program fragment. The expansion process includes changing variables to arrays with the appropriate number of dimensions and

DINTELMAN et al.

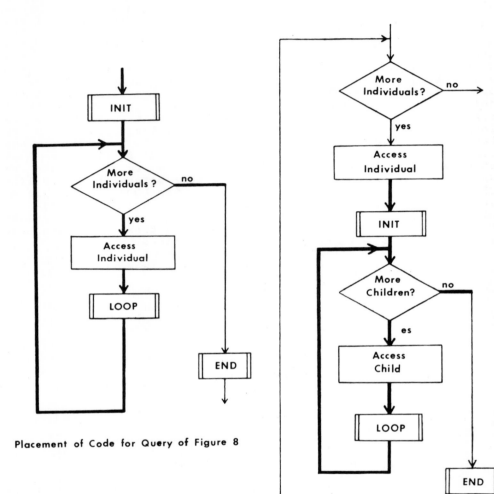

Placement of Code for Query of Figure 8

Placement of Code for Query of Figure 12

FIGURE 14.   Placement of program code.

insertion of code to manipulate these arrays. Code is generated
to be placed after field values (sex, birthyear, etc.)   are
extracted from the record to map the field values to a subscript
value.   These mapping functions are indicated by f1,   f2 and f3
in the expanded code.

```
%  INIT
   REAL COUNT (29,5,2),SUM (29,5,2),AVERAGE (29,5,2)
   DO 10 I = 1,29
   DO 10 J = 1,5
   DO 10 K = 1,2
   COUNT (I,J,K) = 0
   SUM (I,J,K) = 0
10 CONTINUE

%  LOOP
   I = f1 (birthcounty)
   J = f2 (birthyear)
   K = f3 (sex)
   SUM (I,J,K) = SUM (I,J,K) + ageatdeath
   COUNT (I,J,K) = COUNT (I,J,K) + 1

%  END
   DO 15 I = 1,29
   DO 15 J = 1,5
   DO 15 K = 1,2
   AVERAGE (I,J,K) = SUM (I,J,K)/COUNT (I,J,K)
15 CONTINUE
```

FIGURE 15.   Expanded program fragment.

     The ability to define program fragments permits applica-
tion programmers to develop new algorithms independent of the
specific data to which they may be applied and, at the same
time, the more casual user may make use of existing algorithms
without being concerned with the adaptations of the algorithm to
their data.

4.6. User Interface

     GQL and other GENISYS features are accessed through the
User Interface. The User Interface contains the facilities for
creating and editing queries, synonyms, macros and program fragments. Queries may be processed and results displayed in user-
specified formats using commands in the User Interface.

5. Applications

5.1. Examples of Applications in Demographic Analysis

The GQL examples of the previous secton illustrate some of the features of the language. The following examples will illustrate the use of GQL and other features of GENISYS to produce results of specific interest to demographers. The first example produces the sex ratio information displayed in Figure 16. The User Interface session used to produce the table is shown in Figure 17. The first step in the process is to create a query that will accumulate the frequency counts for each birth cohort. The PROCESS command causes the data access program to be generated and executed, creating the result file SEXCOUNT with 35 records. Each record contains the values of total individuals, total males, total females and birth cohort designation for each cohort group. The DEFINE command allows the user to name the fields in the result file so they may be used in further processing. The second query created and processed uses the result file of the first query to produce the column of ratios. The TABLEDISPLAY command is then used to format the output with the titles and headings shown.

The second example produces the table of age at marriage information shown in Figure 18. The User Interface session shown in Figure 19 begins with the definition of the synonyms used in the query. Because the text of the synonyms is not used until the PROCESS command is invoked, they may be defined either before or after the query text is created. The query text also makes use of the globally defined synonyms 'AGEATMARRIAGE', 'UTAHGENEALOGY' and 'FEMALE'. The synonym 'UTAHGENEALOGY' specifies the set of people who were born or who died in Utah or who had a spouse who was born or who died in Utah. STAT1 is a program fragment which contains the code for computing the mean, median and standard deviation of a given variable, in this case AGEATMARRIAGE. TABLEDISPLAY is used to produce the printer-ready version of the table. The table is stored with the dialog used to create it, so that if TABLEDISPLAY is invoked with the table name, the user may re-display his response and may change any items. This allows the user to change titles and headings without having to respecify all the required information. The PRINT command is used to produce the printed copy of the table.

Figure 20 is an infant mortality table produced from the results of the two queries shown in Figure 21. Note that the total number of births in each cohort group was obtained from the result file formed by a query in the session shown in Figure 17.

The final example is a table of female lifetime stability ratios. These ratios are shown in Figure 23 and are produced by the queries of Figure 22. The lifetime stability ratio compares those women who were born and who died in a certain locality with all women who were born there.

BIRTHYEAR	TOTAL	MALES	FEMALES	RATIO
1800-1804	249.	128.	121.	1.058
1805-1809	407.	217.	190.	1.142
1810-1814	549.	300.	249.	1.205
1815-1819	853.	454.	399.	1.138
1820-1824	1323.	668.	655.	1.020
1825-1829	2136.	1125.	1011.	1.113
1830-1834	3325.	1720.	1605.	1.072
1835-1839	4498.	2235.	2263.	.988
1840-1844	6107.	2993.	3114.	.961
1845-1849	7762.	3895.	3867.	1.007
1850-1854	10472.	5350.	5122.	1.045
1855-1859	14114.	7100.	7014.	1.012
1860-1864	17106.	8322.	8784.	.947
1865-1869	20272.	10162.	10110.	1.005
1870-1874	23906.	11997.	11909.	1.007
1875-1879	28011.	14113.	13898.	1.015
1880-1884	32732.	16417.	16315.	1.006
1885-1889	37300.	18734.	18566.	1.009
1890-1894	39462.	19887.	19575.	1.016
1895-1899	40963.	20841.	20122.	1.036
1900-1904	43290.	21982.	21308.	1.032
1905-1909	45849.	23346.	22503.	1.037
1910-1914	45442.	22994.	22448.	1.024
1915-1919	45577.	23059.	22518.	1.024
1920-1924	44751.	22808.	21943.	1.039
1925-1929	40508.	20984.	19524.	1.075
1930-1934	36554.	18673.	17917.	1.040
1935-1939	34486.	17667.	16819.	1.050
1940-1944	35946.	18374.	17572.	1.046
1945-1949	39911.	20266.	19645.	1.032
1950-1954	46463.	23866.	22597.	1.056
1955-1959	47320.	24139.	23181.	1.041
1960-1964	39341.	20131.	19210.	1.048
1965-1969	10672.	5424.	5248.	1.034
1970-1974	954.	479.	475.	1.008

FIGURE 16.   Sex ratio at birth (5 year birth cohorts).

.2.   Other Applications

GENISYS is a general data base system and is useful for pplications other than demographic analyses. The ability of ENISYS to handle familial relationships of any degree makes it particularly useful tool for medical genetic studies.

In addition to containing genealogical information about a arge population, the data base of the Utah Mormon Genealogy roject contains other physical files containing medical infor- ation. One of these files is a statewide tumor registry which as partial ascertainment from 1952 and complete ascertainment f the cases from 1966 to present. Another file is the death

```
+----------------------------------------------------------+
!                                                          !
!     . CREATE/Q SEXCOUNTQ                                 !
!     1 SELECT(COUNT(INDIVIDUALS),COUNT(INDIVIDUALS) BY SEX)!
!     2   BY BIRTHYEAR (1800...1974,5)                     !
!     3 BYE                                                !
!     . PROCESS SEXCOUNTQ INTO SEXCOUNT                    !
!     . DEFINE SEXCOUNT TOTAL, MALEC, FEMALEC, BIRTHCOHORT !
!     . CREATE/Q SEXRATIOQ                                 !
!     1 SELECT SEXCOUNT.MALEC/SEXCOUNT.FEMALEC             !
!     2   BY SEXCOUNT.BIRTHCOHORT                          !
!     3 BYE                                                !
!     . PROCESS SEXRATIQ INTO SEXRATIO                     !
!     . DEFINE SEXRATIO RATIO BIRTHCOHORT                  !
!     . TABLEDISPLAY                                       !
!       tablename ? SEX_RATIO_TABLE                        !
!       title ? SEX RATIO OF BIRTHS (5 YEAR BIRTH COHORTS) !
!       enter headings                                     !
!       column 1 ? BIRTHYEAR                               !
!       column 2 ? TOTAL                                   !
!       column 3 ? MALES                                   !
!       column 4 ? FEMALES                                 !
!       column 5 ? RATIO                                   !
!       column 6 ?                                         !
!       enter source of contents                          !
!       column 1 ? RANGE (1800...1974,5)                   !
!       column 2 ? SEXCOUNT.TOTAL BY SEXCOUNT.BIRTHCOHORT  !
!       column 3 ? SEXCOUNT.MALEC BY SEXCOUNT.BIRTHCOHORT  !
!       column 4 ? SEXCOUNT.FEMALEC BY SEXCOUNT.BIRTHCOHORT!
!       column 5 ? SEXRATIO.RATIO BY SEXRATIO.BIRTHCOHORT  !
!       column 6 ?                                         !
!     .PRINT SEX_RATIO_TABLE                               !
!     .BYE                                                 !
!                                                          !
+----------------------------------------------------------+
```

FIGURE 17.   User   interface   session   to   produce   sex
             ratio table of Figure 16.

certificate file containing cause of death information that i
invaluable in medical genetic studies.   Both the tumor file an
the death certificate file have been linked to the genealogica
data so that the fields from these files may be considered par
of the logical INDIVIDUAL file. Adding fields to logical file
in this manner is easy to do and does not affect existing quer
ies.   Additional data that we plan to add to the data bas
include records of the discharge diagnoses from the hospitals i
Utah and the information from a birth defects registry now bein
developed.

     The study of a particular disease often begins by askin
if individuals with that disease are more closely related tha
would normally be expected. If they are more closely related

Year	1800–1809	1810–1819	1820–1829	1830–1839	1840–1849	1850–1859	1860–1869	1870–1879	1880–1889	1890–1899
Median	21.70	21.74	21.96	21.11	19.85	19.54	20.14	20.86	21.06	21.13
Mean	22.260	22.551	22.576	21.911	20.552	20.108	20.687	21.415	21.619	21.718
St Dev	4.425	4.415	4.610	4.625	4.061	3.580	3.679	3.741	3.625	3.648
N	329	608	912	1268	1949	3715	5824	7163	8360	9318
Age 10	5	6	16	21	68	98	83	63	35	22
15	6	8	14	40	102	193	172	124	88	72
16	15	16	29	64	166	321	401	310	243	238
17	17	41	59	107	215	486	606	568	601	554
18	27	49	72	144	211	505	753	830	912	1057
19	32	66	98	136	250	472	793	906	1116	1278
20	36	62	99	109	186	410	755	910	1118	1041
21	38	76	72	121	170	323	600	811	1041	1162
22	32	50	85	105	152	250	433	662	843	931
23	32	43	78	73	102	172	362	523	629	749
24	15	42	62	69	78	128	245	382	462	571
25	58	111	170	206	188	302	492	880	1030	1124
30	12	30	47	61	48	44	98	158	203	214
35	2	8	6	8	10	8	24	31	32	39
40	1	0	4	1	2	2	4	3	6	14
45	0	0	0	2	1	0	3	1	1	4
50	1	0	1	1	0	1	0	1	0	1

FIGURE 18. Age at marriage of females by birth cohort.

```
+-----------------------------------------------------------+
|                                                           |
|  . CREATE/S AGERANGE                                      |
|  1 ((>=10,<15),(15...24,1),(25...54,5))                   |
|  2 BYE                                                    |
|  . CREATE/S ONCEMARRIED                                   |
|  1 COUNT (MARRIAGE) = 1                                   |
|  2 BYE                                                    |
|  . CREATE/Q AGEATMQ                                       |
|  1 SELECT(STAT1 (AGEATMARRIAGE), COUNT (INDIVIDUALS),     |
|  2    COUNT (INDIVIDUALS) BY AGEATMARRIAGE AGERANGE),     |
|  3    BY BIRTHYEAR (1800...1899,10)                       |
|  4 WHERE SEX = FEMALE AND ONCEMARRIED,                    |
|  5    AND MARRIAGE HUSBAND ONCEMARRIED,                   |
|  6    AND UTAHGENEALOGY                                   |
|  7 BYE                                                    |
|  . PROCESS AGEATMQ INTO AGEATM                            |
|  . DEFINE AGEATM MEDIAN, MEAN, STDEV, TOTAL,              |
|                       COUNT (1...17), BIRTHCOHORT         |
|  . TABLEDISPLAY                                           |
|    table name ? AGEATM_TABLE                              |
|    table ? AGE AT MARRIAGE OF FEMALES BY BIRTHCOHORT      |
|    result file name ? AGEATM                             |
|    column 1 ? "YEAR"                                      |
|    column 2 ? - 11 RANGE   (1800...1899,10)               |
|    column 12 ?                                            |
|    enter source of contents                              |
|    column 1 ? "MEDIAN," MEAN," "STDEV," "N," AGE 10,"     |
|              (15...25,1), (30...50,5)                     |
|    column 2 ? - 11 (MEDIAN, MEAN, STDEV, TOTAL,           |
|              COUNT(I), I=1,17) BY BIRTHCOHORT             |
|    column 12 ?                                            |
|  . PRINT AGEATM_TABLE                                     |
|                                                           |
+-----------------------------------------------------------+
```

FIGURE 19. Creation of age at marriage table.

the possibility of a genetic cause is raised.   Using GENISYS,
family clusters can be extracted and studied in detail.   By
calling individuals in such families into screening clinics, the
detailed medical data necessary for understanding the underlying
mechanisms of disease causation may be collected and added to
the data base for further studies.

GENISYS will be used for the selection and analysis of
specific data sets required for each project.   The advantage of
GENISYS is that any data file, no matter what type of information it contains (laboratory results, answers to questionaires
or hospital records), may be described to the system and the
complete query capabilities of GQL and the analysis capabilities
of existing program fragments may be used.   In addition, if the
new data are linked to existing genealogy information, familial
relationships may be studied.

BIRTH YEAR	-TOTAL- NUMBER	RATE	-MALE- NUMBER	RATE	-FEMALE- NUMBER	RATE
1800-1804	4.	16.06	2.	15.63	2.	16.53
1805-1809	15.	36.86	5.	23.04	10.	52.63
1810-1814	12.	21.86	6.	20.00	6.	24.10
1815-1819	26.	30.48	11.	24.23	15.	37.59
1820-1824	25.	18.90	11.	16.47	14.	21.37
1825-1829	76.	35.58	39.	34.67	37.	36.60
1830-1834	117.	35.19	58.	33.72	59.	36.76
1835-1939	247.	54.91	124.	55.48	123.	54.35
1840-1844	376.	61.57	192.	64.15	184.	59.09
1845-1849	549.	70.73	286.	73.43	263.	68.01
1850-1854	643.	61.40	331.	61.87	312.	60.91
1855-1859	813.	57.60	447.	62.96	366.	52.18
1860-1864	1174.	68.63	547.	65.73	627.	71.38
1865-1869	1412.	69.65	741.	72.92	671.	66.37
1870-1874	1625.	67.97	856.	71.35	769.	64.57
1875-1879	1757.	62.73	897.	63.56	860.	61.88
1880-1884	2043.	62.42	1092.	66.52	951.	58.29
1885-1889	2466.	66.11	1348.	71.95	1118.	60.22
1890-1894	2653.	67.23	1405.	70.65	1248.	63.75
1895-1899	2486.	60.69	1357.	65.11	1129.	56.11
1900-1904	2601.	60.08	1411.	64.19	1190.	55.85
1905-1909	2413.	52.63	1345.	57.61	1068.	47.46
1910-1914	1924.	42.34	1082.	47.06	842.	37.51
1915-1919	1761.	38.64	948.	41.11	813.	36.10
1920-1924	1749.	39.08	962.	42.18	787.	35.87
1925-1929	1296.	31.99	717.	34.17	579.	29.66
1930-1934	982.	26.86	559.	29.99	423.	23.61
1935-1939	768.	22.27	442.	25.02	326.	19.38
1940-1944	575.	16.00	317.	17.25	258.	14.68
1945-1949	512.	12.83	281.	13.87	231.	11.76
1950-1954	544.	11.71	341.	14.29	203.	8.98
1955-1959	482.	10.19	276.	11.43	206.	8.89
1960-1964	385.	9.79	227.	11.28	158.	8.22
1965-1969	86.	8.06	48.	8.85	38.	7.24
1970-1974	7.	7.34	4.	8.35	3.	6.32

FIGURE 20.   Infant mortality.

```
+-------------------------------------------------------------+
| R1: SELECT(COUNT(INDIVIDUALS), COUNT(INDIVIDUALS) BY SEX)|
|          BY BIRTHYEAR (1800...1974,5)                       |
|          WHERE AGEATDEATH << 1                              |
|                                                             |
| R2 : SELECT((R1.TOTAL/SEXCOUNT.TOTAL) * 1000.               |
|          (R1.MALEC/SEXCOUNT.TOTAL) * 1000.                  |
|          (R1.FEMALEC/SEXCOUNT.TOTAL) * 1000.                |
|      BY BIRTHCOHORT                                          |
+-------------------------------------------------------------+
```

FIGURE 21.   Queries to produce data for Figure 20.

DINTELMAN et al.

```
+-------------------------------------------------------+
|                                                       |
| PLACES:  BIRTHCITY ('LEHI','SALT LAKE CITY','HYRUM',  |
|          ('KANAB','GLENDALE'), ('ROCKVILLE','TOQUERVILLE'), |
|          'LOGAN','PROVO','MANTI','FAIRVIEW')          |
|                                                       |
| R1:  SELECT COUNT (INDIVIDUALS) BY PLACES             |
|          BY BIRTHYEAR (1850...1919,10)                |
|      WHERE SEX = FEMALE AND BIRTHSTATE = 'UTAH'       |
|          AND DEATHCITY = ¬ NULL                       |
|                                                       |
| R2:  SELECT COUNT (INDIVIDUALS) BY PLACES             |
|          BY BIRTHYEAR (1850...1919,10)                |
|      WHERE SEX = FEMALE AND BIRTHSTATE = 'UTAH'       |
|          AND DEATHCITY = BIRTHCITY                    |
|                                                       |
| R3:  SELECT (R2.COUNT/R1.COUNT) * 1000.               |
|          BY CITIES BY BIRTHCOHORT                     |
|                                                       |
+-------------------------------------------------------+
```

FIGURE 22. Queries to produce lifetime stability ratio.

BIRTHYEAR	LEHI	SALT LAKE CITY	HYRUM	KANAB/ GLENDALE	ROCKVILLE/ TOQUERVILLE	LOGAN	PROVO	MANTI	FAIRVIEW
1850-1859	152.78	256.27	.00	.00	.00	.00	232.67	178.57	.00
1860-1869	318.58	393.66	311.48	.00	.00	421.49	370.69	230.09	264.15
1870-1879	329.79	576.98	229.51	236.84	54.05	426.57	477.01	328.13	243.90
1880-1889	255.56	562.99	208.33	350.00	.00	324.50	474.86	220.93	357.14
1890-1899	233.33	569.05	235.29	347.83	.00	430.38	324.32	187.50	205.13
1900-1909	214.29	515.34	181.82	400.00	.00	147.06	315.79	125.00	150.00
1910-1919	266.37	462.59	246.51	309.73	60.34	378.79	371.73	237.69	254.24

FIGURE 23. Lifetime stability ratios for women by BIRTHCITY and BIRTHCOHORT.

6. Conclusion

        The design goals of GENISYS include:

    1. The development of a high level language for use by
        researchers with no programming background.

    2. Facilities for the development of statistical meth-
        ods utilizing data from the data base, and

    3. Providing run times that would allow, at worst,
        overnight response to queries.

GENISYS has met these goals and has proven to be more general
and therefore more useful than originally planned. The use of
the relational-like language provides not only a high-level language for our specific application, but allows for changes in
our application and the definition of other applications very
easily. The use of program fragments allows statistical methods
to be developed by applications programmers without their having
to worry about the details of data access. The use of bitmaps
for access paths and the use of the technique of automatic program generation to produce efficient low-level data access programs does allow the best possible response time for our situation.

        In this paper we have shown examples of demographic
results produced from the Utah Mormon Genealogy data base using
GENISYS. It is our hope that these examples give the reader a
feeling for the ease of data retrieval and analysis using this
data base system. Each result could be designed in a short
interactive session. Furthermore, the queries may be easily
modified to use other data sets or perform other analyses on the
same data set. Such a capability is in considerable contrast
with the more usual processes of writing FORTRAN programs for
data retrieval and utilizing standard statistical packages for
analysis.

ACKNOWLEDGMENTS

        This research was supported by NIH Grants HD-10267,
HL-21088, and CA-16573, Public Health Services, DHEW.

REFERENCES

Chamberlin, D.D., M.M. Astrahan, K.P. Eswaran, P.P. Griffiths,
    R.A. Lorie, J.W. Mehl, P. Reisner and B.W. Wade 1976.
    SEQUEL 2: A unified approach to data definition, manipula-
    tion, and control. IBM Journal of Research and Development
    20(6): 560-575.
Codd, E.F. 1970. A relational model of data for large shared
    data banks. Comm. ACM 13(6): 377-387.

Lorie, R.A. and B.F. Wade 1977. "The Compilation of a Very High
     Level Data Language". San Jose, California: IBM Research
     Laboratory, RJ2008 (28098).
Maness, A.T., S.M. Dintelman and M.H. Skolnick 1979. Automatic
     program generation for processing a high level relational-
     like query language. "Proceedings ACM19". In press.
Skolnick, M., L.L. Bean, S.M. Dintelman and G. Mineau 1979. A
     computerized family history data base system. Sociology
     and Social Research. In press.
Tsichnitzis, D. 1976. LSL: A link and selector language. In
     "Proceedings of the 1976 ACM-SIGMOD Conference". Washing-
     ton, D.C. 123-133.

MIGRATION AT MARRIAGE IN COLONIAL NEW ENGLAND: A COMPARISON OF RATES DERIVED FROM GENEALOGIES WITH RATES FROM VITAL RECORDS

John W. Adams
and
Alice B. Kasakoff

This paper presents several rates which have been computed from genealogies related to migration at marriage, an important component of all migration, and compares these with similar rates of researchers who have done "town studies" in Colonial New England using primarily published vital records (1). Our findings offer a striking contrast on the issue of stability of the population.

We chose genealogies as a useful data source because the task of genealogies is pre-eminently one of "following" members of a family as they move through space, over time. The area selected is one on which there is an abundance of genealogical information, and is thus a kind of laboratory for studying differences between rates derived from sets of records which pertain to specific locations and rates derived from family histories, which seek to include all progeny regardless of where they reside. This highlights a general problem in studies of demography and migration: the degree to which a given population can be considered "isolated." The choice of unit to be studied may introduce a serious bias in the rates reported, a bias which is, of course, especially severe when the rates are to be used as evidence about social stability.

Our Sample

We chose three bilaterally descending genealogies for an initial sample to represent families which first settled in different parts of Massachusetts in the 17th century: William White of Plymouth (Kellogg, 1975), Henry Farwell of Concord (Farwell, 1929), and Andrew Greely of Salisbury/Amesbury (Greely, 1905) (2). The numbers of useful marriages, arranged by generation, are given in Table 1.

Age at Marriage

Since "age at marriage" has been computed several times by researchers doing town studies, we decided to compute such a rate from our sample of genealogies in order to see if the sample were representative of the population of Colonial New England. Results are given in Table 2 and Figures 1 - 4.

Genealogical Demography

115

TABLE 1.   Marriages sampled.

Number of marriages in generation

Family	1	2	3	4	5*	Total
Henry Farwell	0	6	25	101	50	182
Andrew Greely	1	5	32	109	64	211
William White	0	3	12	51	48	114
Total marriages by generation	1	14	69	261	162	507
Range of dates of marriage by generation	1644	1640 to 1695	1669 to 1796	1689 to 1800	1718 to 1820	1640 to 1820

*   We sampled every 10th person in Farwell and Greely,
every 5th person in White.

TABLE 2.   Mean age at first marriage.

Date of Marriage	Males	Marriage Cohorts N	Females	N
Before 1700	25.8	31	23.2	29
1700 - 1719	25.9	32	22.5	39
1720 - 1739	25.4	80	21.3	89
1740 - 1759	26.2	51	21.9	44
1760 - 1779	28.3	26	23.4	35
After 1779	26.2	16	22.1	11
Grand mean	26.1	236	22.2	247

Date of Birth	Males	Birth Cohorts N	Females	N
Before 1661	27.3	15	22.3	10
1661 - 1680	26.8	25	24.8	25
1681 - 1700	25.8	48	22.5	41
1701 - 1720	26.2	82	21.6	86
1721 - 1740	26.3	38	21.7	51
After 1770	24.6	28	21.4	34
Grand mean	26.1	236	22.2	247

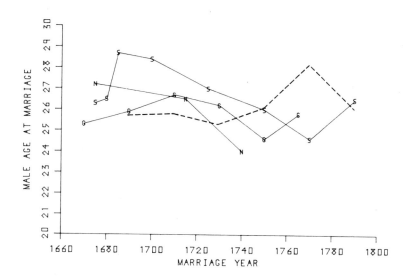

FIGURE 1.   Mean age at first marriage for males by year (mar-
            riage cohorts). *

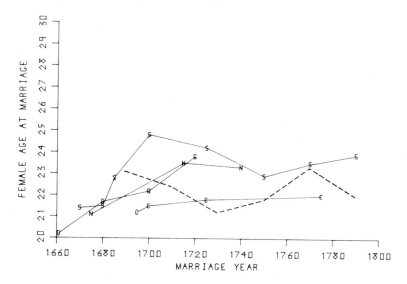

FIGURE 2.   Mean age at first marriage for females by year (mar-
            riage cohorts). *

* Sources: C – Crum, 1914 (genealogies); G – Greven, 1970 (Andover, Mass.); N – Norton, 1971 (Ipswich, Mass.); S – Smith, 1973
(Hingham, Mass.); Broken line – Table 2.

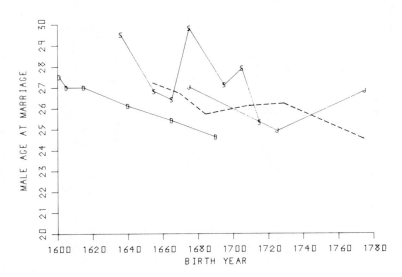

FIGURE 3.   Mean age at   first marriage for males   by year (birth
            cohorts). *

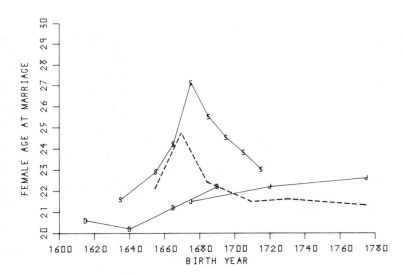

FIGURE 4.   Mean age at first marriage for females by year (birth
            cohorts). *

* Sources: D - Demos, 1970 (Plymouth, Mass.); J -   Jones, 1918
(genealogies); S - Smith, 1973 (Hingham, Mass.); Broken line -
Table 2.

Mean ages are reported in Table 2 in order to provide ready comparability to the results of other researchers. However, because the distribution of ages at marriage is not a Normal one (statistically speaking), statistical tests which compare means are not appropriate. We have therefore used the Kolmogorov-Smirnov test here and throughout the paper where samples were large enough, and Chi-square tests, grouping persons into "earliest marriers", "married at average ages" and "married late", where sample sizes were too small for the other test. For the data arranged by marriage cohorts displayed in Table 2, no tests produced statistically significant differences. However, there were two differences between birth cohorts worth noting. Males born before 1680 were older than those born later; a K-S test had a two-tailed p. of .007, but one of the samples was one less than the number recommended for the test. The Chi-square test of the same data had a p. of .13. With a slightly larger sample it is almost certain that the decline in age for men born after 1680 would be statistically significant. The decline in age at marriage for women born after 1699 was statistically significant; a K-S test had a two-tailed p. of less than .001. The actual dates for the first and last cohorts displayed in Table 2 are: for marriage cohorts, males 1640-1699 and 1780-1808, females 1640-1699 and 1780-1797; for birth cohorts, males 1615-1660 and 1741-1779, females 1619-1660 and 1741-1776.

What is notable about our figures is that they are, comparatively speaking, unremarkable. They fall in the mid-range of reported rates and there are no striking peaks or dips which require special explanation. Taken together with the previously published rates, they all suggest that for females there was a rise in age at marriage during the 17th century, followed by a decline in the 18th century, and that for males there was a steady decline.

We conclude that genealogies provide as useful a rate as do "town studies", one which is furthermore more broadly reflective of the experience of the region as a whole. It might therefore be considered a yardstick against which town study rates could be compared in order to foreground local historical circumstances which may have influenced them. The high ages reported for Hingham and the low ages for Plymouth are two examples and would seem to require further explanation.

Rates of Endogamy and Exogamy

We then computed the frequencies of locally endogamous marriages, using the nominal town of residence of each spouse (3), and found over the entire sample a rate of 53.8 percent, which is what we expected from our previous work on endogamy (Adams and Kasakoff, 1976). The rate of town endogamy fluctuates between 44 percent and 64 percent, and shows neither a clear increase nor a clear decrease over time. In Table 3 endo-

gamy appears to have declined over time and, indeed, a Chi-
square test of the numbers of endogamous and exogamous marriages
occuring before 1740 and those occuring in 1740 or after yields
a p. of .08. However, the result is entirely due to the inclusion of both first and second marriages in the table. Second
marriages are more exogamous than first marriages (see Table 4)
and also tend to occur later in time. In fact, when a similar
table of marriages in which both partners were marrying for the
first time was examined (but not displayed here) and divided
between marriages which occurred before 1720 and those occuring
in 1720 and after (so as to yield as large a difference over
time as possible) it showed an _increase_ in endogamy after 1719,
but the p. of .16 is not statistically significant.

TABLE 3. Endogamy rates: All marriages.

Date of Marriage	Percent Endogamy	Median Dist. Exogamous Marriages	80 Percent Distance*	N
Before 1700	55%	16 miles	16 miles	38
1700 - 1719	48%	9 miles	11 miles	48
1720 - 1739	64%	12 miles	12 miles	102
1740 - 1759	45%	9 miles	15 miles	65
1760 - 1779	56%	8 miles	13 miles	48
After 1779	42%	14 miles	20 miles	24
All dates	53.8%	12 miles	12 miles	325

* Distance within which 80 percent of all marriages
   occur. See text for explantion.

        Ten historians, geographers and anthropologists using pri-
marily published vital records for single towns have computed
142 rates of local endogamy/exogamy for 43 New England towns
during various time periods in the 17th and 18th Centuries,
using a total of 23,998 cases (Bissell, 1973; Greven, 1970;
Jones, 1975; Kelly, 1977; Lemire n.d.; Norton, 1973; O'Keefe,
1976; Smith, 1973; Swedlund, 1971; Swedlund et.al., 1976;
Waters, 1976a) (4). We recomputed their findings by taking
their total numbers of endogamous marriages and showing them as
an overall percentage of all marriages in their aggregated samples. The resulting figure of 68.7 percent, much higher than
our own, will be discussed in the next section.

        Their reported rates of endogamy range from two of 100
percent (Deerfield, 1680's, N = 1; Salisbury, 1660's, N = 36) to
a rate of 13.4 percent (Framingham, 1765 to 1774, N = 30). Several of the authors claim to have found meaningful differences
between the rates but did not perform any tests of significance
on their data. The mean rate of the 142 rates of endogamy which
they reported is 61.8 percent.

TABLE 4.   Endogamy Rates of First and Later Marriages.

	Percent Endogamy	Median Dist. Exogamous Marriages	80 Percent Distance*	N
Both partners' first marriage	59.5%	11 miles	11 miles	200
Either partner's later marriage	44%	12 miles	20 miles	127

* Distance within which 80 percent of all marriages occur. See text for explantion.

A Chi-square test of this table ("both first", "either later", "endogamous", "exogamous") is significant at the .01 level.

A Critique of Two Rates Derived From Published Vital Records

We selected two of the rates -- one high and one low -- for further examination. Of the high rates of endogamy reported, the one for Tewksbury, Massachusetts of 97.7 percent for the period from 1740 to 1749 (Lemire, n.d.) was selected because the sample size (N = 44) and the bulk of the records were manageable. We went to the source used and listed the marriages. These were then searched in the published vital records of a group of neighboring towns where we discovered one of them with residence information which indicated that it was actually exogamous, not endogamous as counted. We also found six additional exogamous marriages involving Tewksbury residents which had not been preserved in the Tewksbury records, or which perhaps had never been reported to the town clerk there. Thus the "true rate" for Tewksbury is undoubtedly much lower.

This indicated to us that there were serious deficiencies in both the original reporting of residence information (5) and in the published records (6). Indeed, the editors of the vital records explicitly state in their prefaces that they have omitted all reference to the community whose records were being published. This renders it impossible therefore for later researchers to decide if the absence of such information indicated that the couple were both from that town, or if the residence information was simply not reported (7). Though the published records are of little use in computing rates of endogamy, the researchers cited above counted a marriage as endogamous whenever no information on residence appeared. Hence it would seem that the high endogamy rate for Tewksbury results from haphazard reporting of exogamous marriages and from improper counting.

We then investigated the lowest rate, that of 13.4 percent endogamy, in the period from 1765 to 1774 for Framingham, Massachusetts (Kelly, 1977). Only one marriage listed was actually performed in Framingham, and that was of a couple who were both from neighboring Hopkinton. All the other marriages took place elsewhere, and in those cases where there was no indication of residence in the Framingham records, we checked the records of the town where the marriage had been performed and discovered that they were all exogamous. Thus, the rate of endogamy reported should have been 0.0 percent, not 13.4 percent. The town history (Barry, 1847) indicated, however, that there had been a resident minister throughout the whole period, so we have concluded that the only register which survived to be included in the published vital records was the one kept of "out-of-town" marriages, which consists either of couples from other towns who were married in Framingham or of Framingham people who married elsewhere. Barry's lengthy genealogies confirmed this by yielding three marriages which were clearly endogamous for the same period of people whose surnames began with "A" alone. All lacked precise dates. The "true rate" remains to be calculated.

The overall rate of 68.7 percent local endogamy computed from the sample of 142 rates reported above is clearly inflated from the miscounting of marriages as endogamous when residence information was lacking. All the rates should be examined, but we suspect that "true rates" fall somewhere within our findings of 55 percent (plus or minus 10 percent) and that it would be difficult to find any statistically significant differences. The variations in rates reported undoubtedly reflect variations in the quality of the published vital records, not variations in rates of local endogamy (8). Therefore, any hypotheses purporting to explain those rates in terms of the age of the town or its location need re-evaluation (9).

Age and Distance and "80 Percent Groups"

We have suggested in another paper (Adams and Kasakoff, 1976) that the most useful measure of endogamy is the area or population size within which approximately 80 percent of spouses are found. This rate is frequently reported in the ethnographic literature, whereas the concept of a 100 percent endogamous group is virtually unworkable except in those very few cases of true isolates. In our genealogical sample, we found that 80 percent of all marriage partners were located within a radius of about 13 miles or less, a distance which included nearly all neighboring towns, and which corresponded to a comfortable day's journey for New Englanders (Allan Kulikoff, pers. comm.). This finding confirms the similar findings of other researchers, though they did not express their figures in quite this way (Kelly, 1977; LeMire, n.d.; Norton, 1973; O'Keefe, 1976; Swedlund, 1971).

We wondered if there was a (statistically significant) difference in age at marriage between those people who married endogamously and those who married exogamously. There was not. (Two-tailed K-S tests: p. = .891 for men and p. = .973 for women.) We wondered also if there was such a difference for those people who found their spouses within a radius of 13 miles (that is, within the 80 percent group) and those who found each other more than 13 miles away. Again, there was not. (A Chi-square test showed a p. of .40 for men and of .94 for women.)

However, when we examined the ages of persons who married in "the middle distance", that is, exogamously but within the 80 percent group, we found a curious "dip" produced by men born in the 18th century but not evident for those born in the 17th century nor for women. Men born in the 18th century whose wives came from this middle distance were significantly younger at marriage than those who married either endogamously or beyond the borders of the 80 percent group (Chi-square p. of .05). Women do not show such a dip because those who married at younger ages tended to marry men who were quite a bit older than they were, while the men who married at younger ages married women closer to their own ages than was usual, women who fell into the "average age at marriage cell" in the table for women. (The average difference in age between husband and wife was about 4.8 years for first marriages.)

This dip in the middle distance, which is evident in marriages made as early as 1720, appears to signal a change in the marriage market caused by the gradual filling in of the countryside with new settlements. Men who married before this in the 17th century appeared to follow a strategy predicated on the principle of least effort, searching close to home first, then in the middle distance and then farther away, which is reflected in an increase in the age of marriage as the distance from which the spouse comes increases. The Chi-square on this table had a p. of .07 for men; .51 for women. The sample size is small (only 25 for men) and a larger one would probably produce statistically significant results for the men.

These findings about age at marriage underscore the fact that the town was not the effective unit for marriage. Not only was a sizeable proportion of marriages made outside the town at all time periods, but during the 18th century men appeared to find their spouses first in the middle distance and only then did they look either at home or farther away. In both periods the important unit for marriages appears to be the "80 percent group", a town and neighboring towns located up to 14 miles away.

Post-Marital Residence

Couples in Colonial New England usually registered their marriage primarily in the town of the wife and only secondarily

TABLE 5.   Mean age at first marriage in endogamous and exogamous
           marriages.   Figures in parentheses are numbers of
           cases.

	All Males		All females	
Endogamy	25.6	(105)	22.5	(116)
Exogamy				
All distances	25.9	(66)	22.9	(73)
13 miles or less	25.1	(42)	21.6	(46)
Over 13 miles	27.3	(24)	25.1	(27)

in the town of the husband, though there was a preference, which
our findings confirm, for virilocal residence of the couple
after marriage.   In fact, twice as many couples making their
first marriage resided virilocally as opposed to uxorilocally.
More surprising is the finding that 11 percent of couples who
married exogamously resided neolocally, as did 9 percent of
endogamous couples (see Tables 6 and 7). This, together with
uxorilocal residence, accounts for the fact that 21 percent of
all men move at the time of their first marriage (10).

     One study which used only vital records attempted to find
out where couples who married exogamously later settled by looking in the birth registers of the town of both husband and wife
for the registration of the births of their children, but was
unable to find children of 58 percent of such couples (O'Keefe,
1976: 12). This failure is further confirmation of the utility
of genealogies as a data source.

Exogamy and Later Migration

     There is a strong relationship in our data between the
distance at which couples find each other and their propensity
to migrate after marriage (see Table 8). Finding a spouse in
another town would therefore seem to be a first step toward
later migration. Indeed, 60 percent of couples who later moved
found each other in separate towns, while only 34 percent of
couples who resided in only one location after marriage had done
so.
     This finding raises the question of whether there was a
division of the population into stayers and movers. To investigate this, we constructed a table of people who either moved (or
stayed put) before, at or during the course of their first marriage. In calculating expected frequencies for each cell of the
table, we assumed that each opportunity to move was independent
of the two others. Our general finding over the entire table is
that by and large, all the cells show greater frequencies than
expected except the cell for one-time movers; i.e., there are
more two- and three-time movers and stayers.   There would,

TABLE 6.   Post-marital residence.

MALES	Median distance moved		N
Movers:			
Neolocal endogamy	14	miles	13
Neolocal exogamy	13.5	miles	8
Uxorilocal	15	miles	22
All movers	13	miles	43
Stayers:			
Endogamous and			
virilocal couples	0		174
		Total	217

FEMALES			
Movers:			
Neolocal endogamy	13	miles	14
Neolocal exogamy	19	miles	11
Virilocal	12	miles	58
All movers	12	miles	81
Stayers:			
Endogamous and			
uxorilocal couples	0		154
		Total	235

The median distance from which a spouse came in the exogamous marriages included here was 11.5 miles. Thus movers moved farther than the distance from which the spouses came at marriage.

therefore, seem to be some justification for a stayer/mover dichotomy (11). We have shown this in Table 9.

In this table the expected frequencies were derived from multiplying the rates of movement at different points in the life cycle (see Table 7; Chi-square for males 12.96, for females 9.64 (d.f. = 1), males significant at less than .001, females between .005 and .001).

Family Dispersion

Though we picked the three families in our sample because they first settled in different parts of (present-day) Massachusetts, by the time of birth of the fifth generation, various family members had moved away, some quite far. The founders of

TABLE 7.   Movement at different times during the life cycle.

	Males	Females
Move before marriage	29%	16%
Move at marriage	21%	34%
Move after marriage (as a couple)	30%	26%

        The small difference here between the per-
centage of males and that of females who move as
couples results from the fact that a slightly
different set of marriages is counted for men
than for women and from the fact that complete
information does not always exist for both partners to a marriage. Also, a small number of marriages are first marriages for one partner but
second marriages for the other. These are based
upon cases for which information on movement at
each of the three times was available. (See
footnote to Table 11 for further discussion.)

TABLE 8.   Relationship between exogamy of couples and their
           movement after marriage.

	Married Endogamously	Married Exogamously
Moved after marriage	22	33
Did not move after marriage	95	48

Corrected Chi-square was 10.4 with 1 degree of
freedom, significant at the .001 level.

each of the families originally settled quite far from each
other, but by the birth of the fifth generation, many of their
descendents were living in the same towns, though we have yet to
find a marriage between descendents of the different founders.
As would be expected, most of the towns in which descendents of
two different founders were born were in the central part of
Massachusetts: both the Greely and White genealogies record a
sib group born in Sutton, Massachusetts; White and Farwell both
have sib groups born in Concord, Stow and Lancaster, Massachusetts. But both Greely and Farwell also have sib groups born in
Hudson, New Hampshire. Movements out of the present boundaries

TABLE 9.   Observed and expected rates of   movement during the
life cycle.

MALES	Observed	Expected	Diff.
Three moves:			
Before, at, and after			
first marriage	9 (1.4%)	5.1	+3.9
Two moves:			
Before and at marriage	17 (6.1%)	11.9	+5.1
Before and after marr.	22 (7.9%)	19.2	+2.8
At and after marriage	10 (3.6%)	12.5	-2.5
All	49 (17.6%)	43.6	+5.4
One move:			
Before marriage	32 (11.5%)	44.7	-12.7
At marriage	23 (8.2%)	29.1	-6.1
After marriage	43 (15.4%)	46.95	-3.95
All	98 (35.1%)	120.75	-22.75
No moves	123 (44.5%)	109.5	+13.5
Total	279 (100%)	278.95	

FEMALES	Observed	Expected	Diff.
Three moves:			
Before, at, and after			
first marriage	8 (3.2%)	3.5	+4.5
Two moves:			
Before and at marriage	8 (3.2%)	10.1	-2.1
Before and after marr.	9 (3.6%)	6.9	+2.1
At and after marriage	20 (8.0%)	18.6	+1.4
All	37 (14.8%)	35.6	+1.4
One move:			
Before marriage	16 (6.4%)	19.5	-3.5
At marriage	50 (20.0%)	52.8	-2.8
After marriage	29 (11.6%)	36.0	-7.0
All	95 (38.0%)	108.3	-13.3
No moves	110 (44.0%)	102.6	+7.4
Total	250 (100%)	250	

of Massachusetts were made by members of all three families. Greelys went to New Hampshire and Maine; Whites to Rhode Island, Connecticut and New Jersey; Farwells to New Hampshire, Vermont and Connecticut (see Table 10).

TABLE 10. Dispersion of birth places of the fifth generation.

Distance from birthplace of founder	Farwell	Greely	White	All
Same birthplace	3 (5%)	30 (30%)	0	33 (16%)
Within 13 miles	12 (21%)	39 (39%)	6 (12%)	57 (27%)
More than 13 mi.	43 (74%)	32 (31%)	43 (88%)	118 (57%)
Totals	58	101	49	208
Median distance for those over 13 miles	16 mi.	48 mi.	48 mi.	48 mi.

Each sibling group was counted only once in each place where a member of it was born. This was done in order to avoid biasing the calculation toward the birth places of the largest sibling groups.

Persistence

Genealogies make it possible to arrive at more accurate lifetime persistence rates than do town studies because they "follow" individuals as they pass through various locations in their lives. Not surprisingly, we find a lower rate of persistence than do most town studies: 41.1 percent for men and 39.9 percent for women (Table 11). However, persistence rates are very difficult to compare with each other since they use different periods of time and different base populations. Further, they must be corrected for life expectancies (12). The rates just quoted for our study are the percentages of people who made a first marriage and who did not move either before, at or throughout that marriage. The rate is much lower than the life-time persistence rates reported by Greven, for example, who states that 78.3 percent of Andover men in the second generation spent their entire lives in Andover (1970: 39). Our highest rate for those men in the group born 1701 to 1720, 49.5 percent, is still considerably below Greven's. Women, by the way, show a general decline in persistence over time (13).

TABLE 11. Changes in persistence rates over time.

Generation	Males	N	Females	N
2	16.7%	12	33.3%	12
3	47.7%	44	47.7%	44
4	43.6%	163	39.1%	169
5	35.0%	100	34.5%	87
All	40.4%	319	38.8%	312
Birth Cohort				
Before 1660	21.1%	19	50.0%	12
1661 - 1680	50.0%	34	50.0%	28
1681 - 1700	41.1%	56	34.1%	41
1701 - 1720	49.5%	95	42.1%	95
1721 - 1740	42.0%	50	37.5%	56
After 1740	21.1%	38	34.1%	44
All	41.1%	292	39.9%	276

Chi-square tests of significant differences in these
tables yielded p = .51 for females counted by generation,
and p = .67 for females counted by birth cohort; the comparable tests for men showed p = .13 when the data was
grouped by generation, and p = .02 for birth cohorts.

These rates are the percentages of persons who did not
move either prior to, at, or during their first marriage.
The differences between the totals for birth cohorts and
generation reflect the absence of exact birth dates for
individuals who were counted in a generation but not in a
birth cohort. The rates are lower than the figure given
for "No moves" in Table 9 because to be included in Table
9, information on whether or not a person moved had to
exist for all portions of the life cycle. A person is
counted as a mover here if he moved at any portion of the
life cycle whether or not information on his activities
during other portions is lacking.

Quality of Genealogies

We feel that the findings which we have presented in this
paper make a very good case for the utility of genealogies as a
data source when researching problems of persistence and migration, and that the vital records of single towns are, comparatively speaking, poorer. But there are several objections to
the use of genealogies which are raised so frequently that they
are worth at least a brief discussion. For instance it is often
asserted that genealogies record only the landed families of

"stayers", but this is patently not the case, as our figures on
persistence show. It is equally often suggested that only the
"rich" are the subjects of genealogies, though it is actually
the case that families which were either "rich" or "poor" in the
initial generations produce lineages of opposite social condi-
tion in the later generations.   "Black sheep" are recorded as
well as "worthies" in an attempt to find literally everyone
(14).

        A genuine problem is the loss of persons from genealogies.
In those for which we have calculated the rate, 10 percent to 30
percent were lost (15). Women are no more likely to be lost
than men. If one assumes a large number of those lost to have
migrated, rates of migration reported in this paper would be
even higher (16). There is no evidence so far, however, that
these persons differ in any other way from those whom the genealogist has been able to trace, and our own unsuccessful
efforts to find them show that the authors of the genealogies
have probably exhausted the resources at their disposal for
doing so.

        What is unclear to us at this time is how to sample from
among available genealogies, and how it might be possible to
sample within one. This latter problem requires some estimation
of the extent to which the life experience of one set of
siblings may be correlated with those of another in the same
family. We would expect this correlation to vary in different
cultures, and, within a culture, over time, and therefore it
must be the focus of subsequent research.

Conclusions

        It is not without a certain sense of irony that, just at
the moment when social anthropologists have begun to question
Kroeber's idea of the village as "the natural unit of study",
social historians of Colonial New England are finding "closed
corporate peasant communities", "stem family households"
(Waters, 1976b) and, above all, a world of "relentless immobil-
ity" (Lockridge, 1966) reminiscent of Levi-Strauss' "cold societies." Nor has this sense of irony completely escaped historians (Rutman, 1977b; Henretta, 1971). The purpose of our criti-
que is to question the design and execution of several studies
which have sought to investigate, in part at least, the topic of
persistence and migration by looking at places through which
migrants passed instead of at the migrants themselves.   Any
study which reports rates of "out-marriage" or "persistence"
using a local community as its focus incurs certain risks, not-
ably an inability to "follow" townsmen across town lines.

        It is unclear why "village" or "town" was so often chosen
as a unit of study in the first place. In a sense, even "parish" is probably better. Yet the vital statistics developed
from a small "closed" set of records are intended to be general-

ized to the experience of a broader region. Why then not sample the region to begin with? Certainly the group of towns within which 80 percent of marriages occurred is a far better unit for studying migration at marriage. Towns are not isolates. Obviously they are units of convenience for the researcher because they coincide with the administrative units which were used for recording and publishing vital records.

Clearly an initial choice of "locale" or "family" will have important consequences for the study of rates which may vary depending on the amount of migration in the population. This study suggests that "regional averages" for rates such as age at marriage, taken from families which have migrated, may foreground specific local rates which by comparison appear "too high" or "too low", and therefore may be subject to local conditions which have not been explored sufficiently. By contrast, a "regional" rate of persistence may aggregate local data in such a way as to obscure actual times and places where rates of persistence are, in fact, quite high or low by comparison.

Above all this, however, we would like to underscore the general finding that the amount of migration in Colonial New England seems to have been much higher than usually reported, and in doing so, to emphasize the potential inadequacy of research which uses data from only one community when the study is used as evidence of stability, whether the community be one with vital records such as those in Colonial New England, or a preliterate one of the sort traditionally studied by anthropologists.

It has not escaped our attention, furthermore, that there may well be important ideological reasons why so many recent researchers have reported "stability" in Colonial New England. If true, it would offer evidence to confirm Zelinsky's hypothesis of a migration transition from a pre-industrial period of great stability to a post-industrial period of "non-stop oscillation" (1971: 247). We have offered evidence that Colonial New England was not a golden age of sedentary people. Allen (1977) has offered evidence that the only other period in our history which would qualify as one of relatively low migration was during the 1930's and 1940's. Ours, by comparison, is actually a time of low though increasing mobility, however much we may feel "uprooted."

ACKNOWLEDGMENTS

This paper was researched and written on an NEH Fellowship at the Newberry Library, 1978-79. We would like to thank Richard Brown, Priscilla Clark, Allan Kulikoff, Chris McGee, Jan Reiff, Daniel Scott Smith, Peggy Sinko and Lawrence W. Towner of the Newberry; Timothy Breen and John Hudson of Northwestern University and Virginia Hunt and Elizabeth White of the General Society of Mayflower Descendents -- for their bibliographic, psychological and financial encouragement.

One version of this paper was given at the Fellow's Semi-
nar at the Newberry Library, Chicago, March 26, 1979. Another
version was given at the symposium "Genealogical Demography" at
the Annual Meetings of the American Association of Physical
Anthropologists, San Francisco, April 5, 1979. We would like to
thank Susan Norton and Alan Swedlund for their comments during
the meetings; and most recently Bennett Dyke and John Justeson.

NOTES

1. Most of the vital records of New England towns have been
    published under the auspices of either the Essex Institute
    or the New England Historic Genealogical Society. Sources
    included not only the records of the town clerks, but also
    family Bibles, family "notes," etc. The information was not
    published in verbatim transcript, however, but was arranged
    alphabetically under "births," "marriages" and "deaths."
    Much family linkage in the original records was thus de-
    stroyed.

2. Published genealogies commonly trace descendents of a single
    male ancestor, either patrilineally or bilaterally, and
    include spouses. They typicaly utilize the vital records,
    church records, family Bibles and information from living
    kin as well as wills and deeds. A few published genealo-
    gies, on the other hand, trace "pedigrees" of a man, woman
    or married couple, ascending bilaterally as far as possible
    but include information on each sib-group and their spouses
    as they go back in time. Several genealogies have included
    illegitimate children, but none has included those who were
    "adopted," insofar as we can recall. "Fosterage," however,
    is quite commonly reported, especially for the 17th century.
    The statistics reported in this paper include the spouses of
    the persons on the genealogy, as well as the ancestor and
    his descendents. The three genealogies used were chosen for
    their quality. The White genealogy, part of the "Five Gen-
    erations Project" of the Society of Mayflower Descendents,
    is very scrupulous about documenting sources. The Farwell
    and Greely genealogies have been cited as works of superior
    quality by a recent genealogist (Colket, 1975).

3. Only marriages that occurred after arrival on this continent
    were counted. One case of an illegitimate birth was entered
    as a marriage with an unknown husband. In coding residence
    prior to a first marriage, children are assumed to be living
    with their parents unless evidence to the contrary is pro-
    vided by the genealogist. Parents' residence is determined
    by one or all of the following:

    a. birth places of later born children
    b. death places of parents or children
    c. genealogist's attempts to trace residence changes
        through deeds, wills, town office holdings, local his-
        tory, etc.

If parents' last child is born in a place and the parents die in the same place they are assumed not to have left
that place unless the genealogist specifies to the contrary.
If one parent dies and the other remarries, we assume that
children go with the remarried parent unless the genealogist
specifies to the contrary. If a person is born and has his
own first child in the same place, we assume he was living
there prior to his marriage. However, if we find cases of
family movement prior to the marriage, we assume that the
person goes with parents unless it is clear from the genealogy that he does not. In the case of second, third or
fourth marriages, the person is assumed to be living in the
town where the couple lived prior to the death of the previous spouse. This is usually determined by the birth places
of the children of the earlier marriages or the death place
of the spouse. Each person is coded as residing in the town
that was legally in existence at the date of the marriage.
Thus if towns divide, the same marriage might be endogamous
before the division but exogamous later. All marriages
listed in a genealogy were compared with the vital records.
Where the vital records had residence information, it was
used in coding endogamy rates and superceded the residence
decided upon by the above rules. We did not assume that the
absence of the entry "of X town" in the records meant that
the person came from the town where the marriage was registered. In such cases we used the above rules. However, if
one of the couple was listed in the records as of a town
different from that where the marriage was registered, but
no residence information was given for the spouse, the
spouse was assumed to be of the town where the marriage was
registered, and the marriage was coded as exogamous.

4.   Unfortunately, there has been some confusion between "migra-
     tion at marriage" and a trip to register a marriage "in
     another town." Since town studies are usually limited to
     studying the latter, it is misleading to label this migra-
     tion at marriage, as some have done (Kelly, 1977; O'Keefe,
     1976). Greven seems to have confused the two when he states
     that men from outside the town whose marriages were recorded
     there resided there after marriage (1970: 210), though a
     search through the published records for Andover lends some
     credence to it in certain cases.

5.   The Massachusetts system of vital registration which was
     instituted in the 17th century began to break down in the
     18th to the point where Lemuel Shattuck, historian of Con-
     cord, Massachusetts and of his own family, reported that it
     was virtually impossible to construct the genealogies from
     data recorded in them after about 1775 (1883: 3). He was so
     upset by this that he campaigned for the eventual reform of
     the vital record system of Massachusetts finally inaugurated
     in 1842. Being interested in computing vital rates, he
     helped form the American Statistical Association. He also

designed the excellent census of Boston taken in 1845, and
was largely responsible, as a result, for the improvements
in the 1850 Federal Census. In addition, he helped found
the New England Historic Genealogical Society as well as
reform the system of public health measures in Boston and,
through its example, of the entire country (Wilcox, 1935).
Somehow, he also found time to publish a set of kinship
terms for New England, using a portion of his own genealogy
to demonstrate their use, fifty years ahead of Rivers (Shattuck, 1847).

6.   The vital records published for Massachusetts towns were not
     accepted uncritically by contemporary reviewers. At least
     one of them pointed out distortions introduced by the edi-
     tors (Putnam, 1905). Early local histories and genealogies
     which used the original sources are, needless to say, closer
     to them than we are when we use the published versions.

7.   The one exception is when "intentions to marry" were pre-
     served, for it is clear from the records of those few towns
     whose records have been published verbatim -- such as Bev-
     erly (also published "alphabetically"), Braintree, Lan-
     caster, Lexington and Weston -- that residence information
     was almost always given in the "intentions," though rarely
     in the actual registrations. In general, those studies
     which have used intentions have found rates of endogamy
     closer to our own than those which have not (Lemire, n.d.;
     Smith, 1973). Most researchers reject marriages which are
     listed in the registers only as intentions (without a subse-
     quent marriage registration) fearing that the marriage never
     actually took place. However, Lemire found by looking in
     the registers of the neighboring towns that almost all such
     persons did actually get married. In using the intentions,
     whether or not they resulted in marriage, one is in effect
     studying engagements. It is our impression, as well as that
     of Daniel Scott Smith (personal communication), that the
     number of broken engagements was few, and that in each
     instance it was caused by a father's disapproval of his
     daughter's choice. Cases in Boston Marriages (1898) suggest
     that those suitors were almost always strangers from far
     away.

8.   This is the same conclusion that Smith (1973: 65 ff.)
     reached about the study of birth records by Higgs and Stett-
     ler (1970).

9.   We have made no effort to sort through the problems of popu-
     lation density and land area of the villages whose rates of
     local endogamy are at issue. Both Prest (1976) and Rutman
     (1977a) discuss this question at length.

10. In marriages in which one or the other of the couple was
     marrying for a second or later time, residence after mar-

riage was more often virilocal than   in those cases in which
both spouses   were making their   first marriage.   But there
was still a high proportion of neolocal residence after marriage (8.7 percent).

11. Even though it   might be expected that   early movement might
delay marriage, this is not the   case.   Movement before marriage has no effect on the age   at first marriage for men or
women.   But men who move <u>after</u> marriage are apt to have married at   a younger age   than those who   did not move   at all
(Chi-square   p =   .01) or   those   who moved   at other   times
(Chi-square p = .035).   The effect is almost entirely due to
men born in the 18th century.   For women, the most striking
effect of   movement on   age at marriage was that   those who
move at least three times   in the life cycle, before, at and
after   marriage, were   older than   those who   did not.   The
effect was not statistically significant, however, doubtless
due to the   rarity of   this type   of movement   pattern (Chi-
square p =   .13).   Those town studies which   did not include
men who moved after marriage   probably report higher ages at
marriage for men born   in the 18th century   than was characteristic of the population   as a whole and,   thus, our findings confirm   Smith's guess that   the differences in   age at
marriage he found between his reconstituted and non-reconst-
ituted families might be due to migration.   For women, however,   results   are   probably   unaffected   by the lack of
migrants   because women   who move   three times   are so   rare
(only 3.2   percent of our   sample fall into   this category).
However, there was no way to have known this before comparing migrants systematically with non-migrants.

12. There is also the problem that many   of the villages of Massachusetts were at first considerably larger than they are a
present, and lost   both territory and people   over the years
as secondary parishes   split off to form   independent towns.
Often, therefore,   a nominal change   of residence   is simply
the artifact of such division and does not signify an actual
migration.   All cases of   this kind on which   no clear decision could be reached have been   discarded from our calculations of   persistence rates.   But those that   had to   be so
discarded were few.

13. Thomas Cole   (1978) who has   studied the dispersion   of Cape
Cod families during the period from   1650 to 1805 also using
genealogies, finds somewhat less dispersion than we do -- if
we read his tables correctly --   as well as greater mobility
than did   Greven, though   less mobility than   do we.   It is
possible that these differences are   due to local geographic
conditions.

14. Beginning as early as the 1820's, genealogists began searching through   the passenger lists   of the first   shiploads of
European immigrants, court and church records, etc., to com-

pile genealogical "dictionaries," which purported to include not only "worthies" (Farmer, 1829), but later everyone of whom there was any trace (Savage, 1860-62; Pope, 1900; Noyes, 1928-39). Occupations are listed, and the available genealogies include many of excellent quality for "poor" families.

15. "Lost" means anyone whom the genealogist knew existed -- usually from a birth registration or from mention in a parent's will -- but was unable to follow at least to marriage although he or she lived to age 21. If a man or a woman was said to be living unmarried after age 50 or, for a woman, if a death record was found in her maiden name, the person was not counted as lost, nor if a death record was lacking but births of children were recorded.

16. Indeed, the information which we have for "stayers" is much more complete than that available for "movers":

Males:	Stayers	Movers	Total
Complete information	123	156	279
Missing information	7	33	40
Total	130	189	319

Chi-square(1 df) = 10.24, p < .001

Females:	Stayers	Movers	Total
Complete information	110	140	250
Missing information	17	50	67
Total	127	190	317

Chi-square(1 df) = 7.36, p = .005 (approx.)

REFERENCES

Adams, J.W. and A. Kasakoff 1976. Factors underlying endogamous group size. In "Regional Analysis, Vol. 2". C. Smith (ed.) New York: Academic Press.

Allen, J.P. 1977. Changes in the American propensity to migrate. Annals of the Association of American Geographers. 67: 577-587.

Barry, W. 1847. "A History of Framingham, Massachusetts". Boston: J. Munroe and Co.

Bissell, L.A. 1973. Family, friends, and neighbors: Social interaction in 17th century Windsor, Connecticut. PhD Dissertation, Brandeis University.

Boston, Massachusetts 1898. Boston marriages from 1700-1751. Report of the Record Commisioners of the City of Boston, Volume 28. Boston.

Cole, T.R. 1978. Family settlement and migration in Southeastern Massachusetts, 1650-1805: The case for regional analysis. New England Historical and Genealogical Register 132: 171-186.

Colket, M.B.,Jr. 1975. "Founders of Early American Families". Cleveland: Order of Founders and Patriots of America.

Crum, F.S. 1914. The decadence of the native American stock: A statistical study. Publications of the American Statistical Association 14: 215-222.

Demos, J. 1970. "A Little Commonwealth, Family Life in Plymouth Colony". New York.

Farmer, J. 1829. "A Genealogical Register of the First Settlers of New England". Lancaster, Massachusetts: Carter, Andrews and Co.

Farwell, J.D. et.al. 1929. "The Farwell Family". F.H. Farwell and Fanny Farwell, Orange, Texas.

Greely, G.H. 1905. "Genealogy of the Greely-Greeley Family". Boston: F. Ward, Printer.

Greven, P.J.,Jr. 1970. "Four Generations". Ithaca: Cornell University Press.

Henretta, J. 1971. The morphology of New England society in the colonial period. Journal of Interdisciplinary History 2: 379-399.

Higgs, R. and H.L. Stettler,Jr. 1970. Colonial New England Demography: A sampling approach. William and Mary Quarterly, Third Series 27: 282-294.

Jones, C.E. 1918. A genealogical study of populations. Publications of the American Statistical Association 16: 201-219.

Jones, D.L. 1975. Geographic mobility and society in Eighteenth-century Essex County, Massachusetts. PhD Dissertation, Brandeis University.

Kellogg, L.M. (ed.) 1975. "Mayflower Families Through Five Generations". Volume I. Plymouth: General Society of Mayflower Descendents.

Kelly, C. 1977. Marriage migration in Massachusetts, 1765-1790. Discussion Paper Series, No. 30, Department of Geography, Syracuse University.

Lemire, R.C.,Jr. n.d. Betrothals and marriages in the Lower Merrimack River Valley, 1660-1790: An example of inter-town contact. Mimeographed.

Lockridge, K.A. 1966. The population of Dedham, Massachusetts, 1636-1736. Economic History Review 19: 318-344.

Norton, S. 1971. Population growth in Colonial America: A study of Ipswich, Massachusetts. Population Studies 25: 433-452.

Norton S. 1973. Marital migration in Essex County, Massachusetts, in the Colonial and Early Federal Periods. Journal of Marriage and the Family 35: 406-418.

Noyes, S. (compiler) 1928-39. "Genealogical Dictionary of Maine and New Hampshire". Portland: Southworth Press.

O'Keefe, D. 1976. Marriage and migration in Colonial New England: A study in historical population geography. Discussion Paper Series, No. 16, Department of Geography, Syracuse University.

Pope, C.H. 1900. "The Pioneers of Massachusetts". Boston: Pub-
    lished by the author.
Prest, W.R. 1976. Stability and change in Old and New England:
    Clayworth and Dedham. Journal of Interdisciplinary History
    6: 359-374.
Putnam, E. 1905. The printed vital records of Massachusetts,
    under the Act of 1902. The Genealogical Magazine 1: 1-10.
Rutman, D.B. 1977a. People in process: the New Hampshire towns
    of the early 18th century. In "Family and Kin in Urban
    Communities". T.K. Hareven (ed.) New York: New View
    Points.
Rutman, D.B. 1977b. Community study. The Newberry papers in
    Family and Community History, No. 77-4J. Chicago: The New-
    berry Library.
Savage, J. 1860-62. "A Genealogical Dictionary of the First
    Settlers of New England". Boston: Little, Brown and Co.
Shattuck, L. 1847. Illustrations of genealogy, names and defini-
    tions of the different degrees of kindred. New England
    Historical and Genealogical Register 1: 355-359.
Shattuck, L. 1855. "Memorials of the Descendents of William
    Shattuck". Boston: Published by Dutton and Wentworth for
    the family.
Smith, D.S. 1973. Population, family and society in Hingham,
    Massachusetts, 1635-1880. PhD Dissertation, Department of
    History, University of California, Berkeley.
Swedlund, A.C. 1971. The genetic structure of an historical
    population: A study of marriage and fertility in Old
    Deerfield, Massachusetts. Research Reports No. 7, Depart-
    ment of Anthropology, University of Massachusetts,
    Amherst.
Swedlund, A.C., H. Temkin and R. Meindl 1976. Population studies
    in the Connecticut Valley: Prospectus. Journal of Human
    Evolution 5: 75-93.
Waters, J. 1976a. Patrimony, succession, and social stability:
    Guilford, Connecticut in the Eighteenth century. Perspec-
    tives in American History 10.
Waters, J. 1976b. The traditional world of the New England peas-
    ants: A view from Seventeenth century Barnstable. New
    England Historical and Genealogical Register 130: 3-21.
Wilcox, W.F. 1935. Lemuel Shattuck. "Dictionary of American
    Biography, XVII". New York: Scribners.
Zelinsky, W. 1971. The hypothesis of the mobility transition.
    The Geographical Review 61: 219-249.

FAMILY RECONSTITUTION IN THE CONNECTICUT VALLEY: PROGRESS ON RECORD LINKAGE AND THE MORTALITY SURVEY

Alan C. Swedlund
Richard S. Meindl
and
Margaret I. Gradie

Introduction

Historical epidemiology (if such a thing exists) probably represents the crossroads of experimentation in nominal record linkage. This is borne out by the variety of disciplines represented by authors in several edited books (e.g. Acheson, 1968; Wrigley, 1973; Hodson, Kendall and Tautu, 1971) as well as by the eclectic groupings of individuals on various research projects. In spite of the progress made since the pioneering efforts of Wrigley (1966; 1969), Henry (1967), Newcombe (1967), Kennedy (1962) and others, there are still numerous obstacles to the adoption of uniform models, approaches and linkage criteria. Perhaps this should not be surprising considering the heterogeneous objectives of those involved.

The purpose of this essay is to briefly describe one particular project that is working on record linkage, to outline some of our major objectives and to describe one example of our preliminary results. In so doing it should become clear where we have borrowed, where we may have comtributed and where obstacles still remain.

The Connecticut Valley Population Ecology Project is investigating twelve historical communities in Western Massachusetts, of which three have been intensively sampled for demographic data. Previous research (e.g. Swedlund, 1975a; 1975b; Swedlund, Temkin and Meindl, 1976; Meindl and Swedlund, 1977; Temkin-Greener and Swedlund, 1978) has described the specific region, communities and major topics examined to date. The overall objective of the research is to describe demographic changes commensurate with agricultural change and industrialization in Western Massachusetts during the 18th and 19th centuries. A major component of this interest is the analysis of fertility decline and mortality trends with respect to their microevolutionary and ecological implications. This involves consideration of a number of economic, sociocultural and environmental variables in addition to the demographic events themselves.

After reviewing our data base and linkage procedures, we will give an example of one question that presently concerns us.

Genealogical Demography

We will employ observations based on both aggregate and linked
data. The question ultimately deals with whether or not a significant "heritable" component can be associated with variations
in mortality during the 18th and 19th centuries. Richard Meindl
(this volume) has more to say about this last topic.

Methods and Materials

        The basic data for our research come from four sources;
vital registrations, genealogies, state and national censuses
and tax valuation lists. Extensive linkage is presently complete on only two towns (Deerfield and Shelburne) and the
sources are as follows:

1.   Vital events -- registration of births, deaths and marriages
      was required by law as early as 1639 in Massachusetts, how-
      ever, enforcement was not effective until additional legis-
      lation was passed in the 1840's. The pre-1849 vital regis-
      ter of both towns had been previously published (Baldwin,
      1920; N.E.H.G.S., 1931) and were simply coded and transfer-
      red to magnetic tape. Vital records for the period 1850 to
      1910 were gathered in their entirety from the Deerfield and
      Shelburne town halls and compiled under a format similar to
      the earlier data (but more extensive to accomodate addi-
      tional information).

2.   The censuses after 1790, including the complete family list-
      ings of 1850 and later, were sorted alphabetically for ease
      of reference.

3.   Family genealogies for Deerfield (Sheldon, 1896) and Shel-
      burne (Bardwell, 1974) were consulted regularly. These are
      derived in part from the vital register, but also drawn from
      other sources as well.

4.   Tax valuation lists exist for various years beginning in
      1781. These are given by taxpayer's full name and the
      assessed value of real property. State censuses have not
      been linked and are used only in the aggregate form; the tax
      valuations are currently only partially linked to the family
      files.

The onset and duration of our data sources are indicated in Figure 1.

        Each record was initially entered into its respective file
in card image with mutually exclusive fields for the vital
events and census categories. All records had surnames and common names in the same columns. We began by linking records for
these periods in which the data appeared most complete.

        Because of the advantages in having decennial censuses,
reconstitution of families was far easier than anticipated.

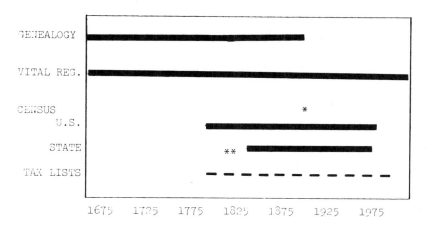

FIGURE 1. Data sources and the relative time periods for which
           they are available, Deerfield, Massachusetts (----
           very sporadic; * 1900, last date of enumeration by
           name; ** used in aggregate form only).

Selection and construction of families proceeded through several
phases. The procedures are summarized in Table 1, and reflect
the semi-automated approach described by Rossman in this volume.

TABLE 1. Major steps in the reconstitution of Deerfield and
          Shelburne families.

Step	Procedure	Method
1	Marriage records sorted by year of event	Mechanical
2a	Birth and Death records linked by concordant names, parents' names, ages, vital dates	Mechanical
b	Non-linked births and deaths sorted, alphabetized and linked manually	Manual
3	Subsequent linked children's file matched to the marriage file	Mechanical /Manual
4	Additional families generated from census observation and reliable registration of children	Mechanical /Manual
5	Deaths of parents, including year, age and cause were traced up to 1950	Manual
6	Each family evaluated for "quality of observation" and ranked	Manual

First,   marriage records   from   1810   in both   towns   were
sorted by year of event.   This is one of the two ways in which a
family   was   initialized   for   our   purposes.   However,   to   be
retained for   further consideration, age   of the woman   at these
marriages (or her   year of birth) had to be   found.   After 1850,
this   item was almost always   recorded on   the marriage   record
itself, but   earlier marriages required additional   work.   This
entailed finding   an undisputed birth   record of a   census which
indicated the year of birth of the woman.

Second, all birth records for each community (1810-1890 in
Deerfield; 1790-1890   in Shelburne) were sorted   alphabetically
within each year.   Next, all neonatal, infant, child and adolescent death records were sorted and listed in the same fashion as
the larger birth   register.   The two computer   files were linked
by means of   a simple   program which   regarded as   a match   any
records   with either   of the   following sets of criteria: (1)
identical   surnames and   names of   parents, concordant age   at
death, year   of birth,   matching sex and   first letter   of first
name, or (2) identical surnames   and first names, and concordant
ages and   events.   Under   ideal conditions,   we would   expect to
match all of the death records to births; however, at this point
in the linkage procedure, only 40% of deaths were matched.

The remaining 60%   of the death records   were alphabetized
within year   of death,   and these   were linked   manually to   the
birth file.   Great variation   in the   spelling of   surnames was
found to   be the   major reason   for a   predominance of   unlinked
death records.   No computer algorithms were devised to deal with
this problem in linking registration data; rather, most of these
remaining records were matched manually.

A second problem in this linkage phase had to do with dis-
cordant ages   derived from   possible links.   In some   cases the
death records indicated   older individuals than did   the births.
This usually   occurred in   early childhood   deaths, ages   two to
six.   In   cases in which the   discrepancy involved a one   or two
year difference, the actual year of birth was taken to be either
that indicated by the   birth record or by an average   of the two
possible years of   nativity.   The decision rested   on inferences
made from the completed genealogy (Sheldon, 1896).   It was found
by examination of all sources available   -- genealogies and censuses -- that the   year of the events of births   and deaths were
almost always   correct, while the age   of death of the   child as
reported by the parents (on the death record) could be in error.
The families of parents which made   a habit of this were usually
eliminated from further consideration.   A three year discrepancy
in such an otherwise good record was   by itself cause for elimi-
nating the family.   Even stronger criteria for   acceptance of a
link were applied to late 19th century data when months of death
and nativity were generally available for all adolescent deaths.

After manual linkage and re-checking of computer links, the proportion of unmatched pre-adult death records remained slightly over 10% for Shelburne and almost 20% for Deerfield. Most of such registration problems in Deerfield were due to two factors: (1) There was considerable mobility in this town in the 1880's and many transient families were in observation only for portions of the reproductive span. Thus, many children were born elsewhere and died in town. These families were generally eliminated although several Irish families -- in observation from some point to the end of reproduction -- were retained for later use. In those numerous instances in which the events of family formation were observed from the beginning (1st child) but not to the end of reproduction, the data were retained. However, these data were accorded a reduced status in the community family files and were dealt with in a different fashion. This classification of families will be described below. (2) The demographic events of families which had recently arrived from Eastern Europe posed considerable problems in reconstruction. A good portion of the unlinked death records of Deerfield is attributed to Polish families after 1880 either because of a great amount of variation in the spelling of their surnames or to an unmeasured degree of mobility of the families themselves. Most of these were saved, along with those poorly observed Irish families.

This terminated the child linkage phase of the operation. Birth record formats were enlarged to accomodate the pre-adult death information where present, and each record received a unique numerical identification. The computerized children's file numbered about 8,000 for Deerfield and less than 5,000 for Shelburne.

Third, the records of this linked children's file were matched to the previous marriage file (which now contained maternal age data). This was accomplished manually by R. Meindl and H. Temkin-Greener. This task was aided by continual reference to decennial household censuses and the Sheldon genealogy. There were frequently instances in which our completed families were more extensive than those found in Sheldon. This observation usually applies only to those families in which the parents were married after 1860. The censuses usually supported our reconstruction over those of Sheldon for this period of time.

For families of those marriages contracted between 1840 and 1860 there was generally close agreement with Sheldon. This was especially true of the older surnames in Deerfield for which Sheldon was an exceptional source. It was noted that Irish and German families as well as transient Yankees were poorly documented in the Sheldon genealogies.

Fourth, additional families were created on the basis of census observation and reliable registration of children. These families, lacking only a marriage record, were retained only if

data existed on maternal age. This constituted the only other
way in which a family could "come into observation." Families
with mothers from this category who did not have their first
child until after age 25 were discarded.

Fifth, death information for parents, including age, year
and cause, was traced up until 1950 in the town registers. This
was done for all families who survived elimination after the
first four phases of linkage.

Last, each family register was evaluated by a variable we
termed "quality of observation." First quality included only
those families fully in observation from the birth of the mother
to the death or survival to adulthood of her last child. Many,
but not all of these, also followed one or both parents to their
death records. First quality families are the completed sibships and constitute less than two-thirds of the Deerfield file
and over three-quarters of the Shelburne file.

Lesser quality observations included those families who
were observed from the birth of the mother to either (1) the
birth of a child previous to a Federal census (which confirmed
the composition of the family at that point), or (2) to the
birth of a child (and no observation at the next census). These
are the incomplete sibships. Note that "completion of a sibship" does not refer to whether both parents survived to age 45
of the mother; rather, it is concerned only with whether these
events are observed. Thus, should a woman die childless at age
thirty after seven years of marriage, the family is regarded as
a completed sibship. On the other hand, if a family of eleven
children does not appear on that census at which the mother's
age was to have been listed as age 38, the sibship is incomplete.

We reserved the option of classifying several completed
sibships as less-than-first quality for a number of reasons.
These included no observation in one census, no observation
after age 43 of the mother or suspicious gaps in fertility histories. Similarly, such units were suspect if individual young
members of the family did not appear on one census. Less than
8% of the 426 completed sibships in Deerfield were classified in
this way. Nearly 10% of the 358 completed sibships in Shelburne
were less than first quality. No major demographic differences
between these groups of completed sibships emerged. For many
analyses they were combined (where no criteria would be vio-
lated).

It is clear that the family files do not constitute a random sample of Deerfield and Shelburne households. Parents of
high mobility are virtually absent from demographic consideration. Eastern Europeans after 1880, and German and Irish
(although these are not very numerous) married before 1850 are
not adequately represented. It is possible that several Yankee

(but probably not Franklin County native) households are not properly observed. Sheldon did not seem to specialize in these, and before 1850 we have no basis with which to confirm the reconstitution of such families.

In Shelburne, the Bardwell genealogy is less helpful. However, the town is far more homogeneous, judging from the surname list. No single group of Shelburne residents seems to be under-represented with the exception of transients.

In. addition to the above families, currently we have approximately 250 reconstituted families from pre-1810 Deerfield, of which 168 are complete, and we are extending the links back in both towns. There still remains the reconstruction of revised genealogies (pedigrees) from these files. It must be kept in mind that a major consideration in this particular study was the availability of a large number of completed sibships for the analysis of longitudinal trends in fertility and mortality. This took precedence over our concern with generational links along family lines.

In defense of the sampling procedure, it must be said that the data are probably quite representative of those individuals who remained in the communities throughout their reproductive lives. It is this portion of the population which before the 1890's reproductively contributed to succeeding generations in these two agricultural communities. This defense of the family files is most appropriate for what is by far the largest portion of the data -- those family histories of farmers who owned and worked their own land.

We think virtually all historical demographers would agree that one of the most consistent perplexities is in the identification of a population at risk for any given demographic event. Not the least of our concerns is how to deal with those individuals who pass from observation or who otherwise appear for only part of a sequence of events. This problem has made cohort methods particularly appealing in historical studies. With events expressed only as a proportion of those individuals who can be legitimately traced through a series of events, registration and enumeration errors can be minimized. This does not, however, eliminate the question of how representative the cohort is of the "real" population from which it is drawn.

In the present study at least three independent sources (vital records, genealogies and censuses) were available to verify events and links, and socioeconomic indicators (census and tax records) are included to aid in the evaluation of group differences and representativeness of samples. The estimation of any particular rate is thus "controlled" in a way that will produce a meaningful outcome.

As indicated, a major purpose in our research has been to
evaluate trends in fertility and mortality, especially as they
occur within the context of the family. Since there were initially good reasons to believe that heritability of fertility
and mortality could account for only a very small amount of the
observable change (see Cavalli-Sforza and Bodmer, 1971; Murphy,
1978), the construction of pedigrees has taken a reduced priority. More important has been the reconstitution of completed
families without regard to their generational depth. We have
had some success in making generational links of families using
patrilineal surnames. This effort is only in its infancy, however, and also necessarily involves utilization of families that
vary greatly in quality of enumeration. The formation of genealogies is part of the current phase of this research project,
and construction of a large number of good pedigrees appears
feasible.

Results

The procedures outlined above have permitted varying levels of inference on mortality as the work progressed. Our first
efforts (Meindl and Swedlund, 1977) were directed at estimating
the traditional aggregate parameters of death in the region.
This included crude death rates, age specific and standardized
rates as well as cohort life tables. The possible effects of
under-enumeration were estimated and the conclusion was reached
that by and large early residents of rural Western Massachusetts
experienced lower death rates and a higher life expectancy than
their urban counterparts (Table 2).

TABLE 2.   Abridged life table suvivorships for the white popula-
           tion by urban-rural residence, United States (ca.
           1830) and Deerfield (ca. 1750). From Meindl and Swed-
           lund (1977: 403).

Age	Early Deerfield	Deerfield	Rural U.S.	Small Cities	Large Cities
5	1000	1000	1000	1000	1000
10	984	929	975	965	938
20	944	839	935	923	877
30	918	668	856	824	725
40	859	566	766	709	513
50	800	467	680	582	311
60	711	387	575	436	164
70	525	288	423	256	49
80	210	105	173	29	--

For sources and data see Jaffe and Lourie, 1942: 357.

It was also possible to evaluate the effect of differing infant and childhood mortality on subsequent survivorship. This was accomplished by identifying childhood cohorts that were subjected to abnormally high mortality by exposure to epidemics. Such incidences have been documented in several towns but we summarize here briefly the case in Deerfield.

Children born within the ten years prior to the dysentery epidemic of 1803 were followed throughout their lifetimes, and control cohorts were constructed for the same approximate time periods (e.g. 1804-1813). The question is, how do the survivors of the stressed cohort compare with the controls? An example of the results is shown in Table 3. Essentially, it was found that an early experience of severe mortality results in an overall higher longevity for the cohort as a whole. This probably occurs as a result of an early "screening" or weeding out of weaker members of the cohort at a very early age, so that survivors display greater longevity. This conclusion was strengthened by comparisons with other cohorts and in other communities.

The next logical question is what mechanism is operating that produces this result. Two tentative explanations were offered (Swedlund and Meindl, 1977: 410): 1) the epidemics selectively screened cohorts with respect to genotype so that the stressed cohort was, on the average, more fit in the face of subsequent stresses, or 2) the survivors were somehow more able to cope with the stress because of their general health or capability for immune response, which might include genetic factors, but is not primarily associated with genetic differences.

In either case the logical questions that arise are whether we can demonstrate mortality patterns in individuals who are genetically more similar than others, and whether certain environmental components (including socioeconomic factors) can be identified which are associated with different patterns of mortality. This issue is addressed, within the limits of the present status of the data, in two parts. The first has to do with using linked pairs of relatives to compare their ages at death; the second (Meindl, this volume) looks at the association of variables within the family and their effect on child mortality.

Family Effects on Mortality

One question that has persisted for a very long time in the study of aging is to what extent longevity is shared by related individuals. Underlying this question, of course, is our concern about possible genetic determinants of aging and life span. The Connecticut Valley data provide a number of possibilities for investigating this issue, some of which we are just beginning to explore.

TABLE 3. Life expectancy and survivorship of the Deerfield
          stressed cohort and control cohort of 1804-1813. From
          Meindl and Swedlund (1977: 407).

Age	l(0)	l(10)	$10Q_x$	E_x
Deerfield stressed cohort (born, 1793-1803)				
0	1000			35.12
1	873		{.370}	39.19
5	695			44.71
10	630	1000	.046	44.06
20	601	954	.133	35.95
30	521	827	.140	30.70
40	448	711	.179	24.89
50	368	584	.217	19.21
60	288	457	.365	13.16
70	183	290	.716	7.84
80	52	83	1.000	5.00
Deerfield control cohort (born, 1804-1813)				
0	1000			32.75
1	875		{.285}	36.38
5	780			36.57
10	715	1000	.084	34.66
20	655	916	.282	27.38
30	470	657	.266	26.19
40	345	483	.226	23.87
50	267	373	.225	19.38
60	207	290	.396	13.55
70	125	175	.584	9.16
80	52	73	1.000	5.00

     The literature on the heritability of longevity in humans,
while not extensive, contains several reviews (e.g. Cohen, 1964,
1965; Rockstein, 1974; Murphy, 1978). A common observation made
by all reviewers is that the data tested in previous studies
tend to be inherently biased. The studies are most often based
on particular family genealogies with few or no controls, or on
samples collected for actuarial purposes in which falsification
of reported age-at-death is a common problem and in which many
relationships and segments of the sample go undetected.   An
exception to these problems are some twin studies (e.g. Kallman,
1957 and Harvald and Haugue, 1965), in which controls are much
better. A further observation which can be made is that these
studies are usually focusing on the question of maximum longevity or the long-lived, rather than on mean longevity or length
of life. It seems that the latter is a more general and perhaps
more interesting problem.

Bearing these past experiences and limitations in mind, we initially conceived a very simple model. We wanted to establish whether or not there is a detectable association between ages at death for a sample of relatives as opposed to non-relatives in the Deerfield population. We decided to control for sex, and because of the ease in tracing male surnames we chose our subjects from the male deaths irrespective of year of death, except that we began observation with 1750 and ended in 1910.

Three samples were drawn, a group of paired sibs, a group of paired individuals who in each case would share the same surname, and a group of random pairs of individuals. Prior to selection, the death file was jumbled so that exceptionally well-represented families would not be over-sampled. The procedure was then as follows: 1. A random number generator was used to select random pairs (N=65); 2. Surname pairs were drawn and the only criteria for a match were that age at death was known and surname was identical (N=77); 3. The sib pairs were identified by searching for two males with identical surnames, identical parents' first names, and known age at death (N=80). We did not, by any means, exhaust all possible pairs of sibs, but attempted to get three relatively small samples (N<100). This procedure included sampling with replacement between groups but not within groups. Because age at death is not a Normally distributed variable and is certainly age-dependent, the measure of interest is the difference between ages at death of the respective members of pairs.

Analysis of variance was used to test mean differences, the null hypothesis being that $S_1 = S_2 = S_3$, where S_1 equals random sample, S_2 surname sample and S_3 sib sample. The between-group contrast of greatest interest is that $1/2(S_1+S_2)>S_3$. The mean difference for random pairs is 38.5; for surnames, 28.5; and for sibs only 13.7 years. The results indicate that the between-group differences are highly significant, and furthermore, that all contrasts are significantly different (Table 4).

The second comparison we chose to make was that between correlation coefficients and their associated confidence limits. In this case we estimated the correlation with Pearson's R, Spearman's rank and Kendall's tau, and provide all three for general interest. However, we consider only Kendall's tau to be appropriate. The reason is that the correlations are on age at death of each member of a pair, and not on pair differences, so that Normality cannot be assumed.

The sib results (Table 5) again suggest a strong familial association, a low correlation between surname pairs and a negative and highly random distribution between random pairs. The

TABLE 4. Analysis of variance and the diferences between ages
          at death for 222 male pairs, Deerfield, Massachusetts
          1750-1910.

		Mean	S.D.
Random	(S_1)	38.5	25.01
Surname	(S_2)	28.5	24.35
Sibs	(S_3)	13.7	14.75

Source*	D.F.	Sum of Squares	Mean Squares	F Ratio	F P<
Between Groups	2	22629.799	11314.399	24.23	.00001
Within Groups	219	102267.412	466.975		
Total	221	124897.212			

* All contrasts significant (P < .0001)

mean age at death, and variation in age at death are very similar among the tested groups, as can be seen in Table 6.

What can we say of these results? There is strong evidence for a family component in mortality. There is a real possibility that the sib correlations are affected by some artifact
of vital registration, but great care was taken to avoid bias in
the sampling procedure. Following all statistical tests, a
listing of the pairs of all three samples was made. There are
no apparent biases in the sib sample and only two cases occurred
of a surname being repeated.

The more provocative question is how much of the variation
in age at death is due to environmental effects and how much to
genetics. Clearly, there is no easy or direct solution to this
question. Nor is it possible at this stage of the analysis to
document the exogenous and endogenous variables of greatest
importance. We know intuitively that the exogenous variables
should include a host of insults that include infectious
disease, nutritional stress and other environmental factors.
Endogenous variables must include non-genetic physiological
diffrences as well as genotypic variation. Cause of death
information is available for several individuals in the sample,
and further refinements in the model that will include other
relatives are anticipated. In future analyses, some improved
inferences about the genetic component can be expected beyond
these preliminary results.

TABLE 5. Correlation coefficients for ages at death for 222
          male pairs, Deerfield, Massachusetts, 1750-1910.

a. All ages

	Sibs (N=80)[1]	Surnames (N=77)	Random (N=65)
Kendall's	.5591**	.1448*	-.0900
Spearman's	.7553**	.1959*	-.1258
Pearson's	.7780**	.2544*	-.1912

b. Age > 5 years

	(N=46)	(N=39)	(N=28)
Kendall's	.4691**	.2327**	-.0561
Spearman's	.6741**	.3315*	-.1046
Pearson's	.7094**	.3886**	-.0685

c. Age > 20 years

	(N=36)	(N=31)	(N=20)
Kendall's	.3355*	.0415	.0160
Spearman's	.4942*	.0716	.0550
Pearson's	.5645**	.0822	-.0646

    1 pairs   * p < .05   ** p < .01

TABLE 6. Mean and standard deviations for age at death in the
          correlated samples.

		N	Mean	S.D.
Sibs				
	Column 1	80	30.20	28.86
	2	80	36.10	29.21
Surname				
	Column 1	77	41.06	30.47
	2	77	31.21	28.95
Random				
	Column 1	65	30.21	27.79
	2	65	37.82	31.16

    Comparison of our results with other studies is also very
difficult. The Danish twin study conducted by the Institute for
Human Genetics estimated the heritability for dizygotic twins
using the equation

$$H = \frac{V_{DZ} - V_{MZ}}{V_{DZ}}$$

where V = variance, MZ is monozygous twins and DZ is dizygous twins. Their estimate based on 209 monozygous pairs and 293 dizygous pairs was that 29% of the variation of the dizygous pairs was due to genetic factors. Problems include that the twins were observed only after survival to age five, and for comparative purposes, as Cavalli-Sforza and Bodmer (1971: 578) point out, we cannot readily relate estimates of H from twin studies to those of other relatives because limiting environmental variation to differences between twins has no direct analogy in other paired comparisons.

Correlation coefficients from other studies (see Cohen, 1964; Murphy, 1978) have not generally been as high as the one for sibs in the present study. Again, however, the whole age distribution is not usually considered, only those who survive to "old age," and sib pairs are less often considered than parent-offspring. In those cases where both have been observed, sibs have tended to have higher correlations than parent-offspring.

One phenomenon that scatter plots of our sib correlations revealed was that many points cluster at the infancy-early childhood ages, and also at ages 60-75. The former was expected, but the latter was less expected. Neither of these clusters appear in the surname and random plots. Obviously, two deaths chosen at random should not be expected to occur at similar ages at a frequency beyond the probability of dying at that given age.

To remove the early childhood effects on the correlation, two additional tests were made. The first eliminated all pairs with an age of less than five years; the second eliminated all pairs with an age of less than twenty years. The results indicate that a significant correlation remains after removing the effects of the early cluster, although the magnitude (and N's) of the correlations decline in expected directions (Table 5 b,c).

We think that these results indicate an important familial component in survivorship. While the correlations cannot be interpreted in the strictest "Pearsonian" sense, the associations are real and sustained beyond the earliest years in the life of sibs. Future tests involving other paired relatives might elucidate more about the potential genetic and environmental contributions to this "family pattern."

Conclusions

We have demonstrated how historical data from the Connecticut Valley are being used to address questions about mortality, while at the same time we continue to improve the precision with which we can address the nature of demographic change. Each step in the linkage process permits a new level of inference which ultimately leads to more definitive statements of causality. However, many interesting and pertinent questions can be asked along the way which, in turn, help clarify appropriate directions for subsequent research.

Our conclusions regarding associations in the age at death must echo those of other previous researchers (see Cohen, 1965; Murphy, 1978). What is clear is that a significant familial effect does exist for mortality but the cause(s) is not self-evident. Twin studies and sib comparisons usually show stronger associations than parent-offspring comparisons. This latter observation is confounded by the fact that parents have to survive to reproductive age in order to be parents, so that earlier ages are not considered, and by the fact that the parent sample is usually drawn from the very long-lived. The test thus tends to be directed at the question of long life rather than overall patterns -- such coefficients should not necessarily be expected to reflect the larger pattern of survivorship. To the contrary, we might actually expect to have more of a genetic component reflected in those individuals who do not survive to "old age."

The fact that sibs do show relatively higher correlations, however, raises the issue of a strong environmental component as cause of the variation. This would especially be true if the result were entirely due to the effect of early childhood deaths from infectious disease, but our preliminary analysis suggests a real correlation at upper ages as well (Table 5 b,c). Moreover, as Murphy (1978) points out, susceptibility to a wide variety of diseases may in itself have a strong genetic component. This might explain why there are not greater similarities in the random and surname pairs for early childhood deaths even though Deerfield went through a couple of childhood epidemics that produced high infant mortality (Meindl and Swedlund, 1977). Finally, the real point of interest is the fact that actual differences apparently do exist between families, other relatives and non-related individuals. Having established that, there are additional models to eliminate some explanations as opposed to others, and the remaining possibilities are important epidemiologically no matter what their origin.

SWEDLUND et al.

ACKNOWLEDGMENTS

    The Connecticut Valley Population Ecology Project has
received support from the National Institutes of Health (NICHHD
08979) and the National Science Foundation (BNS 7907369), which
are gratefully acknowledged. We would also like to thank Alan
McArdle, University of Massachusetts, for programming assistance.

REFERENCES

Acheson, E.D.(ed.) 1968.   "Record Linkage in Medicine". Edin-
        burgh: Livingstone.
Baldwin, T.W. 1920. "The Vital Records of Deerfield, Massachu-
        setts to the Year 1850". Boston: New England Historic
        Genealogical Society.
Bardwell, L.S. 1974. "Vanished Pioneer Homes and Families of
        Shelburne, Massachusetts". Northampton: Gazette Printing
        Company.
Cavalli-Sforza, L.L. and W.F. Bodmer 1971.   "The Genetics of
        Human Populations". San Francisco: W.H. Freeman.
Cohen, B.H. 1964. Family patterns of longevity and mortality. In
        "Genetics and the Epidemiology of Chronic Diseases". J.V.
        Neel, M.W. Shaw and W.J. Schull (eds.) Washington, D.C.:
        U.S. Department of Health, Education and Welfare.
Cohen, B.H. 1965. Family patterns of mortality and life span.
        Quarterly Review of Biology 39: 130-181.
Harvald, B. and M. Haugue 1965. Hereditary factors elucidated by
        twin studies. In "Genetics and the Epidemiology of Chronic
        Diseases". J.V. Neel, M.W. Shaw and W.J. Schull (eds.)
        Washington, D.C.: U.S. Department of Health, Education
        and Welfare.
Henry, L. 1967. "Manuel de Demographie Historique". Geneva:
        Droz.
Hodson, F.R., D.G. Kendall and P. Tautu (eds.) 1971. "Mathemat-
        ics in the Archaeological and Historical Sciences". Edin-
        burgh: The University Press.
Jaffe, A.J. and W.I. Lourie 1942. An abridged life table for the
        white population of the United States in 1830. Human Biol-
        ogy 14: 352-371.
Kallman, F.J. 1957. Twin data on the genetics of aging. In
        "Methodology of the Study of Aging". E. Wolstenholme and
        M. O'Connor (eds.) Boston: Little, Brown and Co., pp.
        131-143.
Kennedy, J.M. 1962. The use of a digital computer for record
        linkage. In "The Use of Vital and Health Statistics for
        Genetic and Radiation Studies". Proc. UN/WHO Seminar,
        Geneva 1960, New York.
Meindl, R. and A. Swedlund 1977. Secular trends in mortality in
        the Connecticut Valley, 1700-1850. Human Biology 49:
        389-414.

Murphy, E.A. 1978. Genetics of longevity in man. In "Genetics of
    Aging". E. Schneider (ed.) New York: Plenum Press.
N.E.H.G.S. 1931. "Vital Records of Shelburne, Massachusetts to
    1850".   Boston: New England Historic and Genealogical
    Society.
Newcombe, H.B.   1967. Record linking: The design of efficient
    systems for linking records into individual and family
    histories. American Journal of Human Genetics 19:
    335-359.
Rockstein, M. 1974. The genetic basis for longevity. In "Theor-
    etical Aspects of Aging". M. Rockstein (ed.) New York:
    Academic Press.
Sheldon, A. 1896.   "A History of Deerfield, Massachusetts",
    Volume II. Deerfield: Pocumtuck Valley Memorial Associa-
    tion.
Swedlund, A.C. 1975a. Isonymy: Estimating inbreeding from social
    data. Eugenics Society Bulletin 7: 67-73.
Swedlund, A.C. 1975b. Population growth and settlement pattern
    in Franklin and Hampshire Counties, Massachusetts, 1650-
    1850. In "Population Studies in Archaeology and Biological
    Anthropology". A.C. Swedlund (ed.) Society for American
    Archaeology Memoir, 30.
Swedlund, A.C., H. Temkin and R. Meindl 1976. Population studies
    in the Connecticut Valley: Prospectus. Journal of Human
    Evolution 5: 75-93.
Temkin-Greener, H. and A.C. Swedlund 1978. Fertility transition
    in the Connecticut Valley: 1740-1850. Population Studies
    32: 27-41.
Wrigley, E.A. 1966. Family reconstitution. In "An Introduction
    to English Historical Demography". D. Eversley, P.Laslett
    and E. Wrigley (eds.) London: Weidenfield and Nicolson.
Wrigley, E.A. 1969.   "Population and History". New York:
    McGraw-Hill.
Wrigley, E.A. (ed.) 1973.   "Identifying People in the Past".
    London: Edward Arnold.

THE USE OF CIVIL RECORDS IN A STUDY OF MIGRATION FROM ST. BARTHELEMY, FRENCH WEST INDIES

Ann W. Brittain

Quantification of migration and migratory patterns is often difficult. Written records of vital events are available for many populations, but these often do not include specific registrations of migration. Lack of this information may seriously limit the utility of the records that do exist, since calculating birth, marriage, and death rates cannot be done with certainty when the complete population at risk is unknown. Census information has proved useful in studies of migration, but it also has limitations. Even when the names and ages of residents are recorded as part of the census, there may be a lack of consistency in reporting, making comparisons between successive censuses difficult. Furthermore, a reliance on census information alone may not allow a distinction between death and emigration, and unless a considerable time-depth is involved, it may be impossible to determine familial relationships between the members of various households. In order to overcome these difficulties, this study is based on information combined from censuses and records of vital events to identify emigrants from the island of St. Barthelemy, French West Indies.

St. Barthelemy (St. Barth) is an island with a population of approximately 2000 for which church and civil records of vital events dating from about 1878 are available. These records have been microfilmed and computerized. Linkage of the birth, death, and marriage records was possible for most individuals, which allowed the construction of genealogies with a depth of several generations. In addition to the records of vital events, census information (in the form of "listes nominatives") was available for the years 1954, 1961, and 1967. By comparing the names, ages, and household composition recorded in the censuses with the information compiled from the records of vital events, it was possible to identify those individuals in the vital records who were actual residents of the island. This was not made easier by the liberal use of male nicknames, nor by the tendency for females to under-report their ages.

Once residents had been identified from the census, it was then possible to compose a list of those individuals who, based on the records of vital events, could also be expected to be living on the island, but who were not. This list of individuals was assumed to represent emigrants from the island. A few of these people were clearly reported to have been living off the island at the time the censuses were taken, but the majority of those missing from the population were simply unaccounted

for. The care with which deaths are recorded on St. Barth makes
it unlikely that individuals would apprear as missing if they
had died while resident on the island.

      Figures 1, 2, and 3 show superimposed population pyramids
of St. Barth in the census years 1954, 1961, and 1967. The
outer pyramid in each case represents the number of births, the
second pyramid births less known deaths, and the inner pyramid
the residents of St. Barth according to the census. The hatched
area between the second and the inner pyramids represents that
portion of the population assumed to have emigrated.

      Once the emigrants were identified in the genealogies com-
piled from the records of vital events, it was possible to do
more than simply count them. Each individual's age and sex were
known, as were marital status at time of emigration and kin
relationships to other emigrants and to the residents of St.
Barth. This made it possible to investigate a number of attributes of demographic and kinship structure which might affect
the likelihood of emigration.

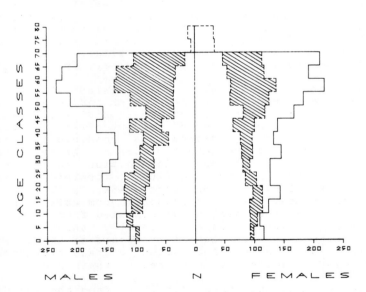

FIGURE 1. Superimposed pyramids for the census year 1954. See
           text for explanation.

      Chain migration is a type of migratory pattern that is
heavily influenced by kinship relationships. One member of a
family, often an oldest child or oldest son, seeks employment in
a new location. If the original move is successful, other
siblings will join him as information about job opportunities
and the capital necessary to migrate become available. Friends

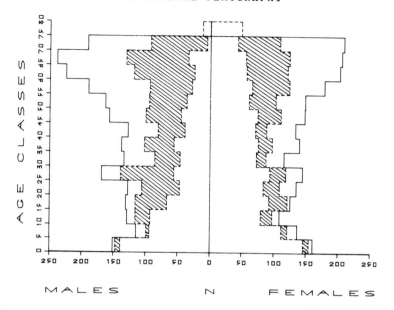

FIGURE 2.   Superimposed pyramids for the census year 1961.   See
            text for explanation.

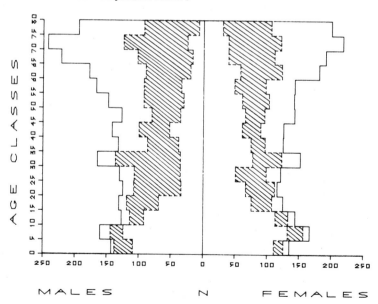

FIGURE 3.   Superimposed pyramids for the census year 1967.   See
            text for explanation.

and neighbors may also be links in migratory chains, particularly in closely knit communities. They may provide information
concerning job opportunities, models of success, or psychological support in the area of destination, though probably not the
financial support that might be available from close family members. Chain migration appears to be a nearly worldwide phenomenon in both internal and external migration. It has been
reported in the United States by Choldin (1973), Hendrix (1976),
Litwak (1960) and Swarzweller, Brown and Mangalam (1971); in
Egypt (Abu-Lughod 1967); in Greece (Friedl 1976); in Subsaharan
Africa (Gugler 1969); and in the British West Indies (Peach
1967) and Montserrat (Philpott 1970).

It is apparent that the chain migration of siblings could
have substantial effects on the kinship patterns of both the
sending and receiving populations. While kinship networks in
the migrant community at the area of destination would be
expanded by the arrival of sibship members, those in the area of
origin would show a corresponding decrease in size and perhaps
in utility.

In interviews conducted in 1975 and 1976, St. Barth residents and emigrants expressed nearly unanimous agreement that
the motive for emigration was seeking employment, describing a
sequential emigration of siblings, particularly brothers, as the
prevailing migratory pattern. In an analysis of the kinship
structure of the St. Barth migrant community on St. Thomas, U.S.
Virgin Islands, Brennan (1974) found a preponderance of parallel
cousins over cross cousins, suggesting that St. Barth migrants
to St. Thomas were more likely to be influenced in their decisions to migrate by siblings of the same sex than by siblings of
the opposite sex.

Given the amount of information available for the St.
Barth population, it should be possible to test the assumption
that demographic characteristics of an individual's family of
orientation will have an effect on that individual's propensity
to migrate to seek employment. People between the ages of 15
and 65 (inclusive) were selected for study as employable adults
capable of making independent decisions. Six family characteristics were used as measures of the influence of siblings on
migratory decisions:

1.   The number of ego's living siblings between the ages of 15
      and 65 regardless of emigration status. Litwak (1960) has
      noted that the larger the group interested in supporting the
      migration of one of its members, the greater the possibili-
      ties of accumulating the resources necessary for the initial
      move to a new area. Furthermore, larger sibship sizes may
      increase pressure on traditional means of family support,
      such as land or family businesses, increasing the need for
      emigration. This measure appears as variable x_1 in equa-
      tion (1) below.

2. The number of ego's living siblings between the ages of 15
    and 65 who were no longer living on St. Barth. This was
    chosen in order to test the assumption that an individual's
    opportunity to migrate increases with the number of siblings
    who are able to help him or her to relocate and find a job,
    since they have already established themselves. (Variable
    x_2.)

3. The proportion of ego's living siblings between the ages of
    15 and 65 who were no longer resident on St. Barth. This
    tests the assumption that the proportion of siblings who
    have migrated rather than the absolute number is important
    in influencing an individual's decision to migrate. It is
    possible that a single successful emigrant would have more
    influence on the individual members of a small family than
    if he or she were a member of a large sibship. (Variable
    $x_3 = x_2/x_1$.)

And, because of the apparent preponderance of like-sexed sibs in
the area of destination mentioned above,

4. The number ego's of living siblings of the same sex between
    the ages of 15 and 65. (Variable x_4.)

5. The number of ego's living siblings of the same sex between
    the ages of 15 and 65 who were no longer resident on St.
    Barth. (Variable x_5.)

6. The proportion of ego's living siblings of the same sex be-
    tween the ages of 15 and 65 who were no longer resident on
    St. Barth. (Variable $x_6 = x_5/x_4$.)

Each of these measures was predicted to have a positive effect
on an individual's decision to migrate.

    The six measures of sibling influence were entered as
independent variables in a step-wise multiple regression using a
program based on an algorithm from Efroymson (1965), and available in the Penn State Computation Center library as program
DNREG. Migration here was treated as the dependent variable and
entered as a dichotomous variable, with a value of 0 indicating
residence on St. Barth and a value of 1 indicating emigration.
Analysis of this type produces an equation representing the
dependent variable as a function of the independent variables of
the form

$$y = a + b_1x_1 + b_2x_2 + b_3x_3 + b_4x_4 + b_5x_5 + b_6x_6 \qquad (1)$$

where

    y   is an individual's migration status

    a   is a constant

b_n is the net effect of each independent variable on the dependent variable when all
other independent variables are statistically controlled, and

x_n is a measure of sibling influence.

Since males between the ages of 15 and 65 were approximately one and one-half times more likely to be missing from the
population in any census year than were females in the same age
range, and since it was assumed that the factors affecting males
in their decisions to migrate might be different from the factors influencing females, the information was analyzed separately for each sex for each of the three census years, giving a
total of six different tests of association. The results of
these tests are presented below in equations 2 through 7.

The step-wise regression procedure has removed from these
equations independent variables that did not contribute significantly (p > .05) to variation in the dependent variable. The
multiple coefficient of determination (R^2) represents the proportion of the variability in the dependent variable that is
explained by variation in the remaining independent variables.

Males

1954 $y = .486 + .651x_3 - .078x_4 + .074x_5$ (2)

$$R^2 = .189$$
$$N = 978$$
$$F = 75.82 \ (df = 3 \times 974) \quad p < .01$$

1961 $y = .596 + .566x_3 - .088x_4 + .072x_5$ (3)

$$R^2 = .143$$
$$N = 920$$
$$F = 50.74 \ (df = 3 \times 916) \quad p < .01$$

1967 $y = .542 + .548x_3 - .062x_4 + .060x_5$ (4)

$$R^2 = .133$$
$$N = 896$$
$$F = 45.43 \ (df = 3 \times 892) \quad p < .01$$

Females

1954 $y = .385 - .064x_1 + .051x_2 + .274x_3 + .501x_6$ (5)

$$R^2 = .248$$
$$N = 1011$$
$$F = 82.74 \ (df = 4 \times 1006) \quad p < .01$$

1961 $y = .324 - .045x_1 + .380x_3 + .513x_6$ (6)

            $R^2 = .189$
            $N = 992$
            $F = 76.70$ (df = 3 x 988) $p < .01$

1967 $y = .339 - .043x_1 + .529x_3 + .321x_6$ (7)

            $R^2 = .179$
            $N = 949$
            $F = 68.90$ (df = 3 x 945) $p < .01$

    Clearly, the factors influencing individual migration decisions are different for males and females. Equally clearly, the direction of association of these factors is not always as predicted. The factors which are seen to have a significant influence are as follows:

Sibship size: The number of living siblings age 15 to 65 (x_1), and the number of living siblings of the same sex age 15 to 65 (x_4).

    The direction of association of the sibship size variables to migration is negative, which is opposite to the predicted direction. It appears that rather than providing a base of financial support for the migration of family members, siblings may be competing with one another for access to the resources that their parents are able to accumulate. That these resources are more likely to be invested in males is shown by the fact that men are influenced to migrate by the number of their brothers (x_4) while women are more heav-

ily influenced by the total sibship size (x_1) than by the number of their sisters.

Number of migrants in the sibship: The number of living siblings age 15 to 65 who were no longer resident on St. Barth (x_2), and the number of living siblings of the same sex age 15 to 65 who were no longer resident on St. Barth (x_5).

    In general the number of migrants in the sibship has a greater effect on the migration of males than of females. For males the significant factor appears to be the number of brothers who have migrated (x_5), indicating that while brothers may be in competition with one another for parental resources, they are potential sources of aid once an initial move has been made. Females were only significantly influenced by the number of their siblings who had migrated in 1954, and this was the weakest of the significant associations of the independent sibship variables with migration

(.05 > p > .01). Since females are less likely to be seeking employment than are males, the number of their contacts
in the area of destination may not be important in their
migration decisions.

Proportion of migrants in the sibship: The proportion of living
siblings who were no longer resident on St. Barth (x_3) and

the proportion of living siblings of the same sex who were
no longer resident on St. Barth (x_6).

Factors x_3 and x_6 explain the greatest part of the
variability in migration. Apparently, the greater the proportion of the sibship that has already migrated, the
greater the probability that the remaining members of the
sibship will migrate as well. This is especially important
for females, for whom the proportion of their sisters who
had migrated (x_6) showed a significant influence beyond the
effects of the proportion of the total sibship between the
ages of 15 and 65 (x_3) who had migrated.

The proportion of the variability in migration explained
by the independent variables demonstrates that females are in
general more influenced by the emigration of their siblings than
are males, and that the influence of siblings on both sexes
decreased between 1954 and 1967. Characteristics of the sibship
accounted significantly for a maximum of 24.8% of the variability in emigration for females in the 1954 census and a miminum
of 13.3% for males in 1967.

Of course, the chain migration of siblings does not
account for the total variability in emigration from St. Barth.
The importance of the aid of siblings in making the decision to
emigrate reported by the people of St. Barth does not exclude
the possibility that more remote family members, such as uncles,
aunts, or cousins, or unrelated friends and neighbors might play
an important role in individual decisions, forming links in the
migrant chain. Factors unrelated to chain migration can also be
expected to influence an individual's decision to emigrate.
These may include educational levels, occupational skills, differences in family finances, local employment opportunities as
alternatives to emigration, and individual personalities.

Problems in the measurement of migration still exist.
Some people who might be expected to follow their siblings in
migration may not have made their final decisions by the time
the censuses were taken, while others may have already returned.
The available data suggest, however, that the chain migration of
siblings plays a significant role in the emigration of the people of St. Barth. The extent to which the actions of individuals correspond to this culturally recognized pattern could not
be evaluated without the combination of information available

from both the records of vital events and the "listes nominatives" to identify emigrants from St. Barth and their family
relationships.

ACKNOWLEDGMENTS

The original data collection and analysis was supported by
DHEW Grant NIMH RO1 MH13964; NSF Institutional Grant for Anthropological Research in Guadeloupe, French Antilles; and NSF Grant
No. GS-27382. Fieldwork was supported by a Hill Fellowship from
the Department of Anthropology, Penn State University. I wish
to thank Dr. James L. Rosenberger of the Penn State Statistical
Consulting Service for advice in the analysis of the data, and
Drs. Bennett Dyke and Warren T. Morrill for their comments on
the manuscript.

REFERENCES

Abu-Lughod, J. 1967. Migrant adjustment to city life: the Egyp-
     tian case. In "Peasant Society: A Reader". J.M. Potter,
     M.N. Diaz and G.M. Foster (eds.) Boston: Little, Brown and
     Co.
Brennan, E.R. 1974. Analysis of first cousin potential mates in
     Northside, St. Thomas, Virgin Islands. Masters paper,
     Pennsylvania State University.
Choldin, H.M. 1973. Kinship networks in the migration process.
     International Migration Review 7 (Summer), 163-175.
Efroymson, M. A. 1965. Multiple regression analysis. In "Mathe-
     matical Methods for Digital Computers". Ralston and Wilf,
     (eds.) New York: Wiley.
Friedl, E. 1976. Kinship, class and selective migration. In
     "Family Structures". J.G. Peristiany (ed.) Cambridge:
     Cambridge University Press.
Gugler, J. 1969. On the theory of rural-urban migration: the
     case of Subsaharan Africa. In "Migration: Sociological
     Studies 2". J.A. Jackson (ed.) Cambridge: Cambridge Univ-
     ersity Press.
Hexdrix, L. 1976. Kinship, social networks, and integration
     among Ozark residents and out-migrants. Journal of Mar-
     riage and the Family 38(1): 97-104.
Litwak, E. 1960. Geographical mobility and extended family cohe-
     sion. American Sociological Review 25(3): 385-394.
Peach, G.C.K. 1967. West Indian migration to Britain. The
     International Migration Review 1(Spring): 34-45.
Philpott, S.B. 1970. The implications of migration for sending
     societies: some theoretical considerations. In "Migration
     and Anthropology", Proceedings of the 1970 Annual Spring
     Meeting of the American Ethnological Society. R.E.
     Spencer (ed.) Seattle: University of Washington Press.
Schwarzweller,H.K., J.S. Brown and J.J. Mangalam 1971. "Moun-
     tain Families in Transition". University Park: Pennsylva-
     nia State University Press.

INTERNAL MIGRATION AND GENETIC DIFFERENTIATION
IN ST. BARTHELEMY, FRENCH WEST INDIES

Paul W. Leslie

Most population genetics models which have been used to investigate the relationship between gene flow and genetic differentiation assume that migration is random with respect to genotype. Consequently migration is expected to reduce the genetic divergence of populations which is produced by random drift and differential selection pressure. This underlying assumption is common to both continuous and discontinuous models of population structure. In island, stepping-stone and migration matrix models (Wright, 1943; Latter, 1973; Malecot, 1950; Kimura and Weiss, 1964; Kimura and Maruyama, 1971; Bodmer amd Cavalli-Sforza, 1968), the individuals leaving a subdivision are taken to be a random sample of the gene pool of that subdivision. Models of isolation by distance permit analysis of continuously distributed populations with uniform density (Malecot, 1950; Wright, 1969). In these models it is assumed that marital distance is uncorrelated with the rate at which an individual's relatedness to other members of the population decreases with their distance from his birthplace.

The implications of migration which is nonrandom with respect to genetically influenced characteristics have been investigated. Mathematical models in which the selection of migrants is based on genotype (Edwards, 1963; Parsons, 1963) and in which the probability of migration depends on the value of heritable metric characteristics (Kempton, 1974; Hiorns et. al., 1976) indicate that this sort of "selective migration" can promote the divergence of populations.

Several authors have pointed out that human migration is often structured along kinship lines--that is, migrants are often groups of related individuals (families, lineages) and therefore are not a random sample of their population's gene pool. This general phenomenon has been referred to as the "lineal effect" (Neel and Salzano, 1967), the "booster effect" (Roberts, 1968), and the "kinship effect" or "kin-structured migration" (Fix, 1975, 1978). Nonrandom migration of this sort has been observed in several human populations, and apparently occurs in some nonhuman primates as well (Koyama, 1970). Like the studies of selective migration, discussions of kin-structured migration have emphasized the potential importance of migration as a factor which <u>increases</u> the differentiation of populations.

Genealogical Demography

167

We thus have two contrasting, though not necessarily contradictory, views of the role of migration in genetic microdifferentiation: the classic migration models consider random migration which results in a decrease in differentiation, while the more recent work on nonrandom migration predicts increasing differentiation. The purpose of this paper is to present some evidence supporting yet another possibility: that under some conditions nonrandom migration may <u>decrease</u> differentiation or promote homogenization to a greater degree than would be expected under random migration. This is the reverse of the effect predicted by previous studies of nonrandom migration.

The Data

St. Barthelemy (St. Barth) is a genetically isolated population of approximately 2000 people in the French West Indies. Civil and parish birth, death and marriage records were originally microfilmed by Warren T. Morrill in 1969, computerized, and then used to construct preliminary genealogies. Subsequently, several workers have conducted a household survey and interviewed selected informants to clarify ambiguities and inconsistencies in the records, and to supplement the residential data. At present, the records extend from 1882 to 1975, and the genealogies are quite complete back to about 1850. Tracing the genealogies to a depth of five generations (back through great-great- grandparents), over 90 percent of the present generation's ancestors are known.

The Study Population

The population of St. Barth is largely rural and is distributed fairly uniformly over the island. There is only one nucleated settlement outside the small port town of Gustavia. Despite the island's small size (approximately 25 sq. km.) and the dispersion of houses, contact among the various parts of the island has always been limited. The rugged terrain and irregular coastline partition the island into a series of steep narrow valleys, bays and small plateaus. These geographical features provide a physical basis for subdividing the island into "quartiers" (quarters or neighborhoods) which, as is shown below, are largely endogamous. Construction of roads began about 25 years ago, and the road network has reached many quartiers only in the last 15 years. Prior to this construction, the quartiers were connected by rather difficult foot paths. Isolation of opposite ends of the island has been sufficient to allow linguistic differences to develop (Benoist and LeFebvre, 1973).

Results

We are concerned here only with that internal migration which may influence the genetic structure of succeeding generations -- that is, migration of individuals who are likely to reproduce. Thus we may define migrants as individuals whose

marital residence is not within their natal quartier. Illegiti-
macy is infrequent enough to be ignored here.

The tendency for individuals to marry within their natal
quartier is reflected in Table 1, a migration matrix for the
1426 individuals who married on St. Barth during the period
1887-1975. The table indicates twelve quartiers plus an additional category, OI, for "off island." The choice of these
thirteen subdivisions is somewhat arbitrary. Many St. Barths
would further divide some of them. However, the written records
do not share the inhabitants' precision in naming places, and
sometimes fail to distinguish between two adjacent areas. It is
unlikely that further division of the quartiers would alter any
conclusions drawn from this study. Table 1 shows that a large
majority (73 percent) of the individuals who married on St.
Barth remained in their natal quartiers. About 93 percent married either within their natal quarter or into a neighboring
one.

From the genealogies and the residential data, it is possible to determine the expected genetic consequences of the
observed migration pattern. In order to have sufficient generational depth to study the relationship between kinship and marital movement, however, analysis must be restricted to a fairly
recent period. The ten year period from 1951 through 1960
represents a compromise between the reduction of genealogical
depth in earlier periods and the increasing mobility allowed by
roads and automoblies in recent years.

Table 2 gives the migration matrix for this chosen period.
Because this matrix is so sparse we cannot determine statistically whether the pattern of marital movement during the restricted period is representative of the general St. Barth pattern. However, the proportions of individuals who marry within
their natal quartier during this period is not significantly
different from those during the rest of the span of the records
(Chi square = 8.09, d.f. = 11), and the destinations of the
migrants appear to be similar in the two matrices. While the
tendency toward quartier endogamy is quite strong, gene flow
among the quartiers is not negligible. The expected effect of
the migration is to reduce inbreeding and random drift within
the subdivisions. The relationships between endogamous and exogamous pairs support this expectation. Mean kinship coefficients between individuals who married during the period
1951-1960 are shown in Table 3.

Endogamous pairs are those in which the mates were born in
the same quartier. Mates born in different quartiers are exogamous pairs. The kinship coefficient for each pair was determined by using Kudo's (1962) method to calculate the inbreeding
coefficient for a hypothetical offspring of that pair. The com-
putations were performed with the genealogies truncated at 3, 4,
5 and 6 generations. The degree of relatedness between mates

TABLE 1. Marital by natal residence for St. Barth individuals married 1878 - 1975.

Natal Quartier

		1	2	3	4	5	6	7	8	9	10	11	12	OI
	1	52	0	6	6	2	6	10	2	0	0	7	0	4
	2	1	13	14	4	0	6	2	1	0	0	0	2	0
M a r r i a g e	3	0	5	124	20	6	2	3	0	0	0	0	1	1
	4	1	2	7	87	21	3	1	0	0	0	0	0	0
	5	0	0	0	26	80	2	0	0	0	0	0	0	1
	6	4	0	4	2	1	91	7	0	1	1	1	2	1
Q u a r t i e r	7	3	1	3	0	0	14	81	3	0	3	3	22	0
	8	1	0	0	1	1	0	3	108	10	9	8	16	5
	9	1	0	0	0	0	0	2	9	138	28	11	2	0
	10	0	0	0	0	0	0	0	0	3	10	0	0	1
	11	0	0	1	0	0	0	0	4	9	1	58	6	0
	12	0	1	0	0	0	1	7	2	1	2	5	67	0
	OI	4	1	5	7	2	3	3	8	1	3	7	3	-
Totals		67	23	165	153	113	128	119	139	178	103	101	121	16

increases with generation depth, since more remote consanguinity and multiple relationships are detected. Little information is gained by including more generations because the genealogies become too incomplete beyond the sixth generation. The difference between endogamous and exogamous pairs including six generations is significant at the two percent confidence level (determined by a two-tailed z-test). Individuals who marry out of their natal quartier are much less closely related to their spouses than are those who marry endogamously. Migration on St. Barth therefore should have a homogenizing effect on the population. However, this analysis does not consider whether the migrants are genetically a random sample of their natal quartier, and thus cannot indicate whether the homogenization is greater or less than what would be expected if migration were

TABLE 2.   Marital by natal residence for st. Barth individuals
           married 1951 - 1960.

Natal Quartier

		1	2	3	4	5	6	7	8	9	10	11	12	OI
M	1	9	0	1	0	0	0	4	1	0	0	2	0	0
a	2	0	2	1	0	0	1	0	1	0	0	0	1	0
r	3	0	0	16	3	0	0	1	0	0	0	0	0	0
r	4	0	0	0	12	2	0	0	0	0	0	0	0	1
i	5	0	0	0	2	14	0	0	0	0	0	0	0	1
a	6	0	0	0	0	0	19	2	0	0	0	0	1	0
g	7	0	0	0	0	0	1	13	1	0	0	0	3	0
e	8	0	0	0	0	0	0	0	13	1	0	1	2	1
Q	9	1	0	0	0	0	0	0	1	23	4	1	0	0
u	10	0	0	0	0	0	0	0	0	3	10	0	0	1
a	11	0	0	0	0	0	0	0	0	3	0	8	1	0
r	12	0	0	0	0	0	0	0	1	0	0	0	5	0
t	OI	1	0	2	2	0	2	0	0	0	0	2	0	-
i e r	Totals	11	2	20	19	16	23	20	18	30	14	14	13	4

random with respect to kinship. To do this we must look not at
the relationships between actual mates, but at the relationships
between endogamous and exogamous individuals and the gene pool
of their natal quartiers. Perhaps the best way to do this in a
sexually reproducing species with overlapping generations is to
determine the average relatedness of individuals to their potential mates   -- that is, all the members of a given subdivision
with whom that individual could have reproduced.   Potential
mates are determined on the basis of sex and age differences:
females may not be more than twenty years younger nor more than
five years older than the male. More than 95 percent of all St.
Barth marriages fall within this range. Since we are concerned
with the relationship between individuals and gene pools, rules
of consanguinity avoidance or preference are not included in the
definition of potential mates.

TABLE 3. Mean kinship coefficient measured between mates: St.
          Barth marriages 1951 - 1960.

		Generation Depth			
		6	5	4	3
Endogamous	Mean	.0119	.0111	.0069	.0012
Pairs (N=52)	Var.	.0002	.0002	.0001	.0001
Exogamous	Mean	.0057	.0056	.0041	.0014
Pairs (N=46)	Var.	.0001	.0001	.0001	.0001

The mean kinship coefficients between individuals who
actually married during the period 1951-1960 and all their
potential mates are shown in Table 4. The difference between
endogamous and exogamous males is significant (p<.05). Those
males who leave their natal quarter to marry are more closely
related to their potential mates in their natal quarter than are
those who remain and marry endogamously. This implies that the
migrants constitute nonrandom samples of the subdivisions' gene
pools. The difference between endogamous and exogamous females
(Table 5) is in the same direction as that for males but is not
statistically significant.

Comparison of the relationship between potential mates
calculated with the genealogies truncated at two generations and
at six generations (see Tables 4 and 5) indicates that a large
portion of the total consanguinity is due to the inclusion of
the nuclear family members in an individual's potential mate
pool. Because of the age difference restrictions and the relatively late age at marriage on St. Barth, the only nuclear
family members that qualify as potential mates are full and half
sibs. The contribution of siblings is greatest, both absolutely
and proportionally, in the case of the relationship between exogamous males and their potential mates from their natal quarter.

The effect of excluding an individual's siblings from his
pool of potential mates may be seen by comparing Table 4 with
Table 6. The most obvious result is the reduction of the average relatedness between potential mates. Note that the figures
in Table 6 are only approximated by subtracting the coefficients
for generation depth 2 from the other columns in Table 4. This
is because siblings, like other individuals, may be related in
more than one way. The relationship between exogamous males and
their potential mates in their marital quartier is not affected
by exclusion of siblings, since all members of a sibship typically are born in the same quartier. Exclusion of siblings as
potential mates also greatly reduces the difference between the
endogamous and exogamous groups.

TABLE 4. Mean kinship coefficients measured between males married in years 1951 - 1960 and their female potential mates.

Type of pair	No. males	No. pairs	Generation Depth				
			6	5	4	3	2
Endogamous males with females from same natal quarter	84	3020	.0232	.0222	.0194	.0148	.0095
Exogamous males with females from same natal quarter	30	1056	.0271	.0266	.0248	.0195	.0124
Exogamous males with females from same marriage qtr.	30	733	.0085	.0083	.0071	.0026	.0000

TABLE 5. Mean Kinship Coefficients measured between females married in years 1951 - 1960 and their male potential mates.

Type of pair	No. females	No. pairs	Generation Depth				
			6	5	4	3	2
Endogamous females with males from same natal quarter	67	2819	.2042	.0236	.0208	.0152	.0091
Exogamous females with males from same natal quarter	36	1404	.0265	.0260	.0235	.0162	.0091
Exogamous females with males from same marriage qtr.	36	1123	.0086	.0083	.0063	.0026	.0001

Discussion

The kin-structured migration which has been discussed in the literature so far deals with situations where groups of related individuals tend to move together. Since the individuals in such a group are genetically more similar to one another

TABLE 6. Mean kinship coefficients measured between males mar-
          ried in years 1951 - 1960 and their female potential
          mates (excluding sisters).

Type of pair	No. males	No. pairs	Generation Depth				
			6	5	4	3	2
Endogamous males with females from same natal quarter	84	2904	.0141	.0131	.0103	.0056	.0000
Exogamous males with females from same natal quarter	30	1003	.0152	.0147	.0130	.0074	.0000
Exogamous males with females from same marriage qtr.	30	733	.0085	.0083	.0071	.0026	.0000

than to the nonmigrants, this sort of migration promotes the
genetic divergence of populations. Rare alleles, for example,
are often concentrated within families or lineages. Migration
of a group of relatives might easily eliminate that allele from
one population while greatly increasing its frequency in
another. The departure of a group of kin will also increase the
average consanguinity among the remaining individuals, which may
increase the level of inbreeding in future generations.

     The pattern of migration observed in St. Barth, however,
works to break up groups of related individuals, and does so
more than would be expected if migration were random with respect to kinship. Rare alleles are thus more likely to be
spread among subdivisions. Relative to the effects of random
migration, the genetic consequences of this sort of nonrandom
migration are:

1. Greater reduction of inbreeding within subdivisions, and

2. Slower differentiation of subdivisions or faster homogeniza-
    tion of previously unrelated populations.

     It appears that a substantial part of the difference be-
tween endogamous and exogamous males in their relatedness to
their potential mates is due to the exogamous individuals having
more siblings. Since nuclear family incest is prohibited on St.
Barths, it may seem that the emigration of individuals who are
more closely related to their natal community because they have
more siblings, whom they cannot marry anyhow, should not reduce
inbreeding any more than would random migration. If we look or⌐

or two generations ahead, however, we see that this is not the case. The number of first cousins an individual has is determined in part by the number of siblings his parents had. Emigration of individuals from large sibships reduces the mean and variance of the sibship size distribution, which implies a reduction in the mean and variance of the numbers of first cousins in the next generation. The opportunity for random and nonrandom inbreeding due to first cousin matings, which do occur in St. Barth, is thus reduced. This effect will be extended to more remote relationships with each succeeding generation. Reduction in the sibship size variance itself implies an increase in effective population size and therefore a reduction in random drift and genetic differentiation of subdivisions.

It is not immediately clear why the difference between endogamous and exogamous females is less than that between endogamous and exogamous males. The discrepancy may be simply an artifact of the small sample sizes. The difference may also have a cultural basis, however. On St. Barth men tend to be more mobile and can search for a mate more actively than can women. A woman with many close relatives among her potential mates may have greater difficulty in finding an acceptable mate than would a man with the same proportion of close relatives among his potential mates. Such women are, culturally, more "stuck" in their natal quartier and would be more likely to remain unmarried.

A related study (Leslie, Morrill and Dyke, 1980) indicates that individuals who fail to contribute to the St. Barth gene pool, due either to celibacy or emigration from the island, are more closely related to their potential mates than are those who do reproduce. On St. Barths, then, internal migration and failure to reproduce on the island are both nonrandom with respect to kinship, and have similar genetic consequences.

Summary and Conclusions

In the partially subdivided population of St. Barthelemy, F.W.I., individuals who marry out of their natal community tend to be more closely related to members of that community than are individuals who marry endogamously. The expected result of this nonrandom migration is to decrease inbreeding and the rate of genetic drift within subdivisions and to decrease genetic differentiation among subdivisions, relative to what would occur if migration were random with respect to kinship. Previous studies of nonrandom, kin-structured migration have emphasized the increased differentiation which may occur.

This phenomenon probably could not have been detected without good genealogical data. It remains to quantify the genetic effects of nonrandom migration. Whether the solution to this problem is reached analytically or by computer simulation, genealogies will again be indispensable.

ACKNOWLEDGMENTS

Support for this research was provided by PHS Grant HD-07618.   I
also thank Dr. Jean W. MacCluer for providing the computer program for calculating inbreeding coefficients.

REFERENCES

Benoist, J. and G. LeFebvre 1973. Organisation   sociale, evolu-
     tion biologique et diversite linguistique a Saint-Barthe-
     lemy. In "L'Archipel Inacheve". J. Benoist (ed.) U. of
     Montreal Press.
Bodmer, W.F. and L. Cavalli-Sforza 1968. A migration matrix
     model for the study of random genetic drift. Genetics 59:
     565-592.
Edwards, A.W.F. 1963. Migrational   selection. Heredity 18:
     101-106.
Fix, A.G. 1975. Fission-fusion and lineal effect: aspects of
     the population structure of the Semai Senoi of Malaysia.
     Am. J. of Phys. Anthro. 43(2): 295-302.
Fix, A.G. 1978. The role of kin-structured migration in genetic
     micro-differentiation. Ann. Hum. Genet. 41: 329-339.
Hiorns, R.W., J. Kirby and G.A. Harrison 1976. Selective out-mi-
     gration -- the genetic effects in human populations. Adv.
     in Applied Probability 8(1): 1-29.
Kempton, R.A. 1974. A model of selective migration. Heredity 33:
     125-131.
Kimura, M. and T. Maruyama 1971. Patterns of neutral polymor-
     phism in a geographically structured population. Genet.
     Res. 18: 125-131.
Kimura, M. and K. Weiss 1964. The stepping stone model of popu-
     lation structure and the decrease of genetic correlation
     with distance. Genetics 49: 561-576.
Koyama, N. 1970. Changes in dominance rank and division of a
     wild Japanese monkey troop in Arashiyama. Primates 11(4):
     335-390.
Kudo, A. 1962. A method for calculating the inbreeding coeffi-
     cient. Am. J. Hum. Genetics 14: 426-432.
Latter, B. 1973. The island model of population differentiation:
     a general solution. Genetics 73: 147-157.
Leslie, P.W., W.T. Morrill and B. Dyke 1980. Genetic implica-
     tions of mating structure in a Caribbean isolate. In
     manuscript.
Malecot, G. 1950. Quelques schemas probabilistes sur la varia-
     bilite des populations naturelles. Ann. Univ. Lyon Sci. A
     13: 37-60.
Neel, J.V. and F. Salzano 1967. Further studies on the Xavante
     Indians. X. Some hypotheses-generalizations resulting from
     these studies. Am. J. Hum. Genet. 19: 554-574.

Parsons, P.A. 1963. Migration as a factor in natural selection.
    Genetics 33: 184-206.
Roberts, D.F. 1968. Genetic effects of population size reduc-
    tion. Nature 220: 1084
Wright, S. 1943. Isolation by distance. Genetics 28: 114-138.
Wright, S. 1969. "Evolution and the Genetics of Populations,
    Vol. 2. The Theory of Gene Frequencies". Chicago.

POPULATION AND SOCIETY IN ÅLAND, FINLAND: 1760-1880

Peter L. Workman
and
Eric J. Devor

Introduction

Early studies in historical demography were often limited to presentations of aggregate statistics based on census data. These aggregate data were used to describe major temporal or spatial trends in mortality and fertility in the past and to describe differences in these parameters with reference to population size and composition, social class, residence, etc. (Glass, 1965; Krause, 1959). Such investigations revealed a diversity of patterns which could not be explained by any simple model of demographic change during the transition from a largely rural, two class peasant society to a complex urban social system dominated by trade and manufacturing.

Subsequent studies of historical populations have been marked by three trends representing a response to the general desire to obtain firmer bases for both theoretical insights and for empirical explanations of the historical processes revealed by analyses of archival material. The focus of research has shifted from larger aggregates to smaller units of social organization (i.e., villages and households) wherein the individual decision process occurs (McInnis, 1978). For example, early efforts to investigate Malthusian questions regarding population and economy provided general correlations between variables describing the mode or intensity of economic activity with those describing regional patterns of population structure (e.g. fertility rates). Contemporary economic models of fertility behavior recognize the necessity of obtaining a detailed knowledge of the micro-environmental context within which fertility decisions are made. (Schultz, 1969; Willis, 1973).

Another clearly seen trend is toward the description of temporal changes, incorporating studies of individual life histories, developmental cycles of households, or of social data extending as far back into the historical past as possible (Berkner, 1972; Segalen, 1977; van de Walle, 1976). Such studies have been advanced in response to the use of rigid typologies confined to cross-sectional data sets which were popularized at the beginning of this decade (Berkner, 1975).

Finally, there is a strong attempt to develop methodology which permits comparisons among studies. This perspective includes not only very sophisticated record linking but also

Genealogical Demography

computer simulation which seeks to unite empirical results with specific causal processes (Hammel and Wachter, 1977). Advances such as these are essential in order that historical demographic research yield not only insights into local history, but also permit the formulation of general models concerning social behavior (e.g. Lee, 1977; Tilley, 1978).

In this report we shall present some of the recent work dealing with the population history of the Åland Islands, an autonomous province of Finland. In order to make clear the larger context within which this work has more general relevance, we shall first describe the nature of the Scandinavian archival material, then sumarize the essential features of Ålandic biosocial history, and finally present some of our current research on changing patterns of household and family size and structure during the period from 1760 to 1880.

Scandinavian Archival Resources

The Swedish ecclesiastical law of 1686 prescribed that Lutheran ministers should keep regular records on all their parishioners (Mielke, 1974). By the early 18th century, this process of population registration was a normal, and well maintained, activity of the parish vicars. Two factors seem to have contributed to the efficiency of this archival development. First, the system included all persons living in any particular region, both Lutheran and non-Lutheran. Thus the vicar played the dual role of ecclesiastic and civil servant in the bureaucratic hierarchy. In addition, each parish covered a clearly delimited geographical area which was regarded also as the civil basis for population registration, military recruitment and taxation (Hofsten, 1970). All persons were necessarily registered in the parish of residence as well as maintained or linked to the records in the parish of birth.

The major records available for Scandinavian historical studies include:

The Church Examination Register/Parish Register: This is the most important source, recording individuals according to family, household, village, and parish. New data were incorporated and the register updated, first at three year intervals and later at five year intervals. Within this document can also be seen individual records of smallpox, vaccination, literacy, and occupational/social class labels.

The Register of Births and Baptisms: A chronological record of individuals born and christened in the parish. Legitimacy and stillbirths are also recorded.

The Register of Published Banns and Contracted Marriages: A chronological record of marriages. In later years, the age at marriage is given, and often occupational/social class labels of the marriage partners or of their parents are included.

<u>The Records of Deaths and Burials</u>: A chronological record, by exact date of death, of persons who died and were buried in the parish. From the mid-18th century, this record contained the ascribed causes of death (where known) permitting detailed studies on mortality.

<u>The Migration Register</u>: A chronological record of all persons or families moving into or out of the parish. This is especially useful for the study of the landless class in a relatively mobile labor pool in farming and fishing regions.

Other records, less widely used, include tax lists, lists of property held at the time of death of a household head, court records, and agricultural information on land use and crop and animal production and holdings.

The parish records were incorporated into a hierarchy of annual summaries (parishes, deaneries, and consistories) which, by 1749, were produced on standardized tables for the entire Kingdom of Sweden. From the first modern census in 1860, the responsibility for production of the annual summaries was taken over by the central Bureau of Statistics. However, the basic data were, and still are, the responsibility of the individual parish vicar (Hofsten, 1970).

In the early period, most of the data were considered to be secret for military reasons, and were not published. This material was, however, summarized by Sundbarg in the early 20th century (Sundbarg, 1905). Historical studies use the microfilm of the original parish records which are maintained in several Scandinavian archives.

<u>The Åland Islands</u>

The Åland Islands are an archipelago between Sweden and Finland, bounded on the north by the Gulf of Bothnia and on the south by the Baltic Sea (Fig. 1). Of the more than 6,000 islands, or skerries, which make up the archipelago, no more than 200 have ever been inhabited. Although archaeological evidence shows habitation from at least 3,000 B.C., the majority of the inhabitants are descended from Swedish migrants who came to the islands in considerable numbers from the 6th century on (Dreijer, 1968). During the Viking period (c. 800 to 1050 A.D.) the main island of Åland (Fasta Åland), about 600 square kilometers, became one of the most densely settled regions in Finno-Scandia. The size of the population at that time has been estimated to have been between 3,000 and 8,000 persons (Mead and Jaatinen, 1974; Dreijer, 1968).

FIGURE 1. A map of Fenno-Scandia showing the location of the
            Åland Islands.

        From the   11th to the   17th century there   were relatively
few   political   or   social disturbances   which   appear   to   have
affected the Ålandic population.   Ålanders during this time settled into a stable peasant economy based on agriculture, stock
raising, and fishing (Dreijer, 1968).   Also, the residents of
the main island developed a considerable forestry trade with
Stockholm (Mead and Jaatinen, 1960).

        Åland is divided into fifteen rural Lutheran parishes or
chapelries.   Ten of these are on the main island and the remaining five are composed of clusters of smaller islands (Fig. 2).
The relatively isolated outer island parishes were densely settled (about 5 to 10 inhabitants per square kilometer) by the
middle of the 17th century.   At that time the total Åland popu-

lation is estimated to have been between 10 and 16 thousand persons (Mielke, 1974). During the late 17th century, however,
population growth in the archipelago was severely affected by
wars and famine which spread through the region. Subsequently,
during the Great Northern War (1700-1721) considerable numbers
of Ålanders moved, temporarily, to Sweden and there remained
less than 8,000 inhabitants in the archipelago (Mead and Jaatinen, 1974; Dreijer, 1968).

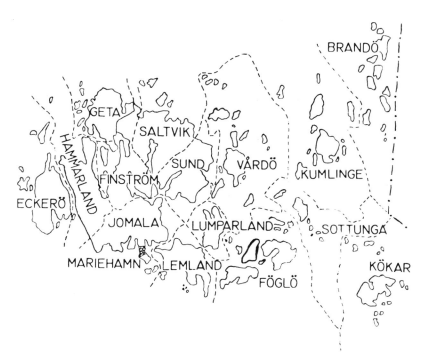

FIGURE 2. Map of the Åland archipelago showing the sixteen
           Lutheran parishes. Note the location of Finström and
           Kökar parish.

        Although the archives are relatively incomplete for the
first half of the 18th century, very precise historical reconstruction can be achieved for the period from 1750 to the present time. For that reason, our research has focused on the past
two centuries of demographic history.

        Overall, Ålandic history in the past two centuries can be
divided into three time periods. Between 1721 and 1808, Åland
was part of the Kingdom of Sweden, though attached to the Duchy
of Finland. During that period, significant changes in the
capacity to subdivide farms led to a marked rise in population

(Nerdrum, 1978). However, our studies show that the predominant increase is in the crofter, or rental farmer class and in the lower class craftsmen and independent farm laborers. Thus, this population growth reflects the development of a demographically substantial "middle class" and a very large lower class.

The Swedish-Russian war of 1808-1809 resulted in the sub-jugation of Åland, along with the Duchy of Finland, to the Rus-sian Empire. During that time, almost one-third of the popula-tion of Åland died as a result of war and epidemic disease and the population did not regain its pre-war size until approxi-mately 1840 (Mielke, et.al., 1976).

Major developments in fishing technology in the middle and late 19th century stimulated an extraordinary growth of popula-tion which reached its maximum, approximately 25,000, in the first decade of the 20th century. Population pressure at that time led to considerable emigration to Sweden and to the United States. At the same time, the founding of the first urban par-ish, Mariehamn, in 1905, initiated a process of urbanization which continues to the present. Currently, Mariehamn contains some 50 per cent of the total Ålandic population of nearly 22,000 persons.

Following World War I, Åland was declared to be an autono-mous province of Finland, governed by its own parliament (Bar-ros, 1968). Development of motorized sea transport, from 1930, permitted much more rapid movement among the islands. Recent patterns of population show that the harshest of the island set-tlements have been abandoned, and a major portion of those remaining in the outer islands are considerably older that those in any other stable region. The permanence of many long-estab-lished, but geographically marginal, villages is now in doubt. In recent decades, tourism has become one of the major sources of income. Thus, service industries are becoming a dominant factor in employment and hence in population distribution.

In many respects, Åland can be viewed as a microcosm within which many features of European demographic history can be seen: the transition from a two class system with a ruling, land owning elite to the development of a large middle class; the impacts of economic diversification; urbanization; and the depopulation of marginally productive territory.

Prior Research on Åland

Intensive studies of Ålandic social history were initiated in the 1950´s by the faculty of Åbo Akademi, the Swedish-speak-ing university in Åbo (Turku), Finland. Simultaneously, demo-graphic, genetic, and medical investigations were started by the population genetics unit at Folkhalsans, a Public Health Insti-tute, oriented toward the Swedish-speaking minority (approxi-mately 7%) of the Finnish population.

Many of the studies thus far completed on the population structure of Åland were summarized by Mielke, et.al. (1976) who noted that "the studies which have been carried out reflect pragmatic concerns with medical problems, the availability of resources for collecting and analyzing data, and the interests of many collaborators who have been involved in Ålandic studies." For example, Eriksson (1973) used the archives to locate all cases of multiple births in Åland from the late 17th century to the present. The twinning rate in Åland in the late 17th century, approximately 19.6 per 1000 births, was one of the highest ever recorded for Caucasian populations. Secular variation over different parishes and over time could be interpreted through the information in the archives on maternal age, parity, legitimacy, the occurence of twinning in the parents of twins, and local endogamy. The most significant factor was found to be maternal age which, with the twinning rate, showed a progressive decline into the 20th century.

Numerous clinical studies have utilized the archives to trace disorders with a genetic basis. The extreme isolation of the outer island parishes (low immigration, high local endogamy) has resulted in the expected pattern, a relatively high frequency of diverse, rare, genetic disorders. The most common of these diseases are the Åland bleeder syndrome (von Willebrand-Jurgens disease), a factor VIII deficiency with frequencies of 10 to 20 per cent in the southeastern part of the archipelago, and the Åland Eye Disease (Forsius-Eriksson Syndrome) (von Willebrand, 1926; Norio, et.al., 1973; Mielke, et.al., 1976). The genealogical reconstruction for those with the eye disorder identified a common ancestor described by his vicar as having "poor eyesight and restless eyes," a classic description of the nystagmus associated with the disorder.

Several studies, past and ongoing, have concentrated on patterns of migration to and within the archipelago (e.g. DeGeer, 1960; Jaatinen, 1960). Mielke (1974) examined patterns of marital migration among parishes. Extremely high parish endogamy was maintained up to the 1930's: 84% from 1750 to 1799; 86% during the 19th century; and above 80% up to 1930. In subsequent decades there was an extremely rapid decline in parish endogamy (41% for 1930-1939 and 31% for 1940-1949), resulting from improved inter-island communication, as well as a marked increase in marriages with non-Ålanders. Patterns of the actual distances involved in marital movement also reflect this decline in endogamy.

These studies show that Åland provides an excellent opportunity to study the process of isolate break-up. Studies at the parish level, however, appear to conceal even more striking local isolation. Present research (Kramer, in preparation) on endogamy and marital distances among individual villages within parishes show that, throughout the period up to the 1930's, there was also a very high degree of village endogamy, and

further, that inter-parish marital exchange was often between
individuals from villages in close proximity, but located in
different parishes. The importance of such hierarchical analyses of mating structure for studies of effective size, inbreeding, etc. is well known.

Longitudinal studies (in progress) have been most influen-
tial in interpreting the social history of the region. Nerdrum
(1976, 1978) examined two cohorts of females born during the
periods 1760-1762 and 1840-1842, respectively. The archives
permitted the reconstruction of individual life histories for
over 90% of each sample. The records provided descriptions of
all houses ever lived in, occupational and marital migration,
marital and fertility history, social class, etc. Similarly,
reconstruction of village histories have been produced by Montin
(1978) and by Sonck (unpublished) for two villages in the parish
of Finström for the period from 1750 to the present. These
studies provide inference on the social arena within which most
decisions are made.

Epidemiological studies examining the impact of epidemics,
particularly smallpox and scarlet fever, also appear to provide
an excellent perspective on social history (Mielke, 1978). The
archives permit one to trace epidemics from household to household and from village to village. The frequency, severity, and
duration of epidemics has been shown to reflect features of
population size and distribution, and the amount of effective
contact between social units. Proposed studies will relate the
epidemic paths and their characteristics to patterns of occupational and marital movement in order to better delineate the
changing size and shape of the units within which the majority
of human interactions have occurred.

In the following section we present some recent results on
the analysis of household and family structure (Devor, 1979),
and show how such material can provide insight both for Ålandic
history in particular, and the European peasant transition in
general.

Household and Family in Åland, 1760-1880

Discussions of households and families concentrate on
understanding the factors involved in determining both the size
of the individual domestic unit and the comoposition of the
family at its core. A simplified category of structures, based
on the scheme presented by Laslett (1972a), includes simple,
extended, and multiple households. The simple household is one
which contains a married couple and their children (if any)
along with various non-related individuals such as servants or
lodgers (if any). The extended household contains, along with
those persons noted above, other related persons such as unmarried siblings, widowed parents, and more distant relations. The
multiple household contains married siblings and their families,

parents, and married offspring and their families. In all of these schemes the degree of relationship of individuals is referred to the head of the household as stated in the record being used. For the purpose of this discussion solitary households, those containing only one person, are considered as a separate class.

Research on historical household and family patterns in Europe appears to have identified two basic forms. The Western European form is characterized by small mean household size (from 3 to 5 persons) and by the predominance of simple family structures (between 60 and 80 per cent of all households). Such a household pattern is exemplified by the 100 English communities dating from 1574 to 1821 presented by Laslett (1972b) and by the 409 English communities abstracted by Wall (1972) which date between 1695 and 1801. On the other hand, the Eastern European form displays larger mean household size (from 7 to as high as 20 or 30 persons) and a high proportion of extended and multiple households (40 per cent or higher). This type of household pattern is reported in the Balkan countries such as Serbia (Halpern, 1972; Hammel, 1972) as well as in Latvia in the Russian Baltic in 1797 (Plakans, 1975a). The apparent dichotomous pattern in Eastern and Western Europe can be seen in the data summarized in Table 1.

Prior research on the Scandinavian peasant family organization has been reviewed by Löfgren (1974). Scandinavian writers typically contrast the "Grand Family," which comprised several co-resident nuclear families, with the modern nuclear family household. Studies in the first decades of the 20th century attempted to provide an evolutionary framework for viewing a gradual, progressive change form larger to smaller households. Unfortunately, their data were often limited to identification of examples of larger household units in the 17th and 18th centuries, and lacked any systematic utilization of the archival material. Later authors noted that larger households often appeared to represent temporary responses to economic factors. Subsequent, more detailed studies failed to confirm any consistent pattern of "Grand Families" in Denmark, Norway, or Sweden. On the other hand, intensive analyses of the Finnish archives identified the highest frequency of larger family units in Scandinavia. As noted by Löfgren (1974), "The majority of Finnish, Norwegian and Swedish grand families have appeared in sparsely populated regions and often show a high degree of economic diversification within the household... a third characteristic of Scandinavian multiple households is that they often represent the upper strata of local peasant society."

Löfgren makes clear that both a more complex typology of household structures as well as a dynamic approach permitting analyses of changes in structure in relation to variations in the socio-economic context within which these units function are required for the analysis of Scandinavian households. Such con-

TABLE 1. Comparison of the "Western" and "Eastern" Family-
          household patterns from selected published data. (MHS
          = Mean household size.)

Location and Date	MHS	Per cent Complex Households	Source
"Western" Pattern			
Ealing, Middlesex, England, 1599	4.75	8.0	Laslett (1977)
Ardleigh, Essex, England, 1851	4.48	14.0	"
Colyton, Devon, England, 1861	4.48	17.0	"
Puddletown, Dorset, England, 1851	4.91	12.0	"
Longuenesse, Pas-de-Calais, France, 1778	5.05	17.0	"
Lesnica, Sileria, Poland, 1720	5.40	5.0	"
"Eastern" Pattern			
Jadar, Podrinje, Serbia, 1895	6.70	----	Hammel (1972)
Daudezewas, Kurland (Latvia), 1797	8.70	75.1	Plakans (1975)
Serbia, 1863	8.30	----	Halpern (1972)
Belgrade, Serbia, 1733-34	7.14	31.8	Laslett (1972a)
Mishino, (Great Russia), 1814	----	84.3	Laslett (1977)
Vandra, Estonia, 1683	----	52.0	Laslett (1977)

siderations were incorporated into the studies of household and
family in Åland during the period from 1760 to 1880. During
this time there is a clear change from a predominantly feudal
"two-class" society to a relatively modern social system with a
substantial middle class containing a non-landowning peasantry
(the crofters) as well as artisans and merchants.

The early 18th century in Åland could almost be described
as a typical feudal system in which a small landowning elite,
together with priests, lawyers and military officers, dominated
the social organization and direction. Inheritance of land was
impartible, by Crown Law, and the peasant farms were complex
economic units. Each farm was involved in agriculture, fishing,
dairying and handicrafts. A large, mobile servant class of male
(drang) and female (piga) farmworkers provided a seasonal labor

force. This labor was required in order to cope with the
diverse economic activities of the households. Population density was relatively sparse and, as shown by Mielke (1974) and by
Workman and Jorde (1979), village sizes were sufficiently small
so that exogamy (by village) was relatively common.   Such features conform exactly to the criteria discussed by Löfgren for
the maintenance of large, complex household structures. Examination of the archives shows that such households could be said
to be typical for Åland during the 18th century.

        In 1747 a Croft Law was passed in Sweden which allowed
peasants to subdivide their holdings and establish tenant
(crofter) farms. In 1757 this law was extended to include so-
called Crown estates (Royally owned lands).   An overview of
household size and structure in the Ålandic parish of Finström
is presented in Table 2.   In the mid-18th century the mean
household size in Finström was 8.86 persons and 56.0% of all
households in this extensively agricultural main island parish
were extended or multiple households.

TABLE 2.   Mean household size and proportion of household types
           in Finström Parish, Åland Islands, 1760-1880.

		1760	1800	1840	1880
Average size of households		8.86	5.29	5.09	4.92
Proportion of household type:					
	Simple	44.03	56.02	66.19	71.61
	Extended	16.35	21.76	20.50	14.32
	Multiple	39.62	22.22	13.31	14.07
Total		159	216	278	391

        Following this time, the number of crofters increased con-
siderably as did the numbers of other non-landowning persons.
The numbers of landowning farmers, on the other hand, remained
relatively constant. This situation is summarized utilizing
data on the occupation of the heads of households in Finström
parish, in Figure 3. It can be seen that, from 1760 to 1880,
the number of households headed by landowning farmers rose only
from 89 to 112, but the proportion of the total number of households occupied by such landowners declined from 54.9% in 1760 to
only 25.7% in 1880.   By contrast the number of crofts rose between 1760 and 1880 from 12 to 101, representing an increase in
proportion from 7.4% to 23.2%, nearly the same proportion as
that of landowning farmer households. It can also be seen that
the most dramatic increase came in the numbers of the "other"
occupations. The economy of Finström became extremely diversified by the late 19th century.

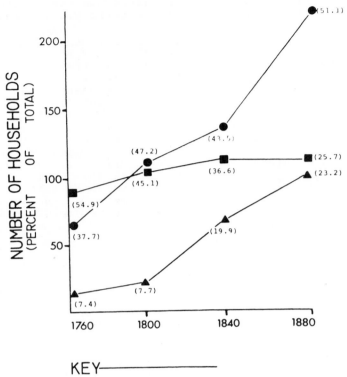

FIGURE 3. A distribution of the proportionate changes among the
           landowning, land-renting, and landless classes of
           Ålandic peasantry between 1760 and 1800. Data are
           for occupation of head of household as listed in the
           tax records (mantal) for Finström parish.

        The effects of this changing population structure on the
mean household size in Finström parish and on the dominant
household form are summarized in Table 3. While the size and
structure of the farmer household remained much the same
throughout the period from 1760 to 1880, the growing numbers of
small simple households among the non-landowning classes produces the effect of an overall reduction in mean household size
and in the proportion of complex household structures. Thus the
decline in mean household size as well as the decrease in the
per cent contribution of complex households to the total does
not necessarily reflect an evolution of household form within

specific residences, but rather a change in the nature of newly formed households in response to changing social and economic conditions.

TABLE 3. Distribution of mean household sizes (MHS) and types by occupational/social class in the Parish of Finström, 1760-1800.

Year	Class	MHS	Simple	Extended	Multiple	Total
1760	Farmer	12.34	12	19	58	89
	Crofter	7.00	7	4	1	12
	Other	4.16	54	3	4	61
1800	Farmer	7.52	30	34	41	105
	Crofter	4.83	12	2	4	18
	Other	3.23	96	11	3	110
1840	Farmer	7.63	39	43	30	112
	Crofter	4.15	48	4	5	57
	Other	3.38	121	10	2	133
1880	Farmer	7.45	50	33	29	112
	Crofter	5.30	76	10	14	100
	Other	3.48	198	13	12	223

The detailed analysis of household composition confirms the dependence of household size and structure on social and economic conditions. In particular, consider the contribution of the servant class to the size of households in Finström parish. In the 18th century the servant in Åland, and indeed in the rest of Scaninavia, lived in the dwelling of his employer and was considered a full member of the farmer's family. Löfgren (1974) points out that, after the beginning of the 19th century there was a radical change in the nature of the servant system. The servant became an independent, seasonal farm laborer with his own household.

In Finström parish in 1760, 54.6% of the households contained servants living in the dwelling (Table 4). Between 1760 and 1880, the proportion of households containing the "live-in" servant declined to 17.0%. The effect of this decline on the average household size is two-fold. First, the average number of servants per household containing servants decreases, and secondly, the proportion of those households declines. In addition, the servants who no longer served in the households of land owning peasants established their own small households.

Thus, the feudal society in 18th century Finström changed over the subsequent one hundred and twenty years to a three class society through the expansion of a demographically substantial middle class. The farmer household, once a larger, self sufficient and economically diverse social unit, began to require the services of specialists to a greater extent than ever before by the middle of the 19th century (Nerdrum, 1978).

TABLE 4. Distribution of servants in households in the Parish
          of Finström, 1760-1880.

	1760	1800	1840	1880
Number of households with servants	89	87	97	74
Proportion of households with servants	54.60	36.16	32.44	16.97
Mean no. of Servants per household	1.73	0.68	0.62	0.35
Mean no. of servants per household with servants	3.17	1.78	1.91	2.06

New laws permitting the subdivision of family farms fostered the
rapid proliferation of crofts, especially after 1800. In response to new economic opportunities presented by crofting and
the expansion of the craft market, the population of Finström,
particularly in the lower classes who were quick to take advantage of these opportunities, grew rapidly after 1800 (Mielke,
1974). Following the Russian take-over of Åland in 1809, restrictions on trade with Sweden imposed by the Russians also
stimulated the development of indigenous craft and merchant
markets. As Löfgren (1974) observed, the conditions favorable
to large complex households were no longer in force after the
turn of the 19th century except in the relatively stable upper
class.

We have also examined the isolated, marginally productive
Åland parish of Kökar (see Figure 2). Kökar does not exhibit
the same decline in mean household size seen in Finström in the
19th century. Nor does the complex household structure decline
into the minority position it does on Finström. The constancy
of Kökar with regard to these parameters is summarized in Table
5.

Appealing to Löfgren's criteria for the presence of large
complex households again, we note that Kökar is a sparsely populated parish, due primarily to a restricted amount of arable
land. Mead and Jaatinen (1974) observe that less than 10% of
the total land surface of Kökar could be farmed, the rest being
classified as impedimenter consisting of intrusive rock, boulder
fields, and standing water.

These conditions prevented subdivision of the farms and
there was no economic demand for specialized craftsmen. Hence,
the farmer household remained self-sufficient and economically
diversified throughout the 19th century. Further, the rocky,
watery land in Kökar could not support any trees other than a
few sparse birch stands. Wood for fuel and heat had to be

TABLE 5. Mean household size and proportion of household types
          in Kökar Parish, 1800-1880.

	1800	1840	1880
Average size of households	7.41	6.71	6.92
Proportion of household type:			
Simple	27.54	41.46	55.81
Extended	24.64	15.86	12.79
Multiple	47.83	42.68	31.40
Total	69	82	86

imported. This probably forced residents to maintain larger
households around a single hearth as an economic necessity.
Taxation at that time also included a hearth tax.

     Our results support the notion that a general model of
population response to changing social and economic conditions
can be monitored by analysis of changes in household and family
size and composition (see also Laslett, 1972b). In general, as
Löfgren has pointed out, if population is sparse and household
activities are diverse, the large complex household is favored.
As population density increases and economic diversification
becomes a societal rather than a household phenomenon, the smaller, simple structure becomes the preferred form for newly
established households. This trend is evident in Finström parish in the 19th century. In Kökar parish, however, where physical constraints inhibit both population growth and economic
diversification, the large complex household persists.

     These results also suggest that the apparent dichotomy
between Eastern and Western European household forms is too sim-
plistic. Variables impinging on the formation and maintainence
of households, such as inheritance strategies, population density, class structure, and economic diversity, interact in ways
which are too complex to be subsumed under an aggregate classification. Where fine-grained analyses of these variables are
possible, as they are in Åland, the result is a process rather
than a typology.

     The elucidation of the social and economic process result-
ing in changes in household and family size and composition lead
to other lines of research. Among those which will be pursued
in Åland are the influence of short-range (intraparish) migration on household formation, the genetic consequences of the
differences in the size and composition of families in Finström
and Kökar, and the implications of the transition from a few
relatively large complex households to many small simple house-

holds for the characteristics of the course of epidemic
diseases. The purpose of these future investigations is to link
social and economic causal processes, through their immediate
consequences such as changes in household size and structure, to
their biological consequences.

ACKNOWLEDGMENTS

        This work was supported, in part, by a grant from the Sig-
rid Juselius Foundation, Helsinki, Finland.

REFERENCES

Barros, J. 1968. "The Åland Islands Question: Its Settlement by
        the League of Nations". New Haven, Connecticut: Yale
        University Press.
Berkner, L.K. 1972. The stem family and the developmental cycle
        of the peasant household: an 18th century Austrian exam-
        ple. Am. Hist. Rev. 77: 398-418.
Berkner, L.K. 1975. The use and misuse of census data for the
        historical analysis of family structure. J. Interdiscipli-
        nary Hist. 4: 721-738.
Devor, E.J. 1979. Historical demography in the Åland Islands,
        Finland: The size and composition of household and fami-
        lies in the parishes of Finström and Kökar from 1760 to
        1880. Unpublished Ph.D. Dissertation, University of New
        Mexico.
Dreijer, M. 1968. "Glimpses of Åland History". Mariehamn,
        Åland: Ålands Museum.
Eriksson, A.W. 1973. Human twinning in and around the Åland
        Islands. Comment. Biologicae 64: 1-159.
Glass, D.V. 1965. Introduction. In "Population in History".
        D.V. Glass and D.E.C. Eversley (eds.). London: Edward
        Arnold. pp. 1-22.
Halpern, J.M. 1972. Town and countryside in Serbia in the Nine-
        teenth century, social and household structure as
        reflected in the census of 1863. In "Household and Family
        in Past Time". P. Laslett and R. Wall (eds.). Cambridge:
        Cambridge University Press. pp. 401-428.
Hammel, E.A. 1972. The Zadruga as process. In "Household and
        Family in Past Time". P. Laslett and R. Wall (eds.). Cam-
        bridge: Cambridge University Press. pp. 335-373.
Hammel, E.A. amd K.W. Wachter 1977. Primonuptiality and ultimon-
        uptiality: their effects on stem-family-household fre-
        quencies. In "Population Patterns in the Past". R.D. Lee
        (ed.). New York: Academic Press. pp.113-134.

Hofsten, E. 1970. The availability of data about the Swedish population. Sartryk Statistisk tidskrift 1: 19-26.

Krause, J.T. 1959. Some implications of recent work in historical demography. Comp. Stud. Soc. Hist. 1: 164-188.

Laslett, P. 1972a. Introduction: The history of the family. In "Household and Family in Past Time". P. Laslett and R. Wall (eds.). Cambridge: Cambridge University Press. pp. 1-89.

Laslett, P. 1972b. Mean household size in England since the Sixteenth century. In "Household and Family in Past Time". P. Laslett and R. Wall (eds.). Cambridge: Cambridge University Press. pp. 125-158.

Laslett, P. 1977. Characteristics of the Western family considered over time. J. Family Hist. 2: 89-115.

Lee, R.D. (ed.) 1977. "Population Patterns in the Past". New York: Academic Press.

Löfgren, O. 1974. Family and household among Scandinavian peasants: An exploratory essay. Ethnologia Scandinavica 1974: 17-53.

McInnis, R.M. 1977. Childbearing and land availability: Some evidence from individual household data. In "Population Patterns in the Past". R.D. Lee (ed.). New York: Academic Press. pp. 201-227.

Mead, W.R. and S.H. Jaatinen 1974. "The Åland Islands". London: David and Charles.

Mielke, J.H. 1974. Population structure of the Åland Islands, Finland, from 1750 to 1950. Unpublished Ph.D. Dissertation, University of Massachusetts.

Mielke, J.H. 1978. Smallpox and scarlet fever epidemics in Åland, Finland, 1750-1860. Paper presented at the 47th Annual Meeting of the American Association of Physical Anthropologists, Toronto, Canada.

Mielke, J.H., P.L. Workman, J. Fellman and A.W. Eriksson 1976. Population structure of the Åland Islands, Finland. In "Advances in Human Genetics, Vol. 6". H. Harris and K. Hirschorn (eds.). New York: Academic Press. pp. 241-321.

Montin, P. S. 1978. Household and family in Vastantrask, a village in Finström parish, Åland. In "Chance and Change: Social and Economic Studies in the Baltic Area". S. Åkerman, H. Chr. Johansen and D. Gaunt (eds.). Odense University Press. pp. 131-135.

Nerdrum, M. 1976. Kvinnan, familjen och det alanska samhallet - en kohortstudie av kvinnor födda i Finströms socken aren 1760-62 samt 1840-42. Unpublished Thesis, Åbo Akademi, Åbo (Turku), Finland.

Nerdrum, M. 1978. Household structure in Finström parish, Åland, 1760-62 amd 1840-42. In "Chance and Change: Social and Economic Studies in the Baltic Area". S. Akerman, H. Chr. Johansen and D. Gaunt (eds.). Odense University Press. pp. 136-142.

Norio, R., H.R. Nevanlinna and J. Perheentupa 1973. Hereditary diseases in Finland: Rare flora in rare soil. Ann. Clin. Res. 5: 109-141.

Plakans, A.   1975. Peasant   farmsteads in   the Baltic   littoral,
     1797.   Comp. Studies Soc. Hist. 17: 2-35.
Schultz, T.P.   1969. An   economic model   of family   planning and
     fertility. J. Political Econ. 77: 153-180.
Segalen, M. 1977. The family cycle and household structure: Five
     generations in a French village. J. Fam. Hist. 2: 223-236.
Sundbarg, G. 1905. Döda efter kön,   alder och civilstand i Sver-
     ige aren 1751-1900 samt medelfolkmangd efter kön och alder
     under femarperioderna för samma tid. Statistisk tidskrift,
     1905.
Tilley, C. (ed.) 1978.   "Historical   Studies of Changing Fertil-
     ity".   Princeton, New Jersey: Princeton University Press.
van de Walle, E. 1976. Household dynamics   in a Belgian village,
     1847-1866.   J. Fam. Hist. 1: 80-94.
von Willebrand,   E.A.   1926.   Hereditar   pseudohemofili.   Finska
     Lak-Sallsk Handl. 68: 87-112.
Willis, R.J. 1973. A new approach to the economic theory of fer-
     tility behavior.   J. Political   Econ. 81   (Suppl. pt.   2):
     514-564.
Workman, P.L. and L.B. Jorde 1979.   The genetic structure of the
     Åland   Islands.   In   "Population   Structure   and   Genetic
     Disease".   A.W. Eriksson, H.   Forsius, H.R. Nevanlinna and
     P.L. Workman (eds.).   London: Academic Press (in press).

MATE CHOICE AND MARRIAGE
ON SANDAY, ORKNEY ISLANDS

Ellen R. Brennan
and
Anthony J. Boyce

Because of their fundamental importance in the social organization of most societies, marriage and the factors which govern the choice of marriage partners are subjects of intense interest to anthropologists. These concerns are likewise of importance in the study of demography and human genetics, since marriage is usually a prerequisite for reproduction.

The determinants of mate choice are many and varied, and they may interact in various complex ways which depend in part on the society in question. Because of these complexities, the analysis of mate choice has usually proceeded in a somewhat fragmentary fashion (see Eckland, 1968 for a review), and few attempts have been made to evaluate the effects of more than a single factor at a time. We present here a preliminary analysis of mate choice as it has occurred in a single small society on the island of Sanday, one of the Scottish Orkney islands, in which we consider the effects of several factors which are known to influence the choice of partners.

It is sometimes convenient to classify the determinants of mate choice into two groups:

1. Structural factors, by which we mean those which are defined by some subdivision of the population. Thus, membership in various classes of age, residence, income, etc. might be expected to influence marriage eligibility.

2. Non-structural factors, or those which are best defined on an individual level, such as personal preferences, values, psychological states, etc.

In this study we have chosen to look at three structural factors: social class, geographical distribution, and kinship, as they affect mate choice on Sanday, Orkney Islands.

THE POPULATION

Sanday is one of the outer Northern Orkney Islands, which are located between the Scotish mainland and the Shetland Islands (Figure 1). The population is isolated geographically and culturally, so that the the effects of urbanization and industrialization were greatly reduced in comparison with most

Genealogical Demography

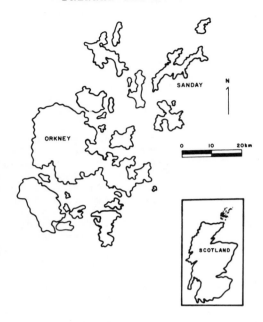

FIGURE 1. Map of the Orkney Islands.

of the rest of Great Britain (see Boyce, et al.   1973). The
primary sources of data for this study are vital statistics and
census records for the period 1855 to 1965. As can be seen in
Figure 2, change in population size was quite pronounced during
this time. Growth rates were positive until 1881, when the maximum size, 2085 was attained. After this time growth rates were
negative and total size decreased rapidly, particularly after
1900. The population size now is less than one third of its
maximum. The demographic structure reflects these changes in
growth rates. Low sex ratios, where females outnumber males,
were characteristic of the population from 1841 through the latter part of the 19th century as the result of excess male migration. After this time, high sex ratios reflect an excess female
outmigration. Throughout the entire period under study, the
population has aged: the proportion of individuals over 60
years of age has increased from 8 percent in 1875 to greater
than 20 percent at present.

        Vital rates underlying these changes in demographic struc-
ture are characteristic of many Western populations experiencing
the demographic transition. Age-specific mortality and fertility rates have decreased from 1860 to the present. In particular, the decrease in fertility is dramatic, as can be seen in
Figure 3. which shows numbers of births, deaths, and marriages
summed over five year intervals.

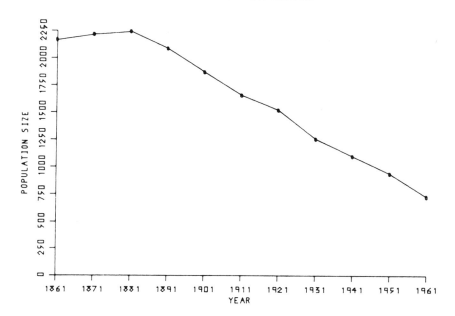

FIGURE 2.   Population size, Sanday.

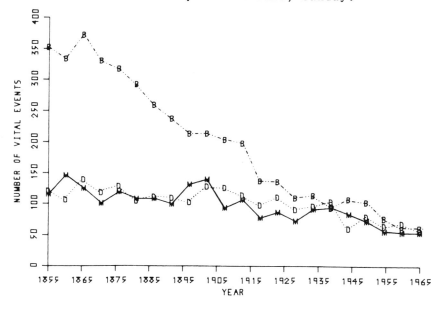

FIGURE 3.   Numbers of vital events, Sanday.

Since 1930, the total number of deaths has exceeded the
number of births, and reproduction has fallen below the replacement level. It is interesting to note, however, that numbers of
marriages have remained remarkably constant in spite of the
drastic decline in overall population size. It is also the case
(although not shown in the figure) that over the entire period,
only 30 to 45 percent of a given cohort ever marry before the
end of the reproductive period. This pattern obviously has
implications for the genetic structure of the population, creating a "bottleneck" effect on the passage of genes between generations such that less than one half of the gene pool of any
birth cohort will potentially contribute genes to subsequent
generations.

Because of the striking changes in demographic structure
which have occurred during the last century, we have divided
marriage cohorts into two groups. Early period marriages occur
between 1855 and 1905, when growth rates were positive. The 605
couples who married during this interval were from large birth
cohorts; the 454 couples who married in the Late period (1906 -
1965) were born at a time of low fertility, and were members of
small birth cohorts. The justification for making this division
can be seen in Table 1, which shows rather large differences in
mean ages at first marriage, and mean age difference of spouses
between the two periods. All tests of significance have been
done using Kolmogorov-Smirnov (K-S) two-sample tests of association.

TABLE 1. Mean age at first marriage and mean age difference
          between spouses (M - F) in Early and Late periods.

	Males	Females	M - F
Early	26.26	23.46	0.74
Late	27.92	24.01	2.06

All differences between periods significant
(P<.001), using a K-S two-sample, two-tailed
test.

We interpret these increases to mean that with the decline
in numbers, individuals search longer, and over wider age range
for their spouses. This pattern may contribute to a delay of
childbearing and lower completed fertility observed in more
recent years.

METHODS

Most of what we know about determinants of mate choice has been inferred from distributions of various characteristics of married couples. Investigations of these distributions have led us to expect associations between age, birthplace, socio-economic class, etc. of husbands and wives. The term "choice" is seldom defined explicitly in these studies, however, so that selection of partners at random from within demographic subdivisions of the population is often confounded with non-random mating. That is, factors of opportunity may play as much of a role as factors of choice (in the traditional sense) in the process of forming a marriage partnership. This confusion is particularly troublesome in populations which are small enough so that "favored" categories of mate are by chance not filled, or that partners of the most appropriate age have already been taken. In order to separate the influence of opportunity afforded by the demographic structure from choice per se, we have adopted a procedure described by Dyke (1971): Samples were taken of males known to have married in each of the two periods described above. Individuals in each of these lists were compared with lists of females who were eligible for marriage during the appropriate period. A female was considered to be a "potential mate" if she was not a member of the same nuclear family as a given male, and if she was no more than five years older, nor 20 years younger than the male. The sampling procedure was necessary because of the very large number of potential couples which would result from matching all individuals over all years. The sample from the Early period consisted of 388 males and 791 females who were available for mating from 1900 through 1905. The Late period sample included 122 males and 274 females who were potential couples from 1960 through 1965. Age, social class, residence, and kinship characteristics were kept for each year that both members of pairs in the samples were of reproductive age (15 to 40 for females, 18 to 50 for males), and single. These characteristics were then averaged over all males and all calendar years for each sample.

By this means we have attempted to define the "structural subdivisions" of the population within which mate choice occurred. Comparison of actual married couples with these potential couples allows us then to evaluate the relative effects of opportunity and of choice.

RESULTS

Social Structure

Social structure as used here implies the subdivision of the population by social status. Following procedures outlined by Kuchemann, et al. (1974), social class was estimated for husbands, their wives, and their potential mates by scoring the occupations of each person's father into five categories using the 1970 Registrar General of the U. K. <u>Classification of Occupations</u>. Classes 1 and 5 represent highest and lowest categories, respectively. Distributions of husbands and wives by social class is shown in Table 2 for two time periods. The highest proportion of both sexes fall into class 4, as might be expected for a rural community. Proportions in the higher classes increase in time, but differences between the two periods are not statistically significant. We can conlude that the social structure of married residents has remained relatively stable over time.

TABLE 2.   Proportions of husbands and wives by social class for two time periods.

	Social Class					
	1	2	3	4	5	Mean
Husbands						
Early	.018	.032	.142	.717	.091	3.80
Late	.023	.084	.157	.634	.102	3.61
Wives						
Early	.020	.059	.156	.699	.066	3.64
Late	.014	.090	.161	.619	.116	3.49

A "social distance" for each married pair and for potential couples was calculated by subtracting the social class estimated for females from that of males. Comparisons of social distance measured between husbands and wives, and between males and their potential mates are shown for two time periods in Figures 4 and 5. The proportion of spouses from the same social class (zero distance) is greater than that expected if mating were at random within the bounds set by our definition of potential mates. This excess is statistically significant (p<.001) only for the Early period, which implies that assortative mating with respect to social class has declined over time.

Geographic Structure

Geographic structure refers here to the subdivision of the population by spatial location. Detailed knowledge of residence locations has made it possible to calculate the distance between birthplaces of husbands and wives, and of males and their potential mates. (Linear distance has been used here, as the island is totally flat, and has no geographical barriers to restrict movement between any two points.) Distributions of these distances for Early and Late periods are shown in Figures 6 and 7, respectively.

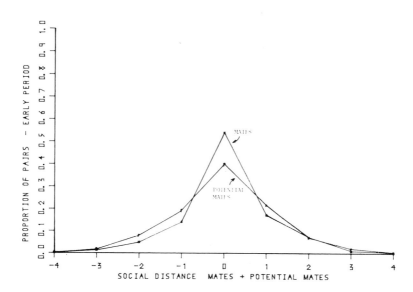

FIGURE 4. Frequency distribution of social distances between
           spouses (husbands - wives) and between potential
           mates (males - eligible females), Early period.

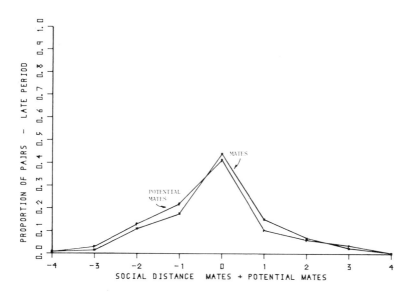

FIGURE 5. Frequency distribution of social distances between
           spouses (husbands - wives) and between potential
           mates (males - eligible females), Late period.

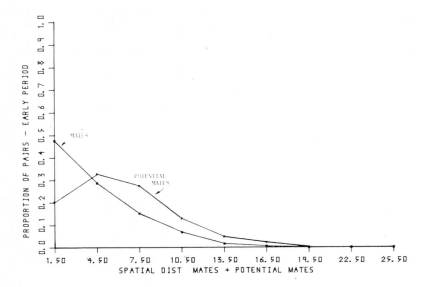

FIGURE 6. Frequency distribution of spatial distances (3 km. intervals) between birthplace of spouses, and of males and their potential mates.

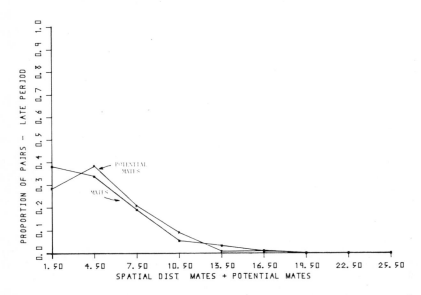

FIGURE 7. Frequency distribution of spatial distances (3 km. intervals) between birthplace of spouses, and of males and their potential mates. Late period.

It is clear that spouses are chosen from closer distances than would be expected from the spatial distribution of potential mates. The difference in means for the Early period is significant (P<.001, by K-S two-sample, one-tailed test).

Although the maximum distance between residences on Sanday is only 28 km., the Late period shows a slight increase in marital distance, which is consistent with similar increases found in most modernizing populations. Mean distance between potential mates decreased in the same period, however, which suggests that as the size of the population has decreased, settlements on the island have become increasingly nucleated.

Kinship Structure

The term kinship structure is defined here as the subdivision of the population by family relationship. A useful measure of this structure is ϕ, the mean coefficient of kinship, which is the probability that two individuals picked at random from a population will have at a single locus, genes identical by descent. Since "identity by descent" can occur only if the two individuals share an ancestor, ϕ serves as a measure of shared ancestry. Table 3 gives the mean kinship of husbands and wives, and of males and their potential mates for both periods.

TABLE 3.   Mean coefficient of kinship of husbands and wives, and of potential couples, in Early and Late periods.

	Married couples	Potential Couples
Early	0.00252	0.00147
Late	0.00146	0.00142

This table shows that actual spouses are significantly more closely related than would be expected from the mean kinship of potential mates in the Early period (P<.001 by K-S two-sample, one-tailed test), but that this pattern disappears in the Late period.

CONCLUSIONS

Each of the structural factors examined can be shown to have an effect on the choice of marriage partners. Comparing characteristics of husbands and wives alone in the two time periods defined, it can be seen that:

1. To the extent that social class is measured by father's occupation, differences between social class of husbands and wives has increased, and that there has developed in the

Late period   a tendency   for women to   marry upwards   on the
social scale.

2.   There has been a slight increase   in distance between birth-
     places of spouses.

3.   There has been a decrease in relatedness of spouses.

     The extent to which these   patterns are due to constraints
of the   demographic structure, or   to assortative mating   can be
determined only   with reference to characteristics   of potential
mates.   By   applying the methods described,   we are able   to say
that:

1.   Despite changes in social structure   which may have occurred
     as the result   of demographic changes over   the two periods,
     couples remain more   alike socially than would   be predicted
     from the distribution of social class in potential couples.

2.   Positive assortative   mating with   respect to   birthplace is
     distinguishable only in the Early period.

3.   Preference for   spouses who are   related has   disappeared in
     the Late period.

These changes have probably occurred   in response to "moderniza-
tion" in some general sense (increased wealth, contact with out-
siders, etc.), but we also feel that a substantial effect is due
simply to decline   in population size: the mate   pool in recent
years has shrunk, making it more difficult for culturally determined preferences to be met.

     We have described here the main features of our investiga-
tion of   mate choice   on Sanday,   but we   should point   out that
further analysis is possible.   For example,   we have examined
interactions of kinship   and social structure, kinship   and geographical   structure, social   and   geographical   structure, etc.
(Brennan 1979).   Although the data   required for   these methods
are difficult to   collect, and the computer   techniques involved
are somewhat   tedious, we feel   that our results   have important
implications for all those fields of study in which it is important to know the determinants of mate choice.

ACKNOWLEDGMENTS

Support for ERB during this study was supplied by PHS Grant 5 T01 GMO 1748 and by a Hill Fellowship from the Department of Anthropology, Penn State University. We thank Bennett Dyke for his comments on the manuscript.

REFERENCES

Boyce, A.J., V.M.L. Holdsworth and D.R. Brothwell 1973. Demographic and genetic studies in the Orkney Islands. In "Genetic Studies in Britain". D.R. Roberts and E. Sunderland (eds.), London: Taylor and Francis, pp. 109-128.

Brennan, E.R. 1979. Kinship, demographic, social, and geographic characteristics of mate choice in a small human population. Ph.D. dissertation, Department of Anthropology, Penn State University, University Park, Pennsylvania.

Dyke, B. 1971. Potential mates in a small human population. Social Biology 18:28-39.

Eckland, B. 1968. Theories of mate selection. Eugenics Quarterly 14:74-84.

Kuchemann, C.F., G.A. Harrison, R.W. Hiorns and P.J. Carrivick 1974. Social class and marital distance in Oxford city. Annals of Human Biology 1:13-27.

VICE IN THE VILLEFRANCHIAN: A MICROSIMULATION ANALYSIS OF THE DEMOGRAPHIC EFFECTS OF INCEST PROHIBITIONS*

Eugene A. Hammel
Chad K. McDaniel
and
Kenneth W. Wachter

Advantages and Disadvantages of Incest Tabus

The cultural regulation of sexuality has long been regarded as one of the most important achievments of mankind, distinguishing us unequivocally from related species. It is certainly reasonable to speculate that the regulation of sexuality evident in tabus of incest and exogamy may go back to the beginnings of human history, emerging coterminously with language, symbolism and the construction of social categories such as that most important one, the family (1).

The "causes" for incest tabus and exogamy have been variously assessed. Six general categories of explanation have been distinguished (2). We list them briefly here by way of background:

1. Inbreeding. Inbreeding produces genetically deleterious results, although these attenuate rapidly as breeding moves outside the immediate circle of primary relatives. For inbreeding to be a factor in the origin or persistence of the incest tabu, selective advantage must favor those societies that for some other reason adhere to a tabu, or the members of a society must realize the effects of close inbreeding from observation and establish or maintain the prohibition.

2. Socialization. It is argued that children must learn to distinguish between familial and extrafamilial roles. A primary distinction between them is the direction of erotic impulses away from family members. This reasoning has seemed confusing to all but the most committed adherents of psychoanalytic explanations. Like the inbreeding theory, it requires either selective advantage or perception of advantage and institutionalization.

3. Family cohesion. It is said that sexual competition within the family would be disruptive and that an incest tabu helps to regulate internal group relations. Like the preceding theories, this one could play a role through selective advantage or through perception and institutionalization. Of the several theories, this is one of the most universally

*An earlier and briefer version of this chapter was published in Science 205, 972-977, September 7, 1979, under the title "Demographic Consequences of Incest Tabus: A Microsimulation Analysis." Copyright 1979, by the American Association for the Advancement of Science

accepted, being associated primarily with the names of Freud, Malinowski, Seligman and anthropologists in general who focus on descent group analysis.

4. Alliance theory. Incest tabus are said to force external political alliances. This theory is the other major attempt to explain the origin (or persistence) of incest tabus, first expressed by Tylor (3) in the phrase "marry out or be killed out". Like the others, it requires acceptance of selective advantage or recognition and institutionalization.

5. Revulsion. Incest tabus are said to be formal expressions of feelings of horror or revulsion at the thought of sexual relations between persons who have been raised in familial intimacy. The theory was proposed by Westermarck (4). The link to establishment or persistence of an incest tabu, however, is as tenuous as with the other theories. The only advantage to be gained from establishment of a tabu would be a reduction in general revulsion, which might benefit the overall fertility rates.

6. Age structure. This theory, propounded by Slater (5), claims that in small primitive societies most of the individuals who would be incestuously linked if they were to engage in sexual relations are probably unavailable to one another by reason of disparity in age. Presumably, incest tabus might emerge simply as rationalizations of what did not occur in most instances anyway. The theory explains why sex between close kin might not occur, but it says little about the tabu itself.

A possible retort to theories that incest tabus confer advantages (selective for the evolutionists or just pleasant for the functionalists) is that they confer a disadvantage more basic and obvious than the supposed advantages. The disadvantage is the demographic cost incurred through the restriction of available mates by the regulation of sexual relations. Individuals barred from certain choices of mates may have longer average waiting times until marriage, and the group to which they belong may lose some of its potential fertility. As an hypothesis it has two special advantages. First, it is tied directly to reproductive success, so that those who wish to speculate on the origin of the regulation of sexuality or the persistence of the rule systems need not forge elaborate logical chains to fit their theories into the regular framework of evolutionary argument. Second, it is subject to sharp enough definition to be modelled and measured. Claims about the likely strength of disadvantages attendant on particular regulations of sexuality are then testable hypotheses. We can call this theory the "marry out or die out" theory, a phrase erroneously attributed to Tylor, who was talking about being killed out in war for want of politically useful marriage alliances. We are talking about withering on the demographic vine.

The larger we measure the demographic cost to be, the greater the burden on advantage theories such as those listed. The broader the class of populations where the cost is measued to be high, the further our attention ought to shift away from advantages, toward possible compensatory behaviors accompanying tabus.

The effect of marriage regulation on the possibility of finding mates has been addressed by Hammel (6) in an analysis of marriage section systems, by Hammel and Hutchinson (7) through computer microsimulation, and by Morgan (8) and MacCluer and Dyke (9), using similar simulation techniques (10). The simulation studies all examine the effect of incest regulations on population viability; that is, they investigate the degree to which a population shrinks in size as a consequence of the difficulties that are generated by the tabu in finding spouses and thus on maintaining fertility. With the exception of Morgan's analysis, which found population viability enhanced by the incest tabu, all the papers suggest that population viability is adversely affected and that this effect is stronger in smaller populations where the exclusion of some particular number of persons (say, siblings) from the marriage market removes a relatively large fraction of the total marriageable population (11).

In a fundamental way, however, these simulation studies all ask the wrong question. Population viability as measured in them is a poor indicator of the effect of incest prohibitions for at least two reasons. First, people faced with a scarcity of spouses created by some cultural rule may create another rule or find some other means of offsetting the effects of the first rule. Second, there is a more direct analytical problem in that these studies all involve a positive feedback between (1) the effect of a tabu in diminishing population and (2) the enhancement of the tabu's effect in small populations. This confounds the effects of the critical variables, severity of tabu and population size.

A Refined Simulation Approach

To avoid these difficulties we developed a different simulation experiment design. Rather than measure the effect of a tabu by allowing it to alter and thus confound itself with population size, we simulate nearly stationary populations and measure the amount of fertility these populations would have to realize outside of normal marriage if their stationarity were to be maintained. The required levels of alternative fertility (AF) can be determined in a straightforward manner: the same input fertility rates are used for both married and unmarried women. The size and growth of a population are thus unaffected by the marital status of its members. The proportion of births to unmarried women, out of all births, is the alternative fertility proportion (AFP); that is, the proportion of fertility that must be realized outside of normal marriage to maintain a

stationary population. Marriage rates are set high so that in
the absence of cultural or demographic impediments to marriage,
the AFP will approach zero. As the difficulties of finding a
spouse increase, the chance that a woman will have a child
before or between marriages increases, and so does the AFP.

Care must be taken in interpreting this AFP measure. It
might be interpreted as "illegitimate fertility", but it need
not be only this. It could be alternative fertility achieved
through any kind of marital or sexual arrangement not explicitly
permitted in the modelling. To allow an initially uncomplicated
evaluation of the problem, we take endogamous monogamy as "normal marriage" in our simulations. Thus any possible means of
realizing fertility outside of endogamous monogamy -- exogamy,
polygamy, promiscuity -- would be a potential mechanism for
realizing the AF levels required. We consider the AFP only as
an indication of the pressure for social change, if such occurs,
or for demographic change if no social change occurs. We suggest that the pattern of our conclusions holds for any base
level of marital arrangements taken as "normal marriage."

Using this measure, we ask three questions about the socio-demographic impacts of incest tabus:

1. Does imposition of a tabu make a large difference in AFP?

2. How does AFP depend on population size?

3. Do different kinds of tabus have different kinds of effects
    on AFP, or are the effects of different tabus sufficiently
    regular to permit generalization?

Assumptions for the Simulation

The computer simulations for this exploration were done
with recent revisions of the SOCSIM microsimulation programs
(12). In order to achieve a range of population sizes, simulation runs were done at three different starting population levels: 50, 100 and 300. Random variation filled out the gaps in
this scale. At each such population level, runs were done at
each of the following levels of incest tabu:

      0 No prohibition

      1 Incest prohibition within the nuclear family

      2 Incest prohibition on first cousins and any
         nearer kin

      3 Incest prohibition on second cousins and any
         nearer kin (13)

To achieve statistical reliability, the number of runs was
substantial. At population level 50, two hundred runs were done
at each level of incest prohibition, and one hundred runs were
done at each level of the incest prohibition at each of the
remaining population levels. There were 1,600 runs in all. The
larger number of runs at the smallest population level was done
because we fully expected some populations to die out simply
because small populations are very susceptible to the vagaries
of random fluctuation. Some of the small ones would have become
extinct by chance alone. Only the 1,503 populations that survived the 200-year simulation period were included in the final
results. The scheme of the experiment is given in Table 1.

TABLE 1. Simulation design.

Simulation Group	Completed Simulations	Starting Population	Incest Level
1	94	50	0
2	89	50	0
3	98	100	0
4	99	300	0
5	99	50	1
6	84	50	1
7	98	100	1
8	99	300	1
9	94	50	2
10	77	50	2
11	99	100	2
12	98	300	2
13	95	50	3
14	83	50	3
15	98	100	3
16	99	300	3

Fertility and mortality rates were set high to mimic the
demographic behavior of the populations in which sexual regulation might be thought originally to have emerged or to have been
important. Mortality rates were taken from Weiss, Table
MT:22.5-50 (14). This table is based on a standard
infant/juvenile mortality curve scaled to give a survivorship to
age 15 of 50% of all live births, and on a mortality schedule
for ages 15 to 55 giving expectation of life at age 15 of 22.5
(further) years (see Table 2).

Fertility schedules were based on Henry's curve of natural
fertility, scaled to achieve a slight annual population increase
of five per 10,000 (15). A lower rate of increase might have
permitted too many cases of random population extinction as
individual populations responded to the stochastic variation in
demographic rates that was actually realized in the simulation.

TABLE 2.   Model life table.*

AGE	Q(X)	l(x)	L(x)	T(x)	e(x)	FB(x)	C(x)	AGE
0	0.2670	100.0	83	2020	20.2	0.0	4.1	0
1	0.1600	73.3	262	1938	26.4	0.0	13.0	1
5	0.1100	61.6	291	1676	27.2	0.0	14.4	5
10	0.0876	54.8	262	1385	25.3	0.0	13.0	10
15	0.1672	50.0	229	1123	22.5	0.060	11.3	15
20	0.1722	41.6	190	894	21.5	0.162	9.4	20
25	0.1774	34.5	157	704	20.4	0.162	7.8	25
30	0.1828	28.4	128	548	19.3	0.131	6.4	30
35	0.1882	23.2	105	419	18.1	0.091	5.2	35
40	0.1939	18.8	85	314	16.7	0.038	4.2	40
45	0.1996	15.2	68	230	15.1	0.008	3.4	45
50	0.2055	12.1	54	162	13.3	0.0	2.7	50
55	0.2434	9.6	42	107	11.1	0.0	2.1	55
60	0.3187	7.3	31	65	8.9	0.0	1.5	60
65	0.4030	5.0	20	34	6.9	0.0	1.0	65
70	0.5162	3.0	11	15	4.9	0.0	0.5	70
75	1.0000	1.4	4	4	2.5	0.0	0.2	75

*   From Weiss, op. cit., p. 137.

Where Q(x) is the probability of dying in the interval.
      l(x) is the number surviving out of the radix 100.
      L(x) is the person-years lived in the interval.
      T(x) is the total person-years remaining to be lived.
      e(x) is the mean expectation of life at age x.
      FB(x) is the annual probability that a female in the
            interval x will give birth to a daughter (in the
            Weiss model).
      C(x) is the percentage of the population in the interval
            x, for a stable population (in the Weiss model).
      AGE defines the beginning of the interval; thus "20" means
            attained age 20 but not yet attained age 25.

A higher rate of increase might have created some enormous populations that would have exceeded our computing capabilities and
would certainly have increased the cost of the simulations.   The
minimum interbirth interval was set to twenty-four months, provided that the last-born infant did not die before two years of
age.   Twenty-four months is not an unreasonable minimum interval
for populations of traditional anthropological interest.   The
resulting realized fertility rates are given in Table 3.

Marriage rates for widowed persons were identical to those
for never-married persons.   A wide range of age differences in
married pairs was permitted, the target central tendency being

TABLE 3.   Five-year fertility rates.

| Age | \multicolumn{8}{c}{Simulation Group} | | | | | | | |
	1	2	3	4	5	6	7	8
15-19	.0515	.0532	.0521	.0524	.0533	.0530	.0531	.0525
20-24	.1493	.1494	.1457	.1469	.1468	.1474	.1477	.1474
25-29	.1467	.1464	.1443	.1455	.1446	.1471	.1468	.1460
30-34	.1400	.1375	.1399	.1398	.1384	.1418	.1434	.1397
35-39	.1285	.1267	.1235	.1267	.1255	.1233	.1265	.1261
40-44	.0877	.0840	.0859	.0846	.0815	.0793	.0862	.0849
45-49	.0078	.0072	.0074	.0077	.0081	.0068	.0077	.0081
50-54	.0000	.0000	.0000	.0000	.0000	.0000	.0000	.0000

| Age | \multicolumn{8}{c}{Simulation Group} | | | | | | | |
	9	10	11	12	13	14	15	16
15-19	.0530	.0527	.0524	.0526	.0524	.0504	.0510	.0525
20-24	.1467	.1450	.1462	.1468	.1426	.1443	.1472	.1466
25-29	.1474	.1475	.1455	.1463	.1443	.1434	.1449	.1472
30-34	.1382	.1423	.1391	.1408	.1369	.1377	.1386	.1404
35-39	.1253	.1253	.1250	.1255	.1227	.1247	.1252	.1258
40-44	.0872	.0818	.0854	.0848	.0852	.0812	.0824	.0866
45-49	.0081	.0079	.0079	.0081	.0057	.0079	.0079	.0080
50-54	.0000	.0000	.0000	.0000	.0000	.0000	.0000	.0000

husbands five years older than wives. These loose constraints on age differences allowed high rates of early marriage and remarriage (16). No divorce was permitted. All these factors make for a conservative estimate of the AFP, although we expect some minimal level of AFP even without an incest tabu under some demographic circumstances because of random fluctuations in mate availability.

Our rates are meant to model the demographic situation we feel many anthropologists have in mind when considering the origin of marriage regulations or in analyzing societies where these have marked effects. No choice of rates can satisfy all potential theoretical interests. Since we possess little precise information on the demography of such groups, any selection of rates can be at best a modestly educated guess.

Each individual simulation within a size category (50, 100, 300) and prohibition level (0, 1, 2, 3) began with the same starting population, one having an age structure appropriate to the anticipated rate of growth. Each run proceeded 100 years to build up genealogical depth sufficient to reckon prohibited relationships. At year 101, a count was begun of births to single and married women. This count was kept up until year 200,

when the simulation stopped. Runs that did not survive until
year 200 were not included in the results. The children of
unmarried females had fathers assigned at random so that each
child would have a full set of ancestors through whom kinship
could be traced for observance of incest tabus. If this had not
been done, the effect of the bilateral incest tabus would have
been halved for children of unmarried women, a negative feedback
that could have masked the consequences of tabus. It must be
remembered that AF children are not necessarily bastards, and
that in small societies paternity is generally known or
assigned.

The demographic results of the simulations are summarized
in Table 4. The expectation of life at birth for females is
narrowly constrained about twenty years, and expectation of life
at age 15 is always very close to 22.3 years. The net reproduction rate is quite close to 1.00, and the total fertility rate
(average number of children expected for women who complete
their reproductive span) is close to 7. The average age at
first marriage for women is between 17 and 20, the mean age at
first birth is about 21, and the average age of mothers over all
births is close to 28. The average growth rate is five per ten
thousand per year, but populations exhibited wide variability in
growth. These results are very close to the expectations of the
input rates and are entirely reasonable for populations of the
kind in which sexual regulation might have emerged. These
rates, where they can be compared, are also close to those in
Weiss' model (Table 2) (14).

The Impact of Incest Tabus

We state first our three main substantive conclusions and
then present the evidence and arguments which lead us to them.

1. In some cases the impact of incest tabus is enormous,
   involving as much as two thirds of all the fertility of a
   population. This finding underscores the importance of considering "demograpic cost" in any theory of incest.

2. The pressure exerted by tabus tapers quickly as population
   size increases, more quickly than has been suggested by
   authors examining these questions from the standpoint of
   population viability. For the most stringent tabu (level
   3), the effect is strong only in populations whose size is
   less than about 250. For the least stringent tabu (level
   1), only populations of less than about 50 are strongly
   affected. The dependence of the AFP on population size
   appears to be extremely regular and can be modelled by a
   simple formula with an intuitive interpretation.

3. The level of AF is regularly dependent on the level of
   incest tabu. Changes in the level of tabu alter only the
   slope of the relationship between AF and population size,

TABLE 4. Realized demographic rates.

Sim. Group	Exp. of life (0)	(15)	NRR	TFR	MACB	MAFB	BAFM	BINT	GROWTH AV	STD
1	20.1	22.4	1.03	7.12	28.3	21.2	18.4	2.83	-.00038	.00045
2	20.0	22.1	1.01	7.02	28.2	21.1	18.3	2.18	.00002	.00034
3	20.1	22.3	1.00	6.99	28.3	21.0	18.1	2.84	-.00043	.00029
4	20.1	22.2	1.01	7.00	28.3	21.0	17.8	2.81	.00002	.00018
5	20.2	22.4	1.01	7.01	28.2	21.1	18.5	2.84	-.00090	.00047
6	20.1	22.3	1.01	7.01	28.2	21.1	18.4	2.85	.00022	.00036
7	20.1	22.3	1.02	7.07	28.3	21.0	18.0	2.83	.00022	.00026
8	20.1	22.2	1.01	7.04	28.3	21.2	17.8	2.81	.00022	.00015
9	19.9	22.1	1.01	7.06	28.2	21.2	18.5	2.84	-.00110	.00049
10	20.1	22.2	1.01	7.00	28.3	21.0	18.5	2.85	.00055	.00040
11	20.0	22.2	1.01	7.00	28.3	21.0	18.1	2.83	.00057	.00029
12	20.1	22.3	1.01	7.04	28.3	21.0	17.6	2.82	.00002	.00018
13	20.0	22.3	0.99	6.85	28.3	21.4	19.6	2.88	-.00177	.00429
14	20.1	22.3	0.99	6.92	28.3	21.3	19.6	2.88	-.00061	.00035
15	20.1	22.4	1.00	7.00	28.3	21.1	18.3	2.83	-.00026	.00028
16	20.1	22.2	1.01	7.06	28.3	21.0	17.8	2.18	-.00026	.00015

Simulation groups are as defined previously. Expectation of life is given for females age zero and fifteen. NRR is the net reproduction rate. TFR is the total fertility rate. MACB is the mean age of mothers at the birth of all children. MAFB is the mean age of mothers at the birth of their first child. BAFM is bride's mean age at first marriage. BINT is the realized interbirth interval. GROWTH AV and STD are the mean and standard deviation of the annual growth rate.

not the form of that relationship. On these grounds, we
believe our findings to be generalizable.

     In support of these conclusions we present first four
plots of the raw data in Figures 1 through 4. In each of these
plots the weighted mean of the population sizes (X-axis) from
five censuses (starting at year 100) at 20-year intervals during
the 100-year observation period is plotted against AFP (Y-axis).
Each plot gives the data for a different level of incest prohibition.

     For populations smaller than 200, the fraction of cases
with AFP greater than one third rises from .01 for no tabu to
.03 for tabu level 1, to .05 for tabu level 2, and to .39 for
tabu level 3. These figures suggest that in populations which
are either habitually small or temporarily so because of random
fluctuations, a strong incest tabu could be a major variable in
the pattern of fertility.

     The tapering of the AFP with population size is obvious
from the absence of points in the upper right regions of all the
plots. This relationship is summarized graphically in the
curves in Figures 1 through 4. These curves represent our best
model of the relationship between AFP and population size for
each level of tabu. In this model, the AFP equals the proportion that a fixed number of people (a number which depends on
the tabu level) bears to the whole population, plus the proportion of exposure to childbearing that women undergo before or
between marriages (because of random delay of marriage even in
an unconstrained marriage market). The formulaic representation
of this relationship is:

$$Y = B/X + A$$

where Y is AFP, B is the fixed number that depends on the
strength of the tabu, A is the AFP for an unconstrained marriage
market, and X is the weighted mean population size. The term
B/X represents the contribution of the incest constraints to the
AFP. We may arbitrarily take the size X at which B/X equals
five percent as our indicator of populations where the fertility
impact becomes important. (The size is halved if we take ten
percent, etc.). These sizes for five percent contribution of
B/X to AFP are 254 people for tabu level 3, 128 for level 2 and
56 for level 1, as compared to a base of 38 for no tabu at all.
Thus, a population must be smaller than about 250 persons for a
strong tabu to depress normal fertility about five percent, and
a population must be smaller than about 50 for a mild tabu to
make as much difference. Another interpretation of these population values is the sizes at which populations one percent
smaller expect AFP's 0.05 percent higher with the same level of
tabu. If population size drops one percent from this point at
any level of tabu, AFP must be about five hundredths of a percent higher to maintain population size.

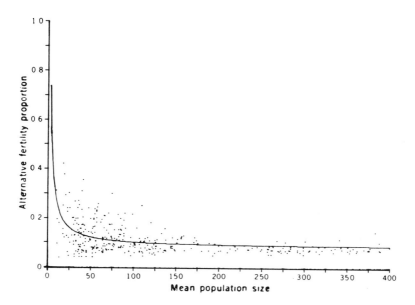

FIGURE 1.   Alternative fertility proportion by mean population
            size for tabu level 0.

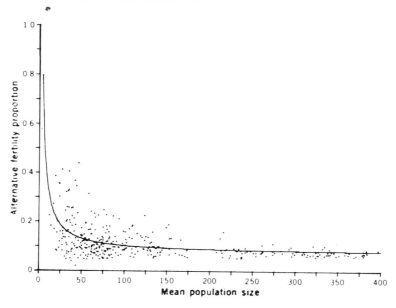

FIGURE 2.   Alternative fertility proportion by mean population
            size for tabu level 1.

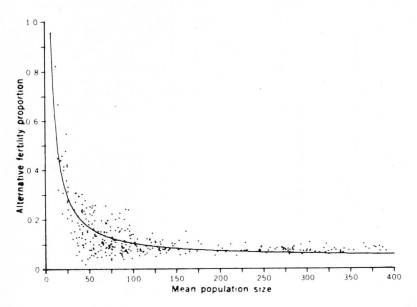

FIGURE 3.   Alternative fertility proportion by mean population
            size for tabu level 2.

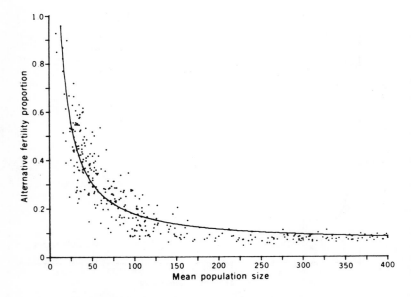

FIGURE 4.   Alternative fertility proportion by mean population
            size for tabu level 3.

That the same form of relationship between AFP and size reappears for the different tabus argues for the generalizability of our claims. This argument would be still stronger if we could elucidate a mechanism which accounts for our formula Y = B/X + A and for the values of B and A which we derive empirically from the data below. The motivating idea for the form Y = B/X + A is that the AFP exceeds a value A for unconstrained marriage by the ratio between a fixed number of kin excluded by the tabu, B, and the whole population, X. A is a base level of AF, and B is a function of the number of kin excluded at a particular tabu level.

This interpretation of A appears viable. For a population of infinite size, B/X must approach zero. Consequently, A must constitute the minimum natural level of AFP for a given study design. We can predict a value for A from the input rates for the simulation using a Markov model of transitions between single, married, widowed, remarried and deceased states for women. Multiplying the resulting numbers of married and unmarried women by age-specific birth rates, summing, and taking the ratio of births to unmarrieds to all births gives A = .070, which agrees well with the minima approached by our curves in Figures 1 to 4.

The quantity B in our model is much harder to interpret or predict. We speculated above that it was some fixed number of persons, dependent on the level of the tabu. It is tempting to interpret it as the number of people excluded by the tabu from marriage with any one person on the average. There are four sets of problems with an interpretation of this kind.

1. The number of people excluded is a complex sum. It consists of the proportion of persons in the population who are of the same sex as the person seeking a spouse, the proportion not of marriageable age, the proportion already married plus the number of persons excluded by the tabu, some of whom might be ineligible on other grounds as well. Only the last of these components of B can be thought of as a fixed number; the rest are all dependent on population size. As will be shown below, even the number of persons excluded by a tabu encompassing certain genealogical positions is dependent on population size, though not in any obvious way.

2. The ratio between births to married and to unmarried women occurs in a way that is not simply related to the number of years spent in the married and unmarried states. The probabilities of giving birth change with age. A woman who fails to find a husband is at a different risk of having a child outside "normal" marriage depending on the age at which her marriage search fails. Widows, for example, contribute quite differently to the AFP than do nubile girls. A non-linearity is introduced into the model.

3. The deficit in years lived in the married state which is
    incurred when certain marriages are prohibited is not simply
    related to the number of people excluded as partners. It is
    combinatorially possible to have every adult in a population
    married, even though each person was prohibited from marry-
    ing anyone else in the population other than the person who
    became the spouse. Achievement of input marriage levels in
    a simulation, or of desired marriage levels in the real
    world, is dependent on the order in which matches are made.
    A simple example is a population with a subset of marriage-
    able persons consisting of three brother-sister pairs and
    having a tabu on sibling mating. All six persons can marry
    if no two sibling sets mutually exchange members. If two of
    them do, only four persons can marry. Social anthropolo-
    gists will recognize the relevance of this mathematical
    point to alliance theory. Unilateral marriage exchange
    allows more marriages to occur in theory. Extreme cases
    like the one described may be unlikely, but milder analogous
    cases must be likely, although their likelihoods defy calcu-
    lation.

4. Finally, the number of people excluded as partners is not
    simply related to the one thing that is reasonably easy to
    count -- the number of kinship positions excluded by a tabu.

    The number of opposite-sex genealogical positions excluded
from a marriage with a given Ego in same and adjacent generations by each of our tabus is easy to count. There are none
excluded at level 0, three (sibling-parent-child) excluded at
level 1, eight more (first cousins, parents' siblings, siblings'
children) excluded at level 2, and thirty-two more (second cousins, grandparents' siblings' children, second cousins' children)
excluded at level 3. Cumulating, zero, three, eleven and forty-
three kinds of kin are excluded at levels 0, 1, 2 and 3 respectively. However, not every person has kin at each of the kinship positions. Full realization of the theoretical membership
of a kinship network requires that every person have a brother
and a sister. For example, in order to have all four kinds of
first cousins (father's brother's child, father's sister's
child, mother's brother's child, mother's sister's child), each
of one's parents must have both a brother and a sister. But if,
for example, mother's brother's child is to have a cousin who is
its own father's brother's child, one's mother's brother must
have a brother too, which means that one's mother must have two
brothers. Extending this, it can be seen that every sibling set
must contain a minimum of four persons, two of each sex, surviving to reproduce if everyone is to have at least one incumbent
in each kinship position. A population with sibling sets of
size four must double every generation. There can have been
very few, if any, human populations so structured for long under
the ecological conditions typical of most societies. The usual
mechanistic kinship analysis rests on a most unlikely behavioral
and demographic base. Indeed, the great advantage of classifi-

catory systems of relationship (in some of which, for example,
all of father's male cousins may be classified together with
father's brother) is that they define kinship statuses sufficiently broadly that most of them will have incumbents most of
the time. Leaving this subject for later exploration in another
work, we remark only that in the kind of society here simulated
which grows slowly if at all, about half of the kinship positions will remain unfilled. Thus, we might expect the number of
persons excluded solely by virtue of the tabu to be 0, 2.5, 4
and 16 or, cumulated, 0, 2.5, 6.5 and 22.5 (18).

    In spite of the problems listed above, we note that the
values of B which we estimate from our data do in fact roughly
parallel these numbers of kinship positions excluded by each
tabu. If this pattern is not fortuitous, then reckoning
excluded persons from excluded kin positions in more refined
ways might allow analytic generation of curves of the same form
appropriate for other tabus, and full interpretation of B might
yet be attained.

    Without a full interpretation of B, the derivation of our
model and of values for A and B remains empirical. The central
claim of our model is that the AFP is a linear function of the
reciprocal of population size. This statement suggests plotting
AFP on the Y-axis not against X, but against 1/X on the X-axis.
Such plots for the four levels of tabu are given in Figures 5
through 8. The soundness of this family of models is reflected
in the similarity between these four plots, which differ from
one another in slope but not to any extent in shape. There is
some flattening at the right and left of each plot, but on the
whole the pattern is linear with variability about the central
line increasing toward the right, as we expect, since population
size decreases in that direction and the variance can be
expected to be greater.

    Each straight line on Figures 5 through 8 corresponds to a
hyperbola on Figures 1 through 4. Since the transformation to
1/X from X has linearized our data, we may use ordinary linear
regression to estimate A and B from the data in Figures 5
through 8. Ordinarily it would be appropriate to use weighted
least squares rather than ordinary least squares for this estimation because the variance increases as 1/X increases. However, the major interest of the model occurs for lower population sizes, toward the right of the graph. For large population
sizes, the effects of the tabus clearly become negligible.
Therefore, we do not downweight the points on the right in spite
of the larger variance, and we use ordinary least squares to
obtain estimates of A and B (see Table 5).

    Referring now back to Figures 1 through 4, it can be seen
that when terms A and B from the regressions are substituted
into the formulae for the model curve, the fit between the data
and the hyperbolic function is quite good. The purpose of Fig-

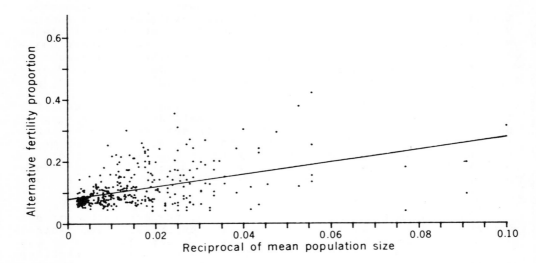

FIGURE 5.   Alternative   fertility   proportion by   reciprocal   of
            mean population size for tabu level 0.

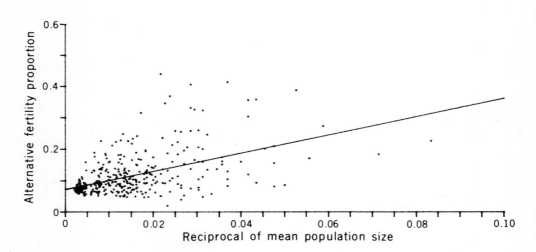

FIGURE 6.   Alternative   fertility   proportion by   reciprocal   of
            mean population size for tabu level 1.

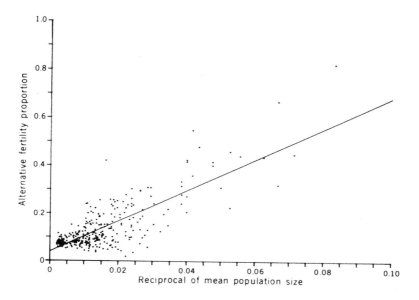

FIGURE 7.   Alternative   fertility   proportion by   reciprocal   of
mean population size for tabu level 2.

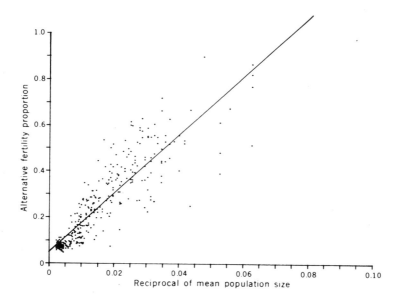

FIGURE 8.   Alternative   fertility   proportion by   reciprocal   of
mean population size for tabu level 3.

TABLE 5.   Regression results.

Incest level	N	Mean(X)	Mean(Y)	S.D.(X)	S.D.(Y)
0	380	.0149	.1097	.0138	.0602
1	380	.0140	.1137	.0117	.0665
2	368	.0138	.1286	.0121	.0962
3	375	.0149	.2407	.0122	.1757

Incest level	a	b	r	r^2	t	d.f.
0	.0804	1.973	.45	.21	9.88	378
1	.0731	2.892	.51	.26	11.51	378
2	.0402	6.408	.80	.65	25.82	366
3	.0508	12.727	.88	.78	36.69	373

ures 1 through 4 is to display the actual data with the fitted model curve. The purpose of Figures 5 through 8 and of the regression results is to measure the effects of the critical independent variables, population size and level of incest prohibition. The base levels of interference (A) are quite close to one another (.080, .073, .040, 0.051) in an expectably irregular way. The AFP for populations with no incest tabu is close to that obtained from the Markov model (.070). The mean AFP of populations larger than 300, in which B/X must approach zero, is about 7 percent or above regardless of the level of tabu. If we had run a larger number of simulations we would expect the values of A to converge even more closely. We judge, therefore, that in populations like those simulated here but of large size, about six to eight percent of fertility would have to come from "alternative" unions if the population were to remain stationary. Of course, minor shifts in the timing of marriage and childbearing could alter that differential. Different estimates of A could be made if other rates, suitable in considering other kinds of populations, were substituted.

The effect of decreasing population size is reflected in the regression coefficient B. The values of B lie in regular progression (1.97, 2.89, 6.41, 12.73). At incest level 0, the number excluded can be only those ineligible by reason of age, sex and marital status. The increment imposed over level 0 at the level 1 tabu is 0.92; at level 2 it is 4.44; and at level 3 it is 10.76. These incremental values scale similarly to those anticipated by virtue of persons thought excludable at the different tabu levels: 2.5, 6.5 and 22.5. For each level of incest tabu, the effect of smaller population size is to increase the interference with "normal" fertility at an increasing rate. All parameters are estimated with some error, of

course; but 95 percent confidence bands for B run 1.5 to 2.4 for
tabu level 0; 2.3 t0 3.4 for tabu level 1; 5.6 to 7.2 for tabu
level 2; and 11.3 to 14.2 for tabu level 3.

        Due to its interaction with population size, the chief
effect of the larger B values for stronger tabus is an earlier
steepening of the curve connecting AFP with size as we move
toward smaller sizes.   Figure 9 illustrates this effect showing
the four model curves for the four tabus on a single plot.   The
model AFP curves are graphed against the population size itself,
as in Figures 1 to 4, rather than against the reciprocal. Here
Level 1 differs little from Level 0, implying that prohibitions
within the nuclear family promote alternative fertility little
more than do constraints of age and sex on marriage with no
tabu.   That Level 2 crosses below Levels 0 and 1 above one hundred persons and hugs Level 0 at very small sizes is probably
not meaningful, since Figure 3 shows our least-squares curve for
Level 2 undershooting the data points at high population sizes.
The AFP tapers quickly at very low population sizes for levels 0
and 1, but more slowly for the first cousin prohibitions at
Level 2, and considerably more slowly for the second cousin prohibitions at Level 3.   Judged by eye, the 5 percent thresholds
quoted above (where the term B/X contributes .05 to AFP, namely
38, 56, 128, 254) are fairly far into the flat region. The 15
percent thresholds of 13, 19, 43 and 85 for the four levels,
however, indicate regions where the excess in AFP over base levels is undeniably pronounced.

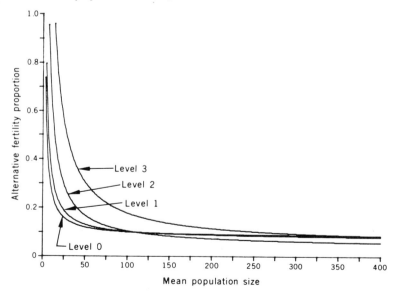

FIGURE 9.   Alternative fertility proportion as a function of
            mean population size: model curves for all incest
            levels.

Discussion

Our findings about the demographic costs of incest prohibitions are the consequences, worked out by the computer in meticulous detail, of theoretical specifications of population structure and dynamics and their interaction with social rules for mating and genealogical position. The modeling effort goes beyond mere assertion that costs are large or small and shows that the broad conclusions to be drawn from our analysis are entirely different depending on what size populations are being considered.

We can distinguish two theaters where scripts dealing with incest might be enacted. One theater specializes in casts of hundreds, the other in casts of dozens. Each cast, of course, stands for an endogamous band with demographic and social characteristics like those in our specifications.

For the theater of the hundreds, we have shown that the demographic costs of incest prohibitions are nearly negligible. Only the strong prohibition against all second cousins and nearer relatives has an impact amounting to as much as 5 percent alternative fertility (in the sense in which we have defined it). This finding contrasts with earlier studies, which found tabus mattering for populations in the low hundreds. In the light of our measurements of alternative fertility in place of viability, we would ascribe the apparent demographic impact of tabus in these earlier analyses to the positive feedback between the effects of tabus and the effects of decreasing size built into them. In this theater, our analysis would illustrate a general claim that the constraints imposed by demography on social structure are loose constraints. For populations of several hundreds, proposed advantages of incest tabus would not have to be set off against demographic difficulties from scarcity of mates, nor would systems facilitating alternative fertility be a logical concomitant of the tabus themselves.

For the theater of the dozens, all our findings are reversed. At all levels of incest prohibition, alternative fertility becomes important. The smallest of the 5 percent thresholds, at Level 0, is 38 people. For prohibition of second cousins and closer relatives, alternative fertility reaches 18 percent for 100 people and 58 percent for two dozen people. In both theaters it is true that prohibition within the nuclear family can scarcely be distinguished from no prohibitions at all, but the impact of the stronger tabus for small populations is clear. In the theater of the dozens, advantage theories of incest have major demographic costs to overbalance or explain away. The presence of a tabu is a prima facie case for the occurrence and importance of alternative fertility outside endogamous monogamous marriage.

So much depends on population size that we should inquire
closely what it means. In societies in which incest tabus may
have emerged, localized kin groups, within which such tabus
would have been most effective, might have been as small as 25
to 50 persons. Thus, they may have been strongly affected by
the consequences of tabus as we have modelled them. On the
other hand, it seems unlikely that such local groups would have
been isolated. More likely they were members of a larger linguistic or cultural grouping, or just co-members of a set of
groups in an ecological zone. How large might such a set of
groups be? Perhaps 500 persons? Perhaps 1,000? Would the
effect of these larger numbers, by our own arguments, reduce the
consequences of imposition of sexual regulation to nothing? The
question is not simple. If a congeries of local groups consisted of 25 units, each averaging 50 persons for a total of
1,250 individuals, it is most unlikely that every marriageable
person in every group was immediately or even periodically
accessible to every other. Population density in the kinds of
societies we are talking about would have been too low to permit
close and continuous social contact, and perhaps even too low to
permit annual contact between all groups. Of course, the kinship network would be territorially dense, and imposition of
tabus would eliminate more persons in neighboring than in distant groups. Looking further afield obviously solves the problem. However, looking further afield means making social contacts and enlarging the socially effective population size,
which takes time -- time during which fertility may be lost. We
cannot provide a hypothetical cost-benefit analysis that closely
models the structure of such societies on the ground, because we
lack the information on which to base one. But our model does
give information on the consequences of <u>socially effective population size</u>. It is up to empirical anthropologists to determine
what the socially effective population sizes in any particular
case may be (19).

   . Interpretation of the more general consequences of these
relations depends on whether selective advantage lies in population growth or in population stationarity (20). We have shown
that at least for small populations, cultural regulation of sexuality either demands alternative avenues for the realization of
fertility, or it impedes growth. When growth is selectively
advantageous, very small societies can tolerate very little
regulation of sexuality without suffering a demographic disadvantage unless they alter their cultural rules to regain their
lost fertility. Somewhat larger societies can tolerate more
sexual regulation. On the other hand, when growth is disadvanta-
geous and stationarity is beneficial, extensive cultural regulation of sexuality makes achievement of stable population size
easier.

   We know little about the actual circumstances of the
growth of early human populations. We should observe, however,
that the primates, like other animal forms, have sometimes

undergone phenomenal adaptive radiation and geographical expansion. Close to the human line, the dryopithecines covered an
area from the Cape of Good Hope to the Alps, and from the Atlan-
tic to the Pacific in a relatively brief geological period.
Similarly, the immediate ancestors of our own species, Homo
erectus, appear to have moved out of a presumably small area of
Africa to cover both that continent and the Eurasian land mass
in about half a million years. Homo sapiens seems to have
spread over the entire globe in about 30-40,000 years.

    One's picture of these expansions differs according to
one's predilection for mono- or polyphyletic origins, but it
does not differ so much as to erase the realization that the
surface of the globe is a considerable area to fill, even if
sparsely, and that expansion of the scope noted cannot have
occurred without population growth at least at the margins of
expansion (from one or several foci). It is certain that some
population growth, however miniscule, was selectively advantageous in establishing the species over a wide area. At the same
time, it is equally likely that stationarity was selectively
advantageous in areas already colonized up to the current limits
of cultural exploitation and resource base (21). The net growth
rates required to reach a world population of 600 million by 1
A.D. would have been about five per ten thousand, assuming the
Garden of Eden to be 40,000 years old, and about eight per ten
thousand given a Cro-Magnon Adam and Eve. These rates are so
small as to be virtually undetectable unless the observer has
tens of thousands of years to watch, as we do. But they are net
rates. If stationarity was selectively advantageous in well-
colonized areas, then population growth must have been higher
than the net rates in pioneer areas, and the larger the area of
established colonization, the greater the disparity between central and peripheral growth rates might have been without alter-
ing the net rates.

    Thus we see that the general consequences of prohibitions
are not determined solely by whether we find ourselves in the
theater of the dozens or the theater of the hundreds. They are
also determined by whether we find the theater on the periphery
of expansion or in areas already colonized. Peripheralness and
centrality are, of course, only two of a myriad of socio-demographic dimensions within which the general consequences of sexual regulation can differ. They serve as well as any, however,
to demonstrate that while the mathematical effects of a given
level of incest prohibition depend in a simple way on population
size, the larger consequences of these effects depend on factors
that include the ecology, technology and social organization of
the population experiencing the effects.

    Still, for those small populations where advantage would
be gained by offsetting lost fertility, it is interesting to
speculate on the utility of socio-cultural responses. Clearly
helpful would be cultural innovation and variety in areas relat-

ing to fertility. We may speculate that the array of marital customs that so titillated Victorian anthroplolgists was a survival mechanism in very small societies, where flexibility of response in the face of random demographic fluctuation, without major institutional revision, may have been important to the maintenance of social continuity. The flexibility of marital arrangements, allowing replacement of fertility loss incurred through the prohibition of certain matings, or its suppression through those prohibitions, would permit small populations to enjoy institutional stability and whatever psychosocial advantages might accrue from incest tabus. This flexibility, we surmise, might have been most important when populations were on expanding peripheries, where maintenance of growth would have been important to the continued geographical expansion of the species, allowing recovery of the necessary fertility lost through other regulations. More broadly, we may observe that intersocietal variation in the cultural regulation of sexuality introduces one more source of heterogeneity of fertility, and thus of population growth rates, beyond those genetic and behavioral sources that may be available to other species. Not only can individual human societies respond to circumstance with altered reproductive behavior; these same societies differ in advance of any presentation of exterior circumstances. The species as a whole thus presents a potentially wider range of responses to differing selective pressures, even though individual populations may be well or badly adapted to any particular pressure.

Conclusion

Our analysis and attendant speculations make three general points clear. First, the mathematical impact of incest prohibitions is simple. It varies directly with the level of tabu and inversely with population size, in a regular and measurable way. Second, however, the impact of any tabu on the growth rate of a population cannot be assessed outside the general socio-demographic and ecological context within which the tabu is implemented. Sexual prohibitions are a few among many factors -- the underlying biological rates, mechanisms for alternative fertility, fluctuations in demographic rates -- that determine the population growth rate. Third, the consequences of any achieved growth rate cannot be assessed outside the broadest cultural and ecological context. Some ecological situations will confer advantage to stationary populations, others to increasing populations, and conceivably others to declining populations. We can suggest no general statement of the meaning of incest tabus for human history, particularly demographic history. What we can do and have done is to identify those populations in which incest prohibitions could have played a significant demographic role, and in them to measure these effects so as to allow clearer examination of their interactions with the numerous other factors at work in the advance of culture (22).

Summary.

    Theories of incest tabus usually stress the psychosocial
advantages of marriage regulation. However, marriage regulation
may produce delays in mating and loss of fertility to a population. Computer microsimulation experiments measure the amount
of fertility that must be achieved outside a normatively specified marriage system in order to keep population constant. This
amount varies directly with scope of tabu and inversely with
population size. For populations of hundreds it is negligible,
yet for those of dozens it can be very great. In the latter,
flexibility of marital arrangements may permit maintenance of
ecologically desirable fertility without repeated revision of
marriage rules.

REFERENCES and NOTES

1. Levi-Strauss, C. 1960. In "Man, Culture and Society". H.L.
    Shapiro (ed.) New York: Oxford Univ. Press.
2. See for example Aberle, D.F., D.R. Miller, U. Bronfenbren-
    ner, D. Schneider, E.H. Hess and J.N. Spuhler 1963. Amer.
    Anth. 65:253.; Cohen, Y. 1978. Human Nature 1:7.
3. Tylor, E.B. 1889. J.R.A.I. 18:245.
4. Westermarck, E. 1921. "History of Human Marriage". London:
    Macmillan. Recent research by Arthur Wolf, 1970. Amer.
    Anth. 72:503, on Taiwanese marriages (in many of which an
    adopted girl, raised with the son of the family, becomes his
    bride) indeed shows lowered fertility in such marriages,
    suggesting that revulsion occurs as Westermarck proposed.
5. Slater, M. 1959. Amer. Anth. 61: 1042; Busch, R.C. and J.
    Gundlach 1977. Amer. Anth. 79: 912.
6. Hammel, E.A. 1960. Oceania 31: 14.
7. Hammel, E.A. and D. Hutchinson 1973. In "Computer Simulation
    in Human Population Studies". B. Dyke and J.W. MacCluer
    (eds.) New York: Academic Press.
8. Morgan, K. 1973. In ibid.
9. MacCluer, J.W. and B. Dyke 1976. Soc. Biol. 23: 1.
10. See also Morton, N.E., Y. Imaizumi and D.E. Harris. 1971.
    Amer. Anth. 73: 1005 for genetic implications of exogamy.
11. Morgan's analysis is based on only five simulations, and the
    stochastic reliability of his estimate is doubtful. It
    seems unlikely that he allowed genealogical relationships to
    build to sufficient depth before observing the effects of
    the incest tabus, so that the tabus imposed may not have had
    a chance to be exercised on persons known to be related. It
    is unclear whether MacCluer and Dyke (9) allowed sufficient
    buildup of genealogical relationships before observing
    effects, and their numerous measures of effect make
    interpretation more complex than the method we will propose.

12. Full details of the original simulation program are given in
    the operating manual [Hammel, E.A., D. Hutchinson, K.
    Wachter and R. Deuel 1976. "The SOCSIM Demographic-Socio-
    logical Microsimulation Program". Inst. of International
    Studies, U.C. Berkeley, No. 27], and illustrated in sev-
    eral substantive papers [Hammel, E.A. and D. Hutchinson
    (7); Hammel, E.A. 1976. In "Demographic Anthropology: Quan-
    titative Approaches". E. Zubrow (ed.) Albuquerque: U. of
    N,M.; Hammel, E.A. and K.W. Wachter 1977. In "Population
    Patterns in the Past". R. Lee (ed.) New York: Academic
    Press; Wachter, K., E.A. Hammel and T.P.R. Laslett 1978.
    "Statistical Studies of Historical Social Structure". New
    York: Academic Press]. Documentation on the revisions is
    available from the authors.
13. "Kinship relations" were defined genealogically. Level 1
    means F, M, B, Z, S, D. Level 2 means Level 1 plus FBC,
    MBC, FDC, MDC. Level 3 means Level 2 plus FFBCC, FMBCC,
    ..., MMDCC.
14. Weiss, K.M. 1973. Amer. Antiq. 38: 2.
15. Henry, L. 1972. "Demographie -- Analyses et Modeles".
    Paris: Societe Encyclopedique Universelle.
16. Our "marriage rates" actually control initiation of searches
    for a spouse by women, not the achievement of marriages. If
    a woman scheduled to search for a mate in a particular month
    failed to find one, she remained at risk of death or of hav-
    ing a child in that same month. If she died, of course,
    that would be the end of it. If she had a child, that child
    would contribute to the AF proportion of births. If she had
    a child, a new event would be scheduled for her at some
    future time according to the probabilities of particular
    events appropriate to her age. If she did not have a child
    in the month in which she failed to find a spouse, she would
    automatically continue her search in the next month. If she
    failed again, she would be subject to the risks of death and
    childbirth again. Thus any woman coming of age for marriage
    or childbearing might have a child before being scheduled to
    seek a husband because the probabilities of childbirth were
    the same for married as for unmarried women and were not
    zero. She would continue to be at risk of bearing a child,
    at the same rates as married women, until she was scheduled
    to seek a husband, and then until she found one.
17. For 100 of the runs at size 50 (at each incest tabu level),
    populations were considered extinct if they fell below size
    10, but for the second 100 runs at size 50 (at each incest
    tabu level) declining populations were permitted to descend
    to zero. (This difference should be noted, although it
    apparently has no important effect).
18. At Level 0, no exclusions. At Level 1, the opposite sex
    parent, the opposite sex child and the expected number of
    opposite sex siblings in sibling sets of size two, namely
    1/2, since Ego is already one sibling of two and the remain-
    ing must be either of the same or opposite sex. At Level 2,
    the additional exclusions are the expected number of oppo-

site sex first cousins in sibling sets of size two (one in
each first cousin set), with one such cousin set descended
from each of the expected number of the siblings of each
parent. There are two parents, each with one expected
sibling; thus, two first cousins are excluded in addition to
the 2.5 exclusions at Level 1. At Level 3, the additional
exclusions are descended from the expected number of
siblings of each grandparent, thus one for each of four
grandparents. Each of these can be expected to have two
children, each of whom will have two children, one of whom
is of the opposite sex from Ego. Thus, eight second cousins
are excluded in addition to the 4.5 at Level 2. These calculations do not include possible exclusions of persons in
intermediate generations, such as the parents' siblings or
nephews and nieces; the calculation is for illustrative purposes and is kept simple.

19. See the interesting explorations of the topic in Birdsell,
    J. 1958. Evolution 12; Peterson, N. (ed.) 1976. "Tribes
    and Boundaries in Australia". Canberra: Australian Insti-
    tute of Aboriginal Studies; King, G. 1978. Cross-cultural
    model for the sociospatial organization of hunters-gather-
    ers. Amer. Anth. Assoc. 77th Annual Meeting.

20. We are indebted to Ronald Lee for asking this question.

21. It should be understood that failure to suppress fertility
    by cultural regulation under some circumstances, such as
    those of populations in already colonized areas pressing
    against their resource base and technological capabilities,
    could result in a myriad of effects, including technologi-
    cal, social, political, economic or other elaboration. See
    particularly Boserup, E. 1965. "The Conditions of Agricul-
    tural Growth". London: Allen and Unwin.

22. We are indebted to R. Lee, N. Howell, B. Benedict, N. Gra-
    burn and others for their comments. This material is based
    upon work supported by the National Science Foundation under
    Grant No. SOC76-10923A02. Any opinions, findings and con-
    clusions or recommendations expressed in this publication
    are those of the authors and do not necessarily reflect the
    views of the National Science Foundation. An earlier and
    shorter version of this paper was published in Science 205:
    972-977, with copyright by the American Association for the
    Advancement of Science. Figures and text reproduced with
    permission.

FAMILY FORMATION AND HEALTH IN 19TH CENTURY
FRANKLIN COUNTY, MASSACHUSETTS

Richard S. Meindl

Factors influencing health in childhood are governed to a large extent by the dynamics of family formation and household composition at the time of each birth. This appears to be the case not only for parts of the underdeveloped world (Omran and Standley, 1976), but for many developed areas as well (Wray, 1971; Dingle, et al., 1964). Thus it might be expected that health differentials of this nature would be reflected by childhood death rates in those historical communities which experienced moderate to high mortality.

It is the objective of this paper to examine in some detail three important sets of variables -- family formation patterns, infant and childhood mortality and economic status -- and their distribution in a rural historical community of western Massachusetts. Characteristics generally associated with high-fertility families include early age at marriage and brief interpregnancy intervals as well as a predominance of high-order births and large mean completed families. It can be shown that each of these variables is correlated to some degree with early childhood mortality risks. In this paper attention will also be directed to the relative strengths of association between each fertility characteristic and early mortality when other variables are controlled. This will involve analyses of correlations within family demographic structure. It will be shown that the fitting of log-linear models is a useful technique for analyzing discrete multivariate data of this nature (Brown, 1976; Goodman, 1971). For example, rapid fertility as measured by close child spacing is often associated with lower socioeconomic scales, certain maternal ages and elevated infant mortality in the study community. It is always desirable to be in a position to generalize to other populations and situations (e.g., other agrarian groups or other populations which lack the benefits of modern health care delivery), and in this paper an attempt will be made to isolate the somewhat separate effects of variation in fertility with survival of children.

Families of mid-19th century Deerfield, Massachusetts (Figure 1) were manually reconstructed on the basis of fertility histories as revealed by the vital register of the town (see Swedlund, Meindl and Gradie, this volume; or Meindl, n.d.). Sheldon's (1896) genealogy served as an independent check as did the 7th, 8th and 9th U.S. Federal Censuses (1850-1870). These decennial lists also ranked inhabitants by taxable wealth, and for these preliminary analyses the Deerfield households were

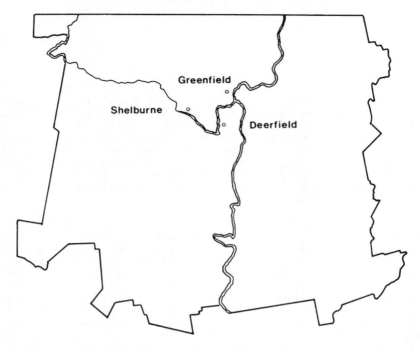

FRANKLIN   COUNTY

FIGURE 1.   Map of Franklin County, Massachusetts.

divided into two classes on the basis of the community medians.
Economic class was assessed by that census which was temporarily
closest to the household head's 30th birthday.   In a longitudinal survey of this data base, it was found that rarely did Deerfield households move up or down among the wealth quartiles
(except for the upper two) and never was there observed a family
which moved two quartiles up or down these wealth scales.   For
the most part, the upper 50% refers to the owners of the larger
farms which had been held by the same lineal families for generations, in addition to several wealthy merchants and self-made
individuals who possessed certain necessary and apparently
expensive skills (Table 1).   This family file by no means con-
stitutes a strictly random sample of Deerfield residents, but it
is probably quite representative of those individuals who
remained in the community throughout their reproductive histories.

     Nearly 700 Deerfield women ranging in year of birth from
1805 to 1845 formed the core of the sample (very few of the
women were born before 1820).   About two-thirds of these families were in full observation, i.e. from the birth of the woman

TABLE 1. Components of socioeconomic classifications within
          samples.

	Upper Class	Lower Class
Farmhands, unskilled laborers	5.7%	28.0%
Skilled laborers, merchants, etc.	25.6%	35.4%
Farmers who own their land	62.6%	31.5%
Unknown	6.1%	5.1%
	100.0%	100.0%

to the death or survival to adulthood of her last child. The
children themselves were traced only to their 21st birthday,
unless of course they later began their own families in town.
Thus, the Deerfield family file is stored only in units of one
and one-half generations at this stage of the project.

Marginal Mortality Frequencies

     The presentation of marginal distributions of categorical
data is the first step in the description of Deerfield early-
childhood mortality structure. Marginal frequencies, or margins, are simply collapsed tabular data which ignore unspecified
variables, and these are useful both in presenting specific summaries and also as an introduction to a multivariate analysis
(see below).

     For instance, consider the simple division of all the
children in the file into four subclasses. Each child is classified by gender and also by another dichotomous scale -- the
position of the father relative to median taxable wealth. These
four cohorts in turn generate four composite life tables (Figure
2). In this, and in subsequent comparisons, only mortality for
the first 12 months of life, and total mortality by 60 months,
of which infant deaths are a part, will be reported (see key in
Figure 3). Almost all of the variation in mortality attributed
to socioeconomic status is due to male survivorship differentials (Figure 3). Not only are the differences in the female
curves nonsignificant, but mortality in this sample is actually
somewhat greater for the higher-class female adolescents after
age ten (Figure 2). Again, these four subclasses were grouped
without regard to other fertility variables and as such represent marginal distributions. But these data clearly suggest
that only males benefited from the conditions in households of
the higher economic class.

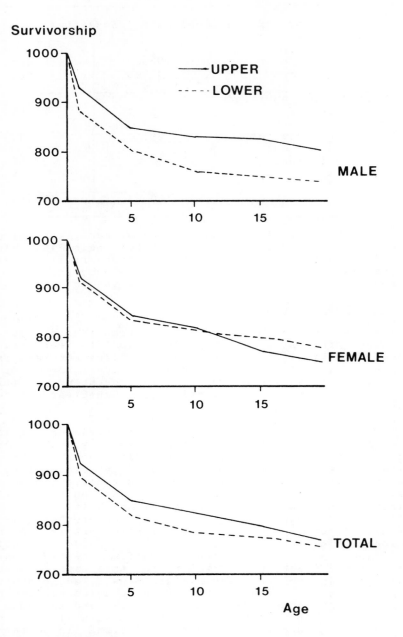

FIGURE 2.   Composite survivorship   curves by   sex and   socioeco-
            nomic class.

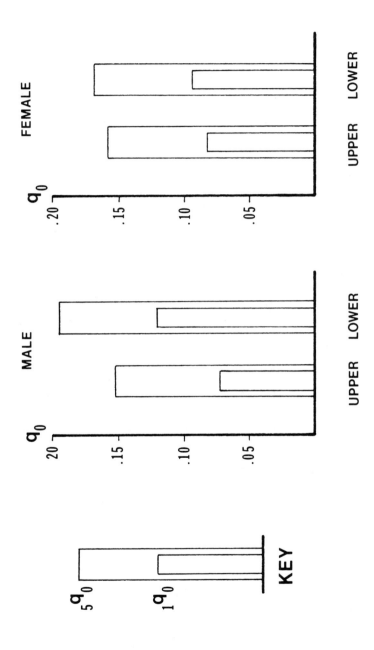

FIGURE 3. Probability of dying in the intervals 0 – 1 years (inner bar) and 0 – 5 years (outer bar) by sex and socioecomic class.

Historical data permit observation of birth and subsequent childhood death or survival as such events occurred within various sizes of completed sibships. Persistent problems emerge from studies of family health and family size. These include the difficulty with which correlated variables such as maternal age, birth order and others are controlled. Neverthless, the notion that the risk of child loss frequently increases faster than the final future size of the family has not been invalidated by any major study (Stettler, 1970). While this holds in the aggregate for Deerfield, different patterns emerge within wealth classes.

The following analysis describes essentially the same children as before. However, gender is here ignored, and the children are grouped into ten cohorts based on two wealth classes and five family size classes (Figure 4) Remember, this scale is not the same as birth order; that is, all children of a given family would be given the same value, an integer equal to the ultimate size of the completed sibship. In the upper half by censused wealth there is a linear increase in risk (per birth) of dying within the first five years of life. The relationship with mortality ($_1q_0$; again, this is the enclosed histogram) was "J-shaped" because of a higher frequency of infant deaths in small families.

The lower class demonstrated a somewhat different pattern. Both infant ($_1q_0$) and total childhood ($_5q_0$) mortality were distributed in reverse "J-shaped" curves because of unusually high risk in very small families. Since the number of lower class families with a total of one or two children is not very large (28), no reliable inferences can be made.

Many workers contend that the opportunity for infection in children increases with family size (Spence, et al., 1954; Douglas and Blomfield, 1958; Dingle, et al., 1964; Wray, 1971; Omran and Standley, 1976). This suggests a similar relationship to mortality itself. However, few of these studies have attempted to control for other fertility variables, and the possibility remains that correlates of family size are perhaps better predictors of early mortality. If contagion and crowding are important determinants of childhood mortality, then birth rank, which indicates the number of older siblings, should show a more accurate relationship with childhood death rates. However, the Deerfield margins for birth rank and mortality gave no such indication (Figure 5). There is considerable variability about a linear model in the wealthier half of the population. In addition, an estimated slope for either infant or total child mortality is only weakly positive. The lower class of the population shows no relation of birth order to child loss. The finding that early mortality is associated strongly with ultimate family size and not significantly with birth order is in agreement with the work of Joel Cohen (1975) who utilized parish registers of pre-industrial France. Additional Deerfield analy-

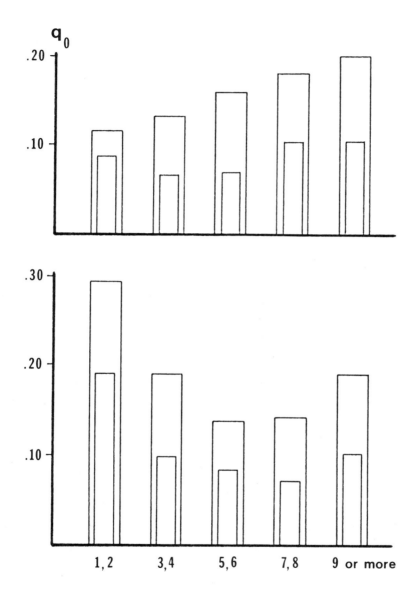

COMPLETED FAMILY

FIGURE 4. Probability of dying in the intervals 0 - 1 (inner bar) and 0 - 5 (outer bar) by completed family size. Upper socioeconomic class top graph, lower class bottom graph.

ses (see below) suggest that birth order explains very little.
That is, birth rank only weakly conditions the probability of
death within families of given sizes. Perhaps mortality (within
various family size classes) is determined by yet another fertility characteristic.

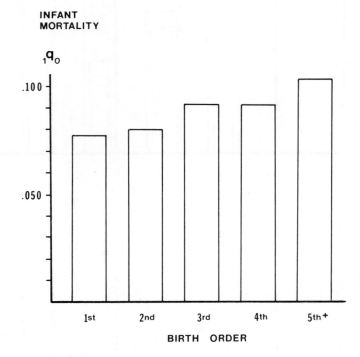

**INFANT
MORTALITY**

FIGURE 5.   Probability of dying in the interval 0 - 1 by birth
             order.

        Maternal age at pregnancy and its relation to late fetal
deaths, perinatal and childhood mortality, and prematurity
should be discussed as a separate fertility entity to emphasize
the importance of timing in the life-history phases of reproducing individuals. The fertility of women gradually increases
with age to a peak rate and then diminishes to age 45 (Weiss,
1973). Rose Frisch addresses the problem of reproductive fitness in her survey of early medical views and 19th Century fertility data from English and Scottish populations (Frisch,
1978). She contends that nutrition, hard work and disease may
affect fertility because reproduction requires energy and
because reproductive ability is synchronized with physical
development and maturation. Whether reproductive errors and
other age-related factors, as reflected by mortality, are more
frequent at the beginning and end of the reproductive span is
examined in the Deerfield family data.

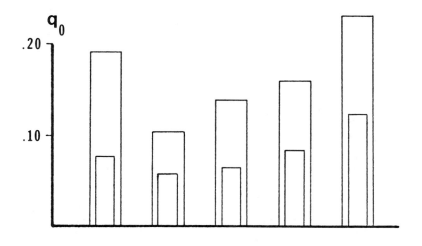

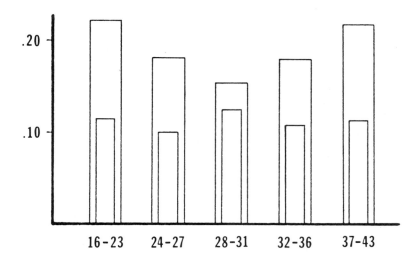

MATERNAL   AGE

FIGURE 6.   Probability of dying in the intervals 0 – 1 (inner
bar) and   0 – 5 (outer bar) by maternal   age. Upper
socioeconomic   class top graph, lower class   bottom
graph.

The next margin ignores family size, birth rank and gender. Children are divided into ten cohorts on the basis of economic class and the age of the mother at the time of the birth
(Figure 6). The association of child loss by the fifth year
($_5q_0$) with the five ordered maternal age classes is similar for

the two groups. The higher risk to children of young mothers in
the lower age class modifies the more usual "J-shaped" pattern,
as seen in the wealthier class, to a "U-shaped" curve. Note,
however, the weak association in the lower class between maternal age and infant death rates ($_1q_0$). It is interesting to

speculate that the overall effects of maternal age on children
only become apparent some time after infancy in this population.

A different factor may have elevated infant mortality in
the 28 to 31 year maternal age class (and other ages as well) in
the poorer segment of the Deerfield population. While these
women were surely of best demographic fitness for reproduction
by the standards of Frisch, the now greater <u>rate</u> of fertility,
coupled with the quality of life in the lower class, may have
had an adverse effect on each child. This is illustrated by
reference to one final cohort comparison.

Membership of a birth in one of four cohorts is now
defined solely by the number of months that the previous sibling
preceded him. Therefore, this scale also indicates the age of
the next older sib at the time of this birth and serves as an
index of fertility rate (per unit time). While total child survival ($_5q_0$) is virtually independent of child spacing, infant

mortality is clearly dependent upon the absolute rate of childbearing (Figure 7). Although the independence of child loss by
age five is difficult to explain, the important point is that
children born less than a year and a half apart may be high risk
infants regardless of other demographic parameters. It should
be noted that this fertility rate threshold was only rarely
attained this late in Deerfield's history, and the appearance of
such narrow birth intervals is largely confined to poorer women
of the middle reproductive years.

Some Log-Linear Models

Many of these fertility variables are, of. course, well-
correlated, and each of the direct associations of various fertility measures with child loss has not been isolated. The need
to control for covariates in noncontrolled or "natural" experiments may become evident from an example (see Cohen, 1975: 35).
Suppose that within any family (of given ultimate size) mortality risks are identical for all birth orders; however, the larger the family the lower the survival rate. Then it can be said
that in the population being sampled survival is independent of
birth order and contingent upon final family size. But if

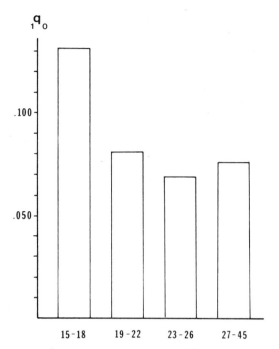

$_1q_0$

PRECEDING BIRTH INTERVAL, MONTHS

FIGURE 7.   Probability of dying in the interval 0 - 1 as a func-
             tion of the number of months since birth of previous
             sibling.

births   are randomly   drawn from this population, there   would
appear   an inverse   relation between birth rank   and   survival
because of the higher proportion of late births in larger families. Yet each set of marginal frequencies (birth order against
mortality; family size against mortality) will appear significant, and it should be clear that such bivariate comparisons can
be misleading.

     One solution is to limit the analysis of, say, birth order
to large families.   However, this simple procedure becomes
unworkable as additional demographic variables are successively
included in the analysis. A more useful approach involves the
screening of interactions in a multi-way contingency table.
General log-linear procedures are outlined by Goodman (1970;
1971), and the following analyses employ a shortcut advocated by
Morton Brown (1976).

     Each Deerfield birth is classified by rank, maternal age,
sex, wealth of the household head, and whether the child reached

its fifth birthday. Survival, wealth and gender remain dichotomous variables. Birth order is collapsed into three classes
(early, middle, late), and the continuous variable, maternal
age, is condensed into four discrete categories. This yields a
five-way table composed of 96 cells, and the design is similar
to the factorial, or "fully-crossed" analysis of variance. One
difference is that the cells contain frequency counts rather
than continuous, normally distributed variates. Another is
that the interactions are of more interest than the main
effects.

TABLE 2.   Partial associations of birth order, maternal age, and
           mortality.

| | | Likelihood ratio | |
Interaction	d.f.	chi-square	Pr.
Birth order with maternal age	6	604.27 *	.001
Mortality with maternal age	3	8.33 *	.05
Mortality with birth order	2	.22 (ns)	.90

           * significant   (ns) not significant

TABLE 3.   Partial associations of family size, maternal age, and
           mortality.

| | | Likelihood ratio | |
Interaction	d.f.	chi-square	Pr.
Family size with maternal age	12	27.41 *	.01
Mortality with maternal age	3	9.03 *	.05
Mortality with family size	4	5.02 (ns)	.29
Third order effect	12	9.60 (ns)	.65

           * significant   (ns) not significant

     Of the 26 second- and higher-ordered interactions
(effects) that were examined in this analysis, only three sec-
ond-order effects, and only one test of each, are presented
(Table 2).   Obviously, there is a strong association between
birth order and maternal age. Any log-linear model with a reasonable chance of fitting these data would have to include this
two-variable margin. Note, however, that maternal age is more
strongly associated with child mortality than is birth order.
Other tests of these same effects (see Goodman, 1970; 1971, for
other tests; the "partial" association is defined in Brown,

PERCENTAGES OF TUBERCULOSIS DEATHS BY MONTH

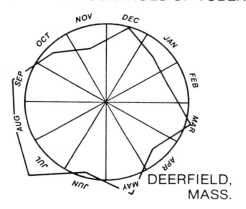

DEERFIELD, MASS.

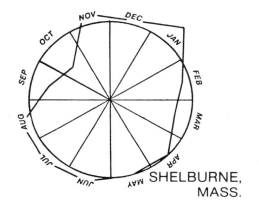

SHELBURNE, MASS.

FIGURE 8.   Seasonality of death from tuberculosis.

1976) gave similar results. Another table was constructed to
test the association of family size with childhood mortality in
the presence of the maternal age variable (Table 3). Again, the
first effect listed is of little interest. However, the child-
mortality/maternal-age interaction is significant; mortal-
ity/family size is not. In fact, the structure of the Deerfield
data can be adequately fitted without the latter margin.

     Stephen Feinberg (1977) cautions that the average number
of counts per cell in log-linear analyses should remain well
above five, perhaps ten or more. Elaborate tables with minimal
data have low statistical power, and even worse, may generate
test statistics that are simply not distributed as chi-square
when the null hypotheses are true. While the tables here all
averaged just over ten per cell, there is limited provision for
additional measures. In fact, the birth-order variable had to
be removed for the analysis of family size. The only point was
that maternal age seemed to be more important than either of
these. It is unfortunate that nominal data must be so numerous
to be informative, because a number of questions remain unan-
swered. One concerns the seasonal distribution of deaths in the

PERCENTAGES OF DEATHS BY MONTH
(DEERFIELD ONLY)

DYSENTERY

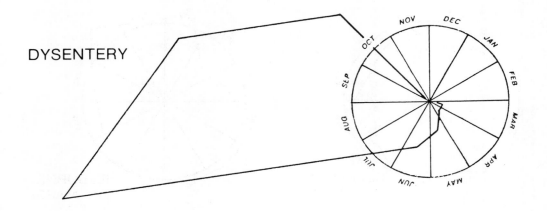

CHOLERA INFANTUM

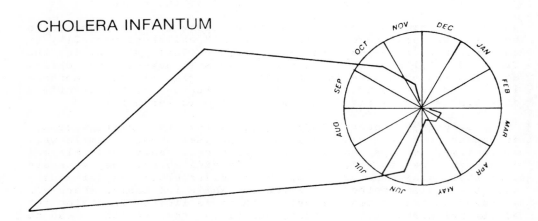

FIGURE 9.   Seasonality of death from dysentery and cholera
infantum.

19th century. Monthly averages for specific diseases were computed for the period 1850 to 1900 for several western Massachusetts communities. As an example, tuberculosis, a common disease confined mostly to young adults, was <u>not</u> seasonal as measured by monthly death rates in Deerfield or in nearby Shelburne (Figure 8; the radius of each circle marks one-twelfth of the total for the fifty years of observation). However, the major killers of children (Figure 9) were very seasonal throughout the 19th century in these communities. It would be of some interest to examine the relationships between the previous set of measures, especially maternal age and birth spacing, and month of birth.

This and other surveys might illuminate the nature of the "U-shaped" maternal-age/mortality function which, it should be noted, is an inverse of the archetypal fertility curve for human females (Weiss, 1973). Frisch quotes (1978) from an 1826 medical text comparing physical growth and the coordinated growth of the female reproductive organs, which "arrive latest at perfection and are the first to become worn out and decrepid." A more complete view of reproductive efficiency, which measures the number of children brought to their fifth year rather than the number of fetuses brought to term, would enrich our understanding of population growth and demographic relationships, both of historic and prehistoric peoples.

ACKNOWLEDGMENTS

Support of grant NICHD 08979 from the national Institutes of Health and BNS 76-83121 fro the National Science Foundation is gratefully acknowledged.

REFERENCES

Brown, M.B. 1976. Screening effects in multidimensional contingency tables. Appl. Statist. 25: 37-46.
Cohen, J.E. 1975. Childhood mortality, family size and birth order in pre-industrial Europe. Demography 12(1): 35-55.
Dingle, J.H., G.F. Badger and W.F. Jordan 1964. "Illness in the Home: A Study of 25,000 Illnesses in a Group of Cleveland Families". Cleveland: Western Reserve.
Douglas, J.W.B. and J.M. Blomfield 1958. "Children Under Five". London: George Allen and Unwin, Ltd.
Feinberg, S.E. 1977. "The Analysis of Cross-Classified Categorical Data". Cambridge, Mass.: M.I.T. Press.
Frisch, R.E. 1978. Population, food intake, and fertility. Science 199(4324): 22-30.

Goodman, L.A. 1970. The multivariate analysis of qualitative
    data: Interactions among multiple classifications. J.
    Amer. Stat. Assoc. 65(329): 226-256.
Goodman, L.A. 1971. The analysis of multidimensional contigency
    tables: Stepwise procedures and direct estimation methods
    for building models for multiple classifications. Techno-
    metrics 13(1): 33.
Meindl, R.S. 1979. Environmental and demographic correlates of
    mortality in 19th Century Franklin County, Massachusetts.
    Unpublished Ph.D. Dissertation, University of Massachu-
    setts, Amherst.
Omran, A.R. and C.C. Standley 1976. "Family Formation Patterns
    and Health: An International Collaborative Study in
    India, Iran, Lebanon, Philippines, and Turkey". Geneva:
    W.H.O
Sheldon, G. 1896. "A History of Deerfield, Massachusetts".
    Reprinted ed., 1972. Somersworth: New Hampshire Publishing
    Co.
Spence, J., W.F. Walton, F.J.W. Miller and F.D.M. Court 1954.
    "A Thousand Families in Newcastle-Upon-Tyne". London:
    Oxford University Press.
Stettler, H.L. 1970. The New England throat distemper and family
    size. In "Empirical Studies in Health Economics". H.E.
    Klarman (ed.). Baltimore: Johns Hopkins.
Weiss, K.M. 1973. Demographic models for anthropology. Amer.
    Antiq. 38(2), part 2.
Wray, J.D. 1971. Population pressure on families: Family size
    and child spacing. Reports on Population/Family no. 9.

INDEX